The Case for
Edward de Vere
as
Shakespeare

GEOFFREY EYRE

Mardle Publications

Also written by Geoffrey Eyre

The Shakespeare Authorship Mystery Explained

ISBN 978-0-9554608-8-3

The Case for Edward de Vere as Shakespeare

First published 2015 by Mardle Publications
www.mardlepublications.com

mardlebooks@gmail.com

Typeset by John Owen Smith, Headley Down

ISBN 978-0-9554608-4-5

Printed by CreateSpace

Contents

Edward de Vere, 17th Earl of Oxford, aged 25.
Unknown artist from a lost original.
National Portrait Gallery, Welbeck Abbey.

Author's Note

The Shakespeare authorship mystery is complex, bound up with British national pride and patriotism. Mass literacy in the 1880s made the plays known to a wide audience of playgoers and readers. Admiration for the humbly born playwright who had prospered by his own ability led opinion formers and educationists to identify strongly with the man from Stratford-upon-Avon. His right to be hailed as the world's greatest dramatist is still staunchly defended by the literary establishment. Yet many people in this country, and others, found it difficult to reconcile the epic nature of the plays with the small-town trader who was supposed to have written them. The search for a more credible author gathered momentum in the last century and produced some strong candidates.

By a long process of elimination Edward de Vere, earl of Oxford, emerged as the best qualified and most probable author of the plays. He was a highly educated and widely travelled aristocrat whose life-span dates of birth and death, 1550–1604, are compatible with the performance and publication dates of the plays, although few of these can be stated with certainty. As a generous patron of writers, actors and musicians he was at the centre of Elizabethan London's cultural and literary renewal.

It must be admitted that no evidence has been produced which would positively identify Edward de Vere as the writer known to the world as William Shakespeare and there is no expectation that such evidence will come to light any time soon. Even so, when the known details of his life are considered in relation to the plays and poetry they make an arguable case. This short study is written in non-academic language as a fair-minded introduction to the case for Edward de Vere as Shakespeare.

Sources

Elizabethan and early Jacobean literary history is well documented. Resources such as the *Dictionary of National Biography* are available online. *William Shakespeare: A Textual Companion* by Wells and Taylor has been frequently consulted, and also Alan Nelson's life of Edward de Vere, Earl of Oxford, *Monstrous Adversary*. The publications of the Shakespeare Oxford Fellowship in the USA and The De Vere Society in the UK have provided much of the information used for the study, in particular *Dating Shakespeare's Plays* edited by Kevin Gilvary.

Dramatis Personae

Brief biographical notes of the main characters are included as an Appendix

Quotations

All the Shakespeare quotations have been taken from *William Shakespeare: The Complete Works*, edited by Wells and Taylor, Clarendon Press, Oxford, Second Edition 2005.

1

The Shakespeare Authorship Mystery

What's in a name?
Romeo and Juliet 2.1.85

Who wrote Shakespeare? It has proved to be an enduring mystery.

Anyone coming new to the authorship debate should be aware of how far back in time the plays were written, and the prevailing circumstances which provided much of their source material. The invention of the printing press in the late fifteenth century allowed for the rapid spread of ideas, many of them revolutionary ideas challenging church and state across Europe. The schism in Western Christianity initiated by Martin Luther and John Calvin, known as the Reformation, led swiftly to the establishment of Protestant churches across Northern Europe.

The Church of England under Edward VI in 1547, and Elizabeth I from 1558, struggled to survive in this time of political and religious convulsion. Latin was the international language of scholarship but its close association with Catholicism presented difficulties for a Protestant ruling establishment. The practical advantages of using English to promote the English church accelerated it from a mainly spoken to a written language. University grammarians began to standardise the spelling and structure of English, and to refine its pronunciation. Among these great scholars were Roger Ascham, John Cheke, William Cecil and Thomas Smith.[1] The cultural self-awareness and patriotism generated by this ambitious undertaking advanced the English language sufficiently to begin replacing Latin as the formal medium of communication.

This position was achieved with remarkable speed. The English of the early Tudors is barely comprehensible today but by the second half of Queen Elizabeth's reign, from the 1580s onward, it began to flourish as a fully-fledged literary language capable of almost infinite expressiveness. This was when the first plays now known to be by William Shakespeare, or earlier versions of them, began to appear.

Records from this period are fragmentary but performances of the plays prior to 1623 were staged at Greenwich Palace, Hampton Court, Richmond Palace and Whitehall Palace. Productions were also staged at Gray's Inn, the Inner Temple and the Middle Temple, and at Oxford and Cambridge universities. To a lesser extent they were performed in the public theatres, these being at the Blackfriars, the Curtain, the Globe, Newington Butts, the Rose and the Theatre.

The London publishing industry was still in an early stage of development and many plays were performed, and manuscripts printed, without naming an author or under a pseudonym. Cheaply printed quarto-sized editions of some of the plays, traditionally sold for sixpence a copy, were issued anonymously from 1594 until 1598.[2] The Shakespeare name first appeared on two long narrative poems, *Venus and Adonis* in 1593 and *Lucrece* in 1594, reissued later as *The Rape of Lucrece.* Beginning with *Love's Labour's Lost* in 1598 it then became associated with the plays as well. No one could possibly have guessed then how famous these plays would later become, or that the name William Shakespeare would be one of the best known in the history of the world.

The two most reliable sources of information on the English Renaissance theatre are the Register of the Stationers' Company and the accounts of the Revels Office. Plays in the form of a prompt-book, had to be registered with the Revels Office for licensing purposes. Prompt books contained everything necessary to stage a production, such as cast lists and contact addresses, exits and entrances for the players, props, costumes, and of course the script. The Master of the Revels,[3] an official subordinate of the Lord Chamberlain, authorised plays for performance by issuing a licence. This licence afforded the acting company legal protection and had to be purchased. In the 1590s this was for the substantial fee of seven shillings.[4]

The first collected edition of the plays, *Mr. William Shakespeares Comedies, Histories, & Tragedies,* was published in late November 1623. It is generally now referred to as the 'First Folio' from its larger page size.[5] Some 750 copies are believed to have been printed, of which just over 200 survive in libraries and corporate collections around the world. In contrast to the cheaper quarto editions, great care and expense was taken to produce the First Folio which was offered for sale at one pound a copy. A puritan diatribe against the theatre by William Prynne,[6] his *Histrio-Mastix* published in 1633, complained that 'Shakespeare's plays are printed on the best Crown paper, far better than most Bibles'.[7] Bound and tooled copies of the First Folio were handsome artefacts in their own right, worthy of the contents between the covers. Each copy would have been a prized possession in any library, perhaps why so many have survived.

The First Folio extended to over 900 pages and the labour of the first editors in compiling, editing and completing such a monumental publishing task compels admiration. It was privately printed and circulated by a syndicate headed by Isaac Jaggard (son of the ageing printer William Jaggard) and sponsored by the earls of Pembroke and Montgomery, these being the brothers William Herbert and Philip Herbert. Of the thirty-six plays contained in the Folio none has subsequently proved attributable in its entirety to someone other than Shakespeare, nor has any play excluded from the Folio proved to be entirely written by him. Five plays show evidence of having been co-authored.[8]

Amazingly the First Folio contained eighteen unregistered plays,[9] among them some of the most famous, including *The Tempest, As You Like It, Twelfth Night, The Winter's Tale* and *Macbeth*. Eighteen previously unknown plays by William Shakespeare appearing in a single package must rate as the most sensational publishing event of all time. How and by whom the manuscripts of these plays had been safely preserved for many years prior to publication adds to the mystery of the Shakespeare authorship.[10]

Reprinted editions followed in 1632, 1663 and 1685 but it is the First Folio of 1623 which defined the Shakespeare canon and continues to do so. Performances of the plays after publication of the First Folio were soon overtaken by events, namely the closure of the playhouses between 1642 and 1660, a period covering the English Civil War 1642–1651 and the puritan regime which followed. The restoration of the monarchy in 1660 inspired a new generation of writers and also introduced a more modern form of theatrical presentation. Enclosed theatres, female performers, moveable scenery, lively dialogue and sexually frank situations acted out on stage changed the way in which drama was acted and produced.

The wordy and poetic Shakespeare plays languished until the actor and impresario David Garrick[11] reintroduced them to a discerning London audience from the 1740s onward. This renewed an interest in the plays and aired the first stirrings of curiosity about the author. The name on the title page led straight back to William Shakspere, a businessman from Stratford-upon-Avon in Warwickshire who had invested some money in the newly built (1599) Globe Theatre in London. The similarity of name and vague references to him as an actor were considered sufficient at the time to establish him as the poet and playwright William Shakespeare.

The first edition to carry brief biographical notes came in 1709 (eighty-six years after the First Folio appeared in 1623) when the publisher Nicholas Rowe wrote a short preface, *Some Account of the Life &c of William Shakespeare*. Although little more than a list of the birth, death and marriage registration dates for William Shakspere and his immediate family in Stratford-upon-Avon, the lapse of time and the lack of a credible alternative author was sufficient to ratify this crucial authorship link, a link that has proved hard to break.

The connection was further strengthened when David Garrick staged a 'Stratford Jubilee' in 1769. The Garrick circus from London arrived in Stratford-upon-Avon five years too late to celebrate the bicentenary of William Shakspere's birth in 1564. Garrick had planned a major celebration with a thirty-gun civic salute and the ringing of church bells but the three-day event 6–8th September 1769 was washed out by incessant rain, and by flooding when the River Avon finally burst its banks. Not one Shakespeare play was performed in Stratford during the so-called 'Jubilee'. Garrick restaged the event in London's Drury Lane Theatre where it was well received, running for ninety-two performances.

Although a commercial success, the Jubilee was mocked for its vulgarity and was seen as a celebration of Garrick rather than Shakespeare. Garrick wrote an Ode to promote the show, it contained the phrase 'our matchless Bard', the origin of the famous sobriquet.

But who exactly was the Bard? The first of the great Shakespearean scholars, Edmond Malone,[12] an Irish barrister resident in London, tried to establish dates of composition for the plays so that they could be arranged in a chronological sequence and thus chart the author's artistic development. Malone's seminal essay *An Attempt to Ascertain the Order in which the Plays of Shakspeare* (sic) *Were Written* was published in 1778, some two hundred years after the first versions of the plays began to appear. His attempts to sequence the plays were unsuccessful, and for a reason that drew attention to a vital component of the gathering authorship mystery. Namely that distinguishing early from late proved not to be possible with any degree of certainty because the plays had been many times revised. Whether the revision was completely authorial or shared by others is still a subject for scholarly debate.

In 1790, twelve years after writing his essay, Malone published his own edition of the Shakespeare complete works, in ten volumes. In the introductory volume he stated his intention to write a 'uniform and connected narrative' of Shakespeare's life. To this purpose he visited Stratford-upon-Avon in 1793, having previously received documents by post, including parish registers. The town Corporation, by permission of the Mayor, allowed him a 'complete rummage through all their papers'.[13] Although he identified previously unrecorded documents relating to Shakspere's business dealings in the area, he discovered nothing that linked him to the plays and so abandoned work on his *Life of Shakespeare*. Malone died in 1812 but his literary executor James Boswell (son of Samuel Johnson's biographer), used the archive material to issue the biography in 1821. This was included as part of a new publication known as the *Third Variorum edition of the Works of Shakespeare*.

Edmond Malone's ground-breaking methods of research triggered an interest in the Shakespeare authorship which has lasted until the present day, and set in motion the greatest literary manhunt of all time. Paradoxically all the subsequent painstaking research into the Stratford man's domestic life, business dealings and litigation suits have only served to disconnect him still further from any association with the poetry and plays attributed to William Shakespeare. From the little that is known about him he seems to have been an astute, energetic and opportunistic businessman, a 'wheeler-dealer' to use a modern expression, but scarcely the chronicler of so many kings and queens.

The Victorian ethos of admiration for the self-made man elevated 'The Bard' to almost mythical status as the supreme literary genius of all time. Shakespeare became a brand which was sold around the world, yet many people in this country and others, the United States of America in particular, found it hard to reconcile the epic nature of the plays with the small-town trader who was supposed to have written them. The Education Act of 1870,[14] and the effects of mass literacy working through in the 1880s, resulted in an even wider audience for the Shakespeare plays, and gave fresh momentum to the authorship quest. By this time it was three hundred years since the plays first appeared so the trail was even harder to follow, and it is now more than four hundred years. Academic reluctance and embarrassment over admitting that they may have been lauding the wrong man could explain why questioning the authorship has always been so sensitive.

Although some authors are able to write convincingly without direct experience of their subject matter, relying instead on imagination, background reading and research, applying such a disclaimer to the works of Shakespeare would present difficulties. As would the case for a collegiate authorship. Anyone who has acted in one of the plays, or studied one for an examination, soon becomes familiar with the distinctive Shakespeare sound patterns and word clusters. These are sufficiently consistent across the canon to conjure up the hidden presence of a single powerful guiding intellect, one responsible for creating the forceful speeches and the deftly written poetry which illuminate play after play. The ability to encapsulate complex ideas in a neatly turned phrase, and the consummate facility with words, imagery and language also point to a central main male author. It is almost beyond belief that his identity should remain a mystery.

Later scholars followed Malone's lead by seeking clues from within the plays. Based on the few dates which are known for certain, for example the publication of the long poem *Venus and Adonis* in 1593, the author would have been born in the last half of the 16th century and died in the first half of the 17th century. Some topical allusions in the plays are traceable within this time frame but none that have proved conclusive. More subjectively the texts of the plays were closely examined to see what the contents might reveal about their author, or what additional information could be gained by extrapolation. There was a broad measure of agreement that whoever wrote the plays was so well informed across a wide range of knowledge that he must have been educated to a high standard and read many books, including books not then extant in English. Even more subjectively it exposed the problem of the feudal and aristocratic cast of mind that distinguishes Shakespeare as an author from the work of other dramatists before and since, something not easy to explain.

Although there have been some strong candidates for the Shakespeare authorship (Francis Bacon, Christopher Marlowe, Henry Neville, Mary Sidney and William Stanley among them), claims made on their behalf do not stand up to prolonged scrutiny. The case for Edward de Vere the 17th earl of Oxford has proved more resilient and for almost a century the Oxfordian movement has continued to provide the most closely argued rationale for a convincing alternative author

The authorship debate can be reduced to this question: what sort of person could have written these chronicles of European high feudalism in which the manners and customs of the senior aristocracy are so accurately portrayed? These would include the indoor pastimes of music, dancing and singing, and the outdoor pursuits of hunting, hawking and martial arts. The patrician mode of speech in which the main characters address one another, and the subtle changes they make when addressing subordinates, would most likely have been written by someone to whom this was the natural way of thinking and speaking.

Similarly for the knowledge of courtly protocol. Edward de Vere had attended the wedding of King Henri III of France in 1575 as the representative of Queen Elizabeth. He was on sufficiently good terms with Henry of Navarre to receive a friendly note from him as King Henri IV of France, written 25th September 1594. His brother-in-law Baron Willoughby d'Eresby (married to his sister Lady Mary Vere) was an ambassador to the Danish royal court at Elsinore. His father-in-law Baron Burghley (formerly Sir William Cecil) wielded immense political influence at the court of Queen Elizabeth. This familiarity with the exercise of international statecraft at the highest level, and similarly with the conduct of national governance, if taken together, would make a persuasive case that a high-ranking palace insider was the true author of the plays.

Edward de Vere started out in life with every imaginable privilege. When he was twelve years old his father the 16th earl of Oxford died and Queen Elizabeth brought him to live in London as a ward of court. He was boarded with the family of her principal secretary Sir William Cecil, who was also appointed as his guardian. With his earldom Lord Edward inherited vast estates and wealth, and also the hereditary title of Lord Great Chamberlain. After completing a long formal education, which included studying law at Gray's Inn, he was admitted into the innermost court circle where he enjoyed Queen Elizabeth's friendship as a favoured courtier with family ties through their mutual Howard connections.[15] On 19th December 1571 at the age of twenty-one he was married to the fifteen-year-old Anne Cecil, daughter of his guardian Sir William Cecil, by then ennobled as Lord Burghley.

Marriages between the sons and daughters of aristocrats were brokered in advance to keep as much money and property in the family as possible. On this occasion it was a double wedding, the other couple being Edward Somerset and Lady Elizabeth Hastings.[16] Elizabeth Hastings had been proposed as a suitable bride for Edward de Vere but lost out to Anne Cecil in the marriage negotiations. The Cecil family were steadily gaining political power and there was every prospect that the young earl would take advantage of this alliance and assume his full responsibilities as the holder of one of the great offices of state. A bright future for this fortunate couple seemed guaranteed.

Exactly the opposite happened. By the age of thirty-six Edward de

Vere, 17th earl of Oxford, was disgraced and ruined. He had dissipated his fortune on foreign travel, on business ventures that failed, by establishing and supporting a literary salon, by underwriting theatrical productions, and by heavy debts incurred as a ward of court. He had to be helped out of his financial difficulties by the grant of a charitable annuity from the Queen, so it was downfall on a grand scale. He had fathered a son with his young mistress, Anne Vavasour, one of the Queen's attendant gentlewomen, had been imprisoned in the Tower and exiled from the court. His marriage to Anne Cecil was wretchedly unhappy and her death at the age of thirty-one left him with few friends at court. By the age of forty his health had begun to fail and his surviving letters reveal him as embittered and reclusive, making no secret either of his increasing infirmity or his deeply depressed state of mind.

It is in these tragic circumstances of his personal life that de Vere differs most from the other authorship contenders. The angry misogyny in some of the sonnets and the dark emotional content of many of the plays, are more readily understood if they are known to originate from someone who had suffered in similar measure himself. Frustrated ambition, fear of betrayal, rage, jealousy, disgust at the human condition, the desire for revenge and the bitterness of failure are written out in the plays for all to see and hear, at length and in painful detail. The downfall of great men is a recurrent theme. Progressive mental deterioration leading to insanity and suicidal despair haunt the great tragic plays of *Hamlet, King Lear, Macbeth, Othello* and *Timon of Athens*. Whoever wrote these plays was supremely gifted. They could also be viewed as the product of a deeply disturbed mind.

It has to be conceded at once that after almost a century of exhaustive research into the life of Edward de Vere no direct evidence has been found that would confirm him as the pseudonymous author of Shakespeare. Conversely no evidence has been found that would comprehensively disqualify him, and there would be little that needed to be explained away if he was ever recognised as the true author. This short study will attempt to provide a simply explained introduction to the case for Edward de Vere as the writer William Shakespeare.

2

Formative Years

The Child is father of the Man
William Wordsworth, from The Rainbow

To produce a writer of Shakespeare's capability much would have depended on his formative years. If the case for Edward de Vere has merit then events in his childhood and adolescence may have helped in the development of his talent. As the beneficiary of time and chance he more than once found himself in the right place at the right time, starting with his birth into a life of wealth and privilege at Hedingham Castle in Essex.

This was on Saturday 12th April 1550, he being the son and heir of John de Vere the 16th earl of Oxford by his father's second marriage to Margery Golding. He had an elder sister Lady Katherine Vere by his father's first marriage, and a slightly younger than himself full sister, Lady Mary Vere, whose date of birth is not known for certain. This was during the reign of King Edward VI, and because no other male Vere had been given the name Edward it is likely that he was so named in honour of the king. Edward's courtesy title as the son of an earl was Viscount Bolbec, anglicised as Lord Bulbeck.

The infant nobleman was born into troubled times. The feudal system of governance which had endured for some seven centuries was slowly breaking down as the rapid population growth in the cities of Northern Europe gathered pace. Aided by print technology, the universities began advocating more modern methods of regulating these large urban societies, based on wider representation. Commercially driven maritime exploration had opened up the world and the Reformation had changed for ever the way in which religion could be taught and practised within a western political system.

Such profound changes were subject to the occasional setback and the early death of the staunchly Protestant King Edward VI in 1553 ushered in his elder half-sister Mary Tudor, whose devotion to the Catholic religion directly affected the education and upbringing of the infant Edward de Vere. Mary was based at Framlingham Castle in Suffolk when the young king died at the age of sixteen. Until then she had enjoyed popular support in East Anglia but her extremist views soon became evident, as did the severity with which she would prosecute them against high profile Protestants.

John de Vere, himself a Protestant, was compromised by his obligations as the Lord Lieutenant of Essex to support the sovereign in these early stages, and he did so, at the same time invoking his hereditary right to the office of Lord Great Chamberlain, which had lapsed. This was granted by the new Queen who also restored the office to the Vere family in its hereditary form. John de Vere duly carried the sword of state at her coronation on 30th November 1553.[1] Four days later Queen Mary introduced the legislation that would repeal all the religious laws passed by her predecessor Edward VI.

To remain a Protestant ran the risk of being accused of sedition and treason. Starting in February 1555 some two hundred and eighty leading Protestants, sixty of them women, were executed in the next three years, mostly burned to death. John Rogers[2] who had made a translation of the Bible into English, was the first to die at the stake during Mary's reign. On 4th February 1555 he was 'tested by fire' at Smithfield. The names of Mary's victims were later listed in John Foxe's *Acts and Monuments of the English Martyrs* published in 1563.

It is not known when or exactly why John de Vere, known as Earl John, sent his young son Edward to the home of his friend and Essex neighbour Sir Thomas Smith, a fellow Protestant. Sir Thomas had been a courtier and diplomat under Edward VI but resigned all his offices when Mary succeeded to the throne in 1553. The simplest explanation could be that Thomas Smith's record of scholastic excellence coupled with his availability rendered him attractive as a private tutor for the young son of an earl. Or it may have been a precautionary move by Earl John whose Protestant sympathies could have put him in danger, both for his life and the sequestration of his estates. Placing his son in a place of safety could have been a compelling motive when the execution of leading Protestants began in 1555.

Sir Thomas Smith was a Greek scholar and polymath whose interests included horticulture and herbal medicine. He had been vice chancellor of Cambridge University in 1543 and also Regius Professor of Civil Law, a new discipline necessary to ensure a smooth transition from the superseded system of ecclesiastical law.[3] Sir Thomas was a Fellow of Queens' College Cambridge, and entered Edward there as a student 1558–59. With his second wife he acquired the large residence of Hill Hall in the village of Theydon Mount in Essex and began a long process of renovation. Edward's tuition was at Sir Thomas Smith's other main residence, the manor of Ankerwicke, a former priory overlooking the Thames near Windsor, opposite Runnymede. Sir Thomas resumed his service to the crown when Elizabeth I became queen and until the end of his life was closely involved in affairs of state, as a Principal Secretary and twice as Ambassador to France.

The Veres were a military family with vast estates and property spread over seventeen counties,[4] many of them in the northern part of their home county of Essex. These had been accumulated one by one since 1066 when the first Veres arrived with William I, known as the Conqueror. Edward's father the 16th earl, and his grandfather the 15th earl, both named John de Vere, also maintained a company of touring actors. These were known as Lord Oxford's Men. In 1561, when Edward was aged eleven, the recently crowned (1558) Queen Elizabeth visited his home at Hedingham Castle in Essex as part of her summer progress in East Anglia. Pageants, dancing and plays in the form of interludes and masques were performed at every stop along the way. The singing and dancing roadshow arrived at Hedingham on 9th August 1561, staying for six days. The castle's spacious banqueting hall with its gallery and huge Norman arch would have provided a fitting backdrop for the spectacle. How much contact Edward had with his family's company of actors as a child, or with John Bale his father's writer in residence, is not recorded but since in adult life he involved himself in a range of theatrical activities it could have provided him with his starting point of interest in the performing arts.

Under the Tudors, beginning in 1485 with Henry VII, the old feudal militias were disbanded and the regional nobility were discouraged from acting as warlords. Their fortified strongholds were abandoned one by one, including eventually Hedingham Castle, the ancestral home of the Veres, and replaced with country mansions. Farming, horticulture, estate management and the country sports of hawking and hunting increasingly occupied their time. Had Edward de Vere inherited his earldom as an adult it is likely that these or similar responsibilities and occupations would have had first claim on his time and attention.

Instead, his father the 16th earl died in his forty-sixth year in 1562, when Edward was twelve years old. At the time of his death Earl John still held the office of Lord Great Chamberlain of the Realm of England. This mostly ceremonial appointment had been first conferred on Aubrey de Vere by King Henry I in 1133. The Lord Great Chamberlain's duties were mainly to ensure that great state occasions were carried out with due ceremony, as distinct from the Lord Chamberlain who was the senior paid official responsible for the day-to-day smooth running of the royal household. Although this high office had in the past been shared among other noble families it was inherited on this occasion by Edward de Vere along with his father's other titles and estates.

As an underage nobleman he was promptly summoned to London and entered into the Court of Wards so that his estates could be managed by the crown until he reached the age of majority at twenty-one. As a 17th earl with a famous name, plus his prestigious inherited office of 'High Chamberlain of England', he had his affairs overseen personally by the Queen, and by her secretary Sir William Cecil who was appointed as his guardian. This was the start of a close association with the Cecil family and other members of the court that lasted until the end of his life.

Four days after his father's funeral (at Earls Colne in Essex) the twelve-year-old earl of Oxford arrived in London, on horseback, complete with a retinue of mounted retainers and baggage train, his destination Cecil House in the Strand. The string of horsemen, over a hundred by some reports,[5] had been to Earl John's funeral and were still in black livery. This allows a glimpse into the extraordinary lifestyle to which the boy was already accustomed. In an age when high birth was regarded almost with reverence Edward de Vere's aristocratic status trumped all the rest. His guardian Sir William Cecil was technically a commoner, as had been Queen Elizabeth's mother Anne Boleyn. They were more in awe of him than he was of them.

Nor was this unjustified. If the origins of Shakespeare can be encapsulated into one single overwhelming event it would be in Edward de Vere's almost miraculous and virtually overnight relocation from an obscure hilltop fort in rural Essex straight into Cecil House, the beating heart and centre of Elizabethan London, and at the peak of the Tudor dynasty's political power. It was the equivalent of 10 Downing Street today. He rarely left London again and for the rest of his life remained close to the ruling elite of this great capital city.

Even so, being a royal ward was not as good as it sounded. Many such heirs had the unpleasant experience of discovering that there was very little left for them to inherit when the time came, usually because those appointed to oversee their estates had plundered them first. The greater part of the Vere estates were entrusted to Robert Dudley, the earl of Leicester, and were never fully returned, a cause of much resentment in Edward's adult life. Crippling management charges were often imposed on wards of court, or other forms of coercion applied, such as forced marriages into the guardian's family. Edward had to enter into a large number of bonds to secure his debt to the Court of Wards, putting up his lands as security. He never entirely freed himself from the debts incurred through his nine years as a ward and money troubles pursued him until the end of his life.

A family dispute arose over his legitimacy. When their father died in 1562 his half-sister Lady Katherine Vere (twelve years his senior) and her husband Edward, 3rd Baron Windsor, disputed his right to inherit the Oxford title and claimed that their young son Frederick Windsor was the rightful heir. They believed that Earl John's sudden second marriage to Margery Golding, Edward's mother, was illegal because his estranged first wife Dorothy Neville, daughter of the 4th earl of Westmorland, was still living at the time. Earl John had a complicated love life with several mistresses, and had even gone through a form of marriage with one of them, so the matter was not straightforward and took almost a year to resolve. On 28th June 1563 a rebuttal document was issued from Sir William Cecil's office and the suit failed. Although the challenge to Edward's title had been lost it had nevertheless carried with it the taint of bastardy, something that never quite goes away. For any young man to have his legitimacy questioned would be an unsettling experience; it must have been even more so for a thirteen-year-old boy with everything to lose.

The rebuttal document had been drafted by Arthur Golding who was employed in a secretarial capacity by Sir William Cecil, more specifically as the receiver for those parts of the Vere estates which had not been ceded to the earl of Leicester.[6] Arthur Golding had attended Jesus College, Cambridge, and was also Edward de Vere's uncle, a half-brother to Countess Margery, Edward's mother. It is possible that Arthur tutored his nephew, or acted in a supervisory capacity to ensure that Sir William's daily regimen of study was strictly followed.

In his biography of Edward de Vere the historian B.M. Ward quotes from a preserved document headed, 'Orders for the Earl of Oxford's Exercises'. These began at seven o'clock in the morning with dancing and prayers, continuing until half-past four in the afternoon with a midday break for food and more prayers. Although based around Latin and French it was a broad curriculum with sufficient variety to maintain a young man's interest. It also listed 'cosmography, writing, drawing, and exercises with his pen'. Cosmography would have included astronomy and world geography (the natural sciences) and was taught by Laurence Nowell, a cartographer. Nowell was also an expert in Anglo-Saxon history and literature.

Other young men who were not royal wards also received their education in Sir William Cecil's house, the soldier–poet Philip Sidney (nephew of Robert Dudley earl of Leicester) being the best known. The royal wards later included Robert Devereux earl of Essex and Henry Wriothesley earl of Southampton but Edward de Vere's almost exact contemporary was Edward Manners. He was a year older than de Vere but inherited his title as 3rd earl of Rutland a year later in 1563.

On 11th November 1565 these two young earls, both named Edward, were pages at the wedding of Ambrose Dudley earl of Warwick, elder brother to the earl of Leicester. The two Edwards were also together when, as former students at the university, they received honorary MA degrees from Cambridge in 1564. Two years later they received similar degrees from Oxford University.[7] Richard Edwards, Master of the Children of the Chapel, was part of the Queen's entourage for the Oxford visit and he staged *Palamon and Arcite*, a two-part play based on Chaucer's *The Knight's Tale*. To what extent the sixteen-year-old Edward de Vere collaborated in this production is not known but it surfaced later as *The Two Noble Kinsmen* with Palamon and Arcite as the main characters. When first published in 1634 the title page gave John Fletcher and William Shakespeare as the joint authors. *The Two Noble Kinsmen* is included in the Oxford Shakespeare Complete Works where the introductory notes are written by Professor William Montgomery. He defends the contributions claimed for Shakespeare (mainly Acts 1 and 5) as 'characteristic of his late style'. A revised version by William Davenant and retitled as *The Rivals* was performed in 1664.

Arthur Golding was also in residence at Cecil House, and while there he began his translation of Ovid's *Metamorphoses*, a work which all scholars agree was drawn on by Shakespeare for many classical allusions.

The first edition was published in 1567 when Golding was thirty-one and his nephew Edward de Vere by this time seventeen. If judged by his early poetry de Vere was a skilful writer in English and even if he did not assist in the translation he certainly knew it line by line when writing plays in adult life. Its inventive felicity of language has ensured an enduring appeal for this early masterwork in English. In the course of his life Golding rendered many other Latin texts into English but Oxfordian supporters consider these to be less inspired translations, lacking the linguistic originality and sparkle of *Metamorphoses*. The extent to which the young de Vere collaborated with his uncle in translating Ovid is a theory which can never be proved but he was on the spot and sufficiently proficient in Latin for it to be offered as a possibility.

The poet and critic Ezra Pound considered Golding's translation, 'the most beautiful book in the English language'.[8] Professor Kenneth Muir in his *The Sources of Shakespeare's Plays* is less complimentary and considered it an imperfect translation, referring to its 'clumsiness' and inaccuracy. Muir also expressed his belief that the author known as William Shakespeare was a better Latinist than Arthur Golding, citing passages from *The Tempest* where the Ovid quotations are from the original Latin rather than from the translation. Muir writes, 'Even at the end of his career, thirty years after he left school, he (Shakespeare) still remembered enough Latin to improve on the accuracy of Golding's translation.' If Edward de Vere is substituted as the author and superior Latin scholar then Muir's observation could be valid.

In July 1567 aged seventeen Edward de Vere killed his guardian's servant Thomas Brincknell in the grounds of Cecil House. Edward had been fencing with another man, practising their use of the newly introduced rapier, a long-range stabbing weapon. It was customary to practise with a protective ferrule on the tip of the blade but apparently not so on this unfortunate occasion. Thomas Brincknell, described in Sir William Cecil's diary as an 'under-cook' and believed to be drunk, had somehow run on to the point of the earl's sword. A coroner's jury considered that the cook had in effect committed suicide and the matter was quickly hushed up.

Raphael Holinshed the historian served on the jury that acquitted de Vere. He was another fellow resident at Cecil House and the first edition of his famous *Chronicles* would be published ten years later in 1577. This links together Arthur Golding's translation of Ovid's *Metamorphoses*, Holinshed's *Chronicles* and the History plays of Shakespeare. They can all be traced back to Sir William Cecil, his well-stocked library, and his extended student family at Cecil House in London.

Sir William's entourage included many university graduates. A formal education was required of all who aspired to rise in the government service, plus legal training for those with estates to administer when their education was complete. Cecil's own legal expertise had been acquired at Gray's Inn in London and this was where the two Edwards were sent to

19

receive theirs, Edward de Vere enrolling in 1567. After this their education was considered to have been completed and as with all students, it was then up to them what they did with the rest of their lives.

In 1568, when he was eighteen, Edward de Vere's mother Countess Margery died at the age of forty-three. Following the death of Earl John in 1562 she had remarried, her second husband being Charles Tyrrell, a retired country gentleman with connections to the earl of Leicester's family. There is no record of any correspondence between mother and son, or written evidence that Edward attended her funeral in Earls Colne where she was entombed with her first husband, John de Vere.

In November 1569 Sir William Cecil masterminded the campaign to subdue the so-called 'Rising of the North'. This was an attempt by the earls of Northumberland and Westmorland as Catholic nobles to depose Elizabeth by declaring for Mary Queen of Scots. Cecil appointed Thomas Radcliffe earl of Sussex to the command of an army, and to demonstrate his commitment to the Protestant cause also sent both his sons. These were Thomas Cecil by his first wife Mary Cheke, and Robert Cecil by his second wife Mildred Cooke. His ward Edward Manners 3rd earl of Rutland was sent as well. Edward de Vere also followed the army north but several weeks later in 1570, having been previously incapacitated with an illness which had kept him housebound for several months. How much actual fighting he saw, or was involved in himself, is not recorded. Even so he had travelled with an army and witnessed the brutal suppression which followed. Towns were burned and castles ransacked as a deterrent to any other dissident faction planning to mount a challenge to the Protestant regime in London.

The nature of the illness de Vere suffered in the winter months 1569–70 is unknown but in view of the mental depression he reveals in his later letters to Robert Cecil this has to be considered a possibility. He went into retreat by renting rooms at Windsor and seems to have occupied himself with buying and reading books. Records of his purchases from the London bookseller William Seres during this period include a Chaucer, a Plutarch in the French translation by Jacques Amyot and a Geneva Bible. This Bible with marginalia in de Vere's distinctive handwriting is now in the Folger Library in Washington.

The privilege of an education in the great houses of Sir Thomas Smith and Sir William Cecil has to be measured against the early deaths of Edward's parents and the loss of a childhood in the family home. The long-term effects on a sensitive mind may be guessed at but can never be known with certainty. Lacking a father as well as a mother the dominant male influence in Edward de Vere's life had been provided by the two stern Protestant grandees mentioned above, in whose households he spent his formative years, and where many hours of every day were occupied in compulsory study. When considering the carefully constructed dialogue in the Shakespeare plays this early exposure to the legal mind and formal manner of speech from infancy onward could provide an explanation for how such dialogue came to be so well and authentically written.

Cecil House in the Strand was huge, a double-courtyard brick-built three-storey palace with corner turrets, standing in grounds extending as far north as Covent Garden. On the west side were a service courtyard and kitchen gardens, to the east were located the stables and also tenement buildings to house the huge number of servants employed. The eastern side of the house featured a long narrow bowling alley and a covered tennis court. Formal quadripartite gardens, a private garden, an orchard with a belvedere, and a covered arcade (loggia), provided recreational facilities for family and friends.

Sir William Cecil, the Queen's principal private secretary, who also happened to be chancellor of Cambridge University, took life and learning seriously. As did his second wife Mildred, a scholar in her own right, and a speaker of classical Greek.[9] As hosts to visiting dignitaries and ambassadors this formidable couple would have created a favourable impression of the calibre of Queen Elizabeth's administration. Opulent, famous and politically astute, William Cecil was the founder of a dynasty that would last until the present time. Edward de Vere dined every day at the great man's table and had only to sit still and listen to learn the language of statecraft at first hand. We hear it in every play.

It is in similarly large, lavishly appointed houses that the Shakespeare plays are mostly set. Learned discourse, the leisure pursuits of the well-to-do, including music and dancing, and the formal botanical gardens where they took their ease, serve as the natural background canvas to many of the plays. Writers write about what they know, and these were the privileged surroundings that the author of Shakespeare knew best. If writers need luck in the provision of an inexhaustible supply of privileged source material then the young earl of Oxford had it in abundance. The poet Ezra Pound, quoted earlier, also wrote, 'All great art is born of the metropolis'. This would prove true for Edward de Vere who found himself in the right place at the right time, the rapidly expanding and cosmopolitan city of London.

By now aged twenty he had reached the end of his formative years. He had received a first-rate education, he had enjoyed access to some of the best privately owned libraries in the land, at Cambridge University, at Gray's Inn in London and in the homes of his two mentors Thomas Smith and William Cecil. He was competent in Latin and French, he had seen service with the military, and would soon come into his inheritance and take his seat in the House of Lords. He was a fortunate young man with many career options.

At the same time it was becoming obvious to those around him that Edward de Vere was not suited to the discipline of a career at court. In a society where rank was strictly observed it was unwise to criticise too openly the behaviour of an aristocrat, particularly one highly placed and the holder of an office, even if a mainly ceremonial office. Those who did so chose their words carefully. Reading between the lines de Vere's detractors seem to be describing what we might today call a 'free spirit', someone impatient of restrictions and determined to go his own way whatever the consequences.

Unflattering references to de Vere's character will be considered in more detail later, as cumulatively they adversely affected his reputation, and have stiffened resistance to his Shakespeare candidacy in modern times. Among those who wrote disparagingly about the earl were the courtier Gilbert Talbot, later 7th earl of Shrewsbury, Charles Arundel a member of the Howard family, and Gabriel Harvey a writer and noted scholar.[10] The French ambassador Bertrand de Salignac Fénélon, seigneur de la Mothe[11] (served 1568–1575) in his *Memoires touchant l'Angleterre* was a shrewd observer of Queen Elizabeth's court, and by publishing abroad was not subject to censorship by the Lord Chamberlain's office.

The concept of maritime England with its indomitable queen and adventurous sea captains has long captured the public imagination. The New World had been discovered, trade flourished as never before, the English language had begun its global march and the professional theatre would soon have an insatiable demand for new material. It is hard to think of a better time, or a better city, in which a gifted young man with a compulsion to write could develop his talent.

3

Troubled Times

Uneasy lies the head that wears a crown.
2 Henry IV, 3.1.31

Edward de Vere's life was bounded by two seismic events, one beneficial, the other less so, but both contributing to his development as a writer of world-class drama. The pan-European Renaissance provided him with the wonderful new world of learning and thought. The Reformation obliged him to live with the grim reality of religious intolerance.

The spread of Protestant churches in northern Europe prompted the Dutch War of Independence, a revolt in the Habsburg Netherlands against the Catholic occupiers led by Philip II of Spain. This proved to be no weekend skirmish but a war that would last for eighty years, from 1568 until 1648.[1] It would claim the lives of Edward de Vere's immediate descendants,[2] also several of his friends and fellow courtiers. News of Spanish brutality against the civilian populations of the northern provinces in the Netherlands provoked anti-Catholic feelings in England. Queen Elizabeth was conciliatory towards her Catholic nobles but the Protestant hardliners led by William Cecil and Francis Walsingham were uncompromising in their hostility to anyone suspected of being insufficiently supportive of their regime.

Cecil's firm handling of the northern rebellion at home triggered an angry response from the Vatican. Pope Pius V issued a Papal Bull (edict) dated 25th February 1570 with the title *Regnans in Excelsis*. This held Queen Elizabeth personally responsible for the brutal suppression of the Catholic uprising in the north of England and Scotland. He excommunicated her as being of illegitimate birth, and a heretic. The edict went further by warning that any Catholics who recognised her position as head of the church in England would be similarly expelled. At the same time absolution was offered in advance to any potential assassin, who would be seen as performing a dutiful act.

It was against this fraught background that Edward de Vere came into his inheritance on 12th April 1571. Eight months later he was married off to his guardian's daughter, Anne Cecil. The marriage of any aristocrat where titles, country estates, town property and large sums of money were at stake could be the subject of lengthy negotiations. In a patriarchal society there was often little consideration for the feelings of the young people involved, the young women in particular, some scarcely more than children. Philip Sidney had been proposed as a suitable husband for Anne

23

Cecil but he was poor, as well as a commoner.

On 25th February 1571 William Cecil was elevated to the peerage as Baron of Burghley, from then on signing himself as William Burghley. Edward de Vere was an eligible bachelor, Anne was now the daughter of a lord, so the disparity in rank was no longer an issue and their wedding took place in December 1571. In a letter from Lord Burghley to Sir Francis Walsingham he gives the date of the wedding as Wednesday 19th and adds that the Queen had honoured the ceremony with her presence.

Edward was twenty-one at the time of his marriage. On 5th December, a fortnight before the wedding, Anne had reached her fifteenth birthday. The new husband and wife were well known to one another since they had both grown up in her father's house but it was not a successful marriage and brought much unhappiness to the Cecil family. Exactly why has never been satisfactorily explained. A contributing factor could have been Edward's annoyance and disappointment when his new father-in-law did not remit or clear his substantial livery fees immediately after the marriage. Whether this was a misunderstanding on his part, or intransigence on Burghley's part as Master of the Court of Wards, the marriage never recovered from this inauspicious beginning.

Even in an age when a bride of fifteen was not unusual, and even if it was an arranged wedding rather than a love match, it is still difficult centuries later to unravel the circumstances surrounding Edward de Vere's unhappy marriage to Anne Cecil or to apportion blame. The bride's parents in this case repay closer scrutiny. William and Mildred Cecil owned and presided over three palatial households, at Burghley House in Lincolnshire, at Theobalds in Hertfordshire and Burghley House in London. They expected and received, instant obedience and deference from the huge numbers of officials and servants they employed. The domestic regime they presided over at their London home was puritanical in the extreme, with the young wards entrusted to their care very firmly kept in their place. It may have been for their own good, and served them well as career preparation, but it is unlikely that any of them found it an enjoyable experience.

Lord Burghley held the purse strings as well as having the whip hand. Neither he nor his wife Mildred was much inclined towards compromise. As a matriarch Mildred was no less intimidating, both as a mother and a mother-in-law, and she too was accustomed to being obeyed. Few would doubt that the docile Anne Cecil was a virgin at the time of her marriage, possibly an unprepared virgin with no expectation of what would be required of her as a wife. Edward had likewise spent his childhood and formative years under constant supervision and surveillance in the stern Protestant households of Sir Thomas Smith and Sir William Cecil. The possibility exists that he too was sexually inexperienced which could explain the failure of the marriage to develop normally.

The young couple's first home was in the Savoy, a former royal palace converted to a hospital and then let out as apartments. A few months later they were mentioned as living at Wivenhoe, an Essex seashore residence forming part of the Vere estates. Some years later when Edward had returned from his continental journeys and rejected his wife, Lord Burghley met the earl in an effort to analyse the reasons for the estrangement and facilitate a reconciliation. In surviving notes Burghley lists de Vere's complaint, among others, that his mother-in-law (Mildred Cecil, Lady Burghley) had earlier removed her daughter Anne from the marital home at Wivenhoe. Lady Burghley's reason for doing so is not specified but as Anne was unhappy and still not pregnant it could indicate that the physical content of the relationship was still inhibiting both partners in the marriage. Anne ended up back with her parents, at their homes of Theobalds House in Hertfordshire and Burghley House in London. Worse was to follow in the years to come as this unhappy marriage ran its course.

A complicating factor could have been the imprisonment of Edward de Vere's cousin Thomas Howard, the 4th duke of Norfolk. This arose as a direct response from the excommunication of Queen Elizabeth by the Vatican. The queen's hold on power, not strong at this stage in her reign, was threatened by the existence of a credible alternative head of state. This was Mary Stuart, Queen Mary I of Scotland and the great-niece of Henry VIII. Mary already had a son (the future James I and VI) and was capable of producing another if a husband of suitable rank could be provided, with the Catholic duke of Norfolk as the leading marriage contender. Sir William Cecil was determined that no such marriage would ever take place. By now appointed as Queen Elizabeth's principal secretary of state, and with his position at court consolidated by his forceful action against the northern rebellion, Cecil perceived the duke as a danger to the Protestant regime and sought his execution. Accused of scheming to marry Mary Stuart, and of complicity in the September 1571 Ridolfi plot[3] to assassinate Queen Elizabeth, the duke was beheaded on Tower Hill on 2nd June 1572 aged thirty-six.

Thomas Howard was Edward de Vere's cousin, the son of his aunt Frances Vere, Countess of Surrey. He was the highest ranking nobleman in the land, the hereditary Earl Marshal and a cousin to the Queen whose grandmother had been Lady Elizabeth Howard, the mother of Anne Boleyn. This did not save him from the block. Edward's friendship and staunch support for his Catholic cousin was a conflict of interest that came at an awkward time, overlapping as it did the marriage negotiations with Anne Cecil and their first year as husband and wife. The incarceration and cruel death of such a close relative, engineered and forced through by his father-in-law, was not calculated to improve what was already a failing marriage, even less so as Anne was likely to have taken the side of her authoritarian father in matters relating to religion and state affairs. Since Burghley did not foresee, or chose to disregard, his son-in-law's appalled reaction to the death of his cousin it follows that he should bear some responsibility for the early breakdown of his daughter's marriage.

The Tudors had always been despotic rulers. Queen Elizabeth and her Cecil henchmen, William followed by his son Robert, were brutal tyrants by today's standards. De Vere's failure to obtain clemency for his cousin exposed the weakness of his position when it encountered the clenched fist of political might. By not pursuing a conventional career at court he had ruled himself out of contention and so would never himself be a member of the governing elite. Nevertheless by not returning to his Essex castle and lording it over his estates, choosing instead to stay on in London, he remained close to the scene of action. Close enough to write convincingly about how crowned heads and their enforcers conducted the nation's business.

The year 1572 had not started well for Lord Burghley whose health was beginning to fail at the age of fifty-two. He was incapacitated by gout and fell ill, most likely from exhaustion after years of constant work and responsibility. But he recovered and in April, following the death of the marquis of Winchester, he was appointed Lord High Treasurer, the top government post, with control of the Exchequer.[4] A Garter Knighthood went with this promotion and on 18 June 1572 he was formally installed into the mystic brotherhood of the Garter Knights gathered for their annual ceremony at Windsor Castle.

A drawing made at this prestigious event by the exiled Flemish painter Marcus Gheeraerts the Elder (1520–1590) shows the earl of Oxford in his capacity as Lord Great Chamberlain carrying the sword of state as he preceded Queen Elizabeth into St George's Chapel. De Vere and the Queen were the last two after a long procession of knights and court-iers. If the drawing is an accurate representation it shows the earl to be fractionally shorter than Queen Elizabeth. Her height is unknown but has been estimated from her costumes and portraits to have been five feet four inches, about

The Earl of Oxford bearing the Sword of State at the Garter ceremony, Windsor Castle, 18 June 1572.

average for the period. This would make Edward de Vere a man of small stature if drawn to scale.

Sir Thomas Smith was promoted into Burghley's former post and became the new Principal Secretary of State. Edward de Vere's two educators and mentors were thus still hard at work, still serving their country and still advancing their careers while their erstwhile pupil at this stage had little to show in return for their efforts on his behalf.

The religious divide widened still further two months later. French Huguenots (Calvinist Protestants) had gathered in Paris for a wedding between the Catholic Margaret Valois and the Protestant Henry III of Navarre. This had been arranged by Margaret's brother Charles IX in an attempt to reconcile these divisions within the church and French society. Four days after the wedding, on 24th August 1572, mob violence directed at the gathered Protestants escalated into a full scale massacre. This spread outwards from Paris, continued for several weeks and resulted in several thousand deaths, most of them Protestant. News of these terrible events, which became known as the St Bartholomew's Day Massacre, made Protestants elsewhere fearful and angry. In England this slaughter hardened attitudes against any form of attempted subversion by Catholic conspirators to topple Queen Elizabeth.

Edward de Vere was sufficiently roused to write an impassioned letter to his father-in-law Lord Burghley, pledging his support for the Protestant cause. This letter, written in September 1572, urged Burghley as the leading English Protestant to guard against any attempt on his life. The brutal suppression in Paris had been sparked by the murder of Admiral Gaspard de Coligny,[5] the Huguenot leader. De Vere feared for the consequences if Burghley, his Protestant counterpart in England, was similarly assassinated.

Although suspicions of Catholic sympathies lingered around de Vere for the rest of his life they were mainly based on his unsuccessful attempts to gain a reprieve for his cousin the duke of Norfolk. That he had acted out of family loyalties rather than for ideological reasons mitigated his perceived offence. Paradoxically this close association and support for his executed Catholic cousin may have helped to facilitate his travels on the continent of Europe 1575–76.

Living through troubled times confers insight and understanding when applying the experiences of the present to events in the past. The eight History plays which chart the dynastic struggles king by king from Richard II murdered in 1400 to Richard III slain in battle 1485 are among the finest in the canon. These stirring chronicles of civil war with pitched battles, murders, treachery and brutal regime change are written in language which is powerful but which also contains long passages of a lyrical nature. The many forward-striding speeches create a brooding sense of momentum as the grim historical events unfold. The ability to marshal the large numbers of noble characters featured in the eight plays, and to make coherent the shifting alliances between them, required theatrical and writing expertise of the highest order.

Whoever wrote these plays about the so-called 'Wars of the Roses' possessed extraordinary creative powers. The Oxfordian case is that de Vere's wide-ranging education, his access to libraries, and the availability of the 1577 edition of Holinshed's *Chronicles*, were sufficient to allow him to write the first drafts as a young man in his twenties. The Veres had a long and proud military tradition and even if Edward's involvement in the campaign led by the earl of Sussex to extinguish the Rising of the North had not been long or noteworthy he had at least witnessed at first hand the harsh reality of military action.

His ancestor the 12th earl of Oxford had been beheaded during a period of Yorkist supremacy. The 13th earl had been an army commander on the winning side at the battle of Bosworth. As a descendant and kinsman of the many noble families locked in these bitter disputes over succession to the throne he was better placed than most to write knowledgeably about them, and to emerge as the most notable chronicler of this greatly troubled time in British history.

4

Early Work

A rare talent!
Love's Labour's Lost 4.2.63

No authenticated juvenilia by William Shakespeare has ever come to light. To account for the missing early work it is necessary to show that Edward de Vere was capable of producing high quality writing in his teens and early twenties.

In 1564 his uncle Arthur Golding had dedicated a translation from a Latin text to his fourteen-year-old nephew. This was his *Abridgement of the Histories of Trogus Pompeius* and he prefaced it with praise for the young earl's knowledge of history. Golding then dedicated his 1567 translations of the first four books of Ovid's *Metamorphoses* to Robert Dudley the earl of Leicester but the exceptionally felicitous quality of this translation has always excited comment. Whether the precocious young earl assisted his uncle in a master and pupil collaboration can only be speculative but the idea merits serious consideration when seeking Shakespeare juvenilia. Golding's reference to his nephew's interest in history may also be relevant because some early anonymous plays are concerned with British history, among them *Edmund Ironside*, a play which contains some Shakespeare fingerprints.

De Vere entered Gray's Inn in London as a law student in February 1567, immediately establishing a link to the plays of Shakespeare where legal terms and concepts are a conspicuous feature of the writing. Still under the stern supervision of his lawyer guardian Sir William Cecil, he could have acquired sufficient legal training to supply an explanation for the knowledge of law contained within the plays, even though he never subsequently practised as an advocate. As a landowner, a grasp of legal capability would have been essential so it is likely that he would have taken his studies seriously.

In 1568 a play with the title *Horestes* was performed at Gray's Inn. This was in part a morality play based on William Caxton's translation from the French of *Historyes of Troye* rather than from Aeschylus and the *Oresteia Trilogy*. Horestes is forgiven for the murder of his mother and her lover in this early Tudor revenge tragedy. (*Hamlet* being the ultimate mother-lover Tudor revenge tragedy). *Horestes* was attributed to a John Pykering about whom nothing is known and so could have been a pseudonym used by de Vere (or another) to conceal the writer's identity. *Horestes* was the first play to make use of the soliloquy as a means of conveying the actor's thoughts to an audience, something which became a feature of Shakespeare's stagecraft writing. The plays of George Gascoigne, a former student at Gray's Inn, were regularly performed there, including his comedy *The Supposes,* translated from Ludovico Ariosto's Italian play *Suppositi.* There were two versions, the first in prose, the second in verse, and they provided the Lucentio–Bianca sub-plot for *The Taming of the Shrew.*

Two foreign translations have Shakespeare connections and Edward de Vere was involved in both cases. The first of these foreign sources was Baldesar Castiglione's *Il Cortegiano* (*The Courtier*) translated in 1572 from Italian into Latin by Bartholomew Clerke.[1] De Vere contributed a prefatory letter, also in Latin. This book had previously been translated into English by Sir Thomas Hoby. He was another Essex landowner, a graduate of St John's College, Cambridge, and had included Italy in his grand tour of the continent as a young man. His wife Elizabeth Cooke was sister to Mildred Cooke, Lord Burghley's second wife. His four volume translation *The Courtyer of Count Baldessar Castilio* was published in 1561 and was intended to provide a complete philosophy of life and conduct for the perfect Elizabethan gentleman. Of interest is that Hoby's second son was named Posthumus, the name used for a main character in the Shakespeare play *Cymbeline.*

Edward de Vere's first published poem, *The Earle of Oxenforde to the Reader,* appeared in Thomas Bedingfield's 1573 translation from the Italian of *Cardanus Comforte,* a collection of philosophical essays by Girolomo Cardano. De Vere commissioned the English translation by Thomas Bedingfield[2] which was published in 1573 as *Cardan's Comfort.* He also contributed a long prefatory letter in English to the book, which Bedingfield had dedicated to him. Textual analysts (Geoffrey Bullough,[3] Harold Jenkins[4]) have identified this as the book Hamlet carries about with him and quotes from in his 'To be, or not be' speech.

The final words spoken by King Richard in the play *Richard II,* 'Mount, mount my soul; thy seat is up on high / While my gross flesh sinks downwards, here to die' (5. 5. 111–112) are similar to the final sentence of Edward de Vere's prefatory letter to Bedingfield's book. 'For when all things shall else forsake us, virtue yet will ever abide with us, and when our bodies fall into the bowels of the earth, yet that shall mount with our minds into the highest heavens.' A penitent King Claudius at prayer in *Hamlet* says, 'My words fly up, my thoughts remain below'. (3.3.97).

These two short pieces of prose writing, the English translation of de Vere's preface in Latin to *Il Cortegiano* and his preface in English to *Cardan's Comfort,* although a slender offering would not be unworthy of a fledgling Shakespeare. Without extrapolating too much from too little these essays have a high seriousness, and are written in an authoritative manner for one so young.

An anthology of poems published anonymously in 1573 with the title

A Hundreth Sundrie Flowres appears to be the work of several young courtiers using their initials, or Latinised pen-names known as 'posies'. The verse is not serious, much of it indelicate allusions to ladies of the court, but some is of a semi-dramatic nature calling for a response. Included are contributions attributed to Edward de Vere, George Gascoigne and Christopher Hatton, who used the posy *'Felix Infortunatus'*. The anthology was quickly pruned to remove offending material and reissued as *The Posies of George Gascoigne, Esquire*. Hatton's pen name identifies him as Malvolio in *Twelfth Night*.

In another anthology eight poems signed 'E.O.' are attributed to Edward, earl of Oxford. This was compiled by Richard Edwards, Master of the Children of the Chapel Royal. Edwards died the next year in 1567 but his anthology with the title *The Paradise of Dainty Devices* was not published until ten years later. The eight Oxford poems it contains would thus have been written when the earl was still a teenager. Three more appeared in *England's Parnassus* published in 1600. Scholars disagree about how many of his other poems can be identified as authentic. Katherine Chiljan in her 1998 collection *Letters and Poems of Edward, Earl of Oxford* lists twenty-six poems obtained from printed and other sources, including the Rawlinson manuscripts in the Bodleian Library. Edward de Vere's biographer Thomas Looney listed twenty poems in his 1921 collection[5] *The poems of Edward De Vere, seventeenth earl of Oxford*. Professor Steven W. May of Georgetown College, Kentucky (not an Oxfordian) limited these to sixteen in a 1980 edition *The Poems of Edward De Vere, Seventeenth Earl of Oxford*.[6] In a later publication, *The Elizabethan Courtier Poets*, published by the University of Missouri in 1992, Professor May considers that the poem 'My mind to me a kingdom is,' attributed to the courtier poet Sir Edward Dyer, was more probably written by Edward de Vere.

No dates of composition are available for any of the poems but they would appear to be early work and some seem intended as song lyrics. How should they be assessed? Are they mediocre and unworthy of William Shakespeare? Opinion varies, but then the poems and song lyrics contained in the Shakespeare plays are also of variable quality. Two Oxfordian scholars, Louis P Benezet an American, and Edward Holmes who was British, both compiled hybrid poems interweaving lines or stanzas taken alternately from the poems of Shakespeare and Edward de Vere and challenged readers to tell them apart. It can't be done. Whether the same hand wrote both remains open to interpretation but the de Vere poems cannot be easily discounted on stylometric evidence alone. They could well pass muster as examples of early work by the writer known as William Shakespeare.

If Edward de Vere, born in 1550, was actively writing for the stage before leaving for Italy in 1575, and resumed soon after his return the following year, then the blossoming of Elizabethan literary talent could have started by the 1580s, preceding Spenser, Sidney, Lyly and later,

Marlowe. Golding's translation of Ovid's *Metamorphoses* had been available since 1567, the first edition of Holinshed's *Chronicles* appeared in 1577, both providing Shakespeare source material. Most of the alternative authors, including the man from Stratford-upon-Avon born in 1564, would have been too young, hence the orthodox preference for the 1590s as the decade in which the Elizabethan literary revolution began to flourish. The case for Oxfordian primacy and leadership is made most strongly by Richard Malim in his book *The Earl of Oxford and the Making of 'Shakespeare'*.

There exists a Shakespeare apocrypha of unattributed early plays, or parts of plays, some of which were later subsumed into the canonical plays. In the American *Encyclopedia of Shakespeare* compiled by Charles Boyce the entry under 'Oxford' reads

> English aristocrat, poet and playwright. Oxford was a patron of poets and players and wrote verse and plays himself. John Lyly was his secretary and wrote plays for his (Oxford's) boys' company. Oxford's own plays are lost.

Lost, or misattributed? Reference has already been made (in Chapter 2) to the early play *Palamon and Arcite* based on Chaucer's *The Knight's Tale*, reappearing later as *The Two Noble Kinsmen*. It was performed before the Queen at Oxford University in 1566, the royal visit to Oxford when Edward de Vere received his MA degree. The play was produced by the choirmaster Richard Edwards, mentioned above for his anthology *The Paradise of Dainty Devices*. Could the young graduate have written or collaborated in writing the earlier play? Francis Meres in his 1598 *Palladis Tamia* links Edwards and Oxford together as 'best for comedy'. Lines from *Palamon and Arcite* also found their way into *Romeo and Juliet*. In an exchange with the musicians in Act 4 the Capulet retainer Peter sings some lines from *Palamon*, 'In Commendation of Music', beginning, 'When griping grief the heart doth wound'. (4.4.152–54). Although tenuous, it remains a link from de Vere to a Shakespeare play.

Edmund Ironside has never found acceptance in the Complete Works but it remains an outside candidate for inclusion. *Edmund Ironside,* or *War Hath Made All Friends* is about the Saxon king Edmund II who succeeded to the throne on the death of his father, known as Ethelred the Unready. This was in April 1016 but seven months later he was overthrown by the Danish king Canute. The play records the ongoing conflict between Edmund and Canute, complicated by a traitorous nobleman named Edricus. This play has no discernible Italian influence and so could be dated as written prior to Oxford's continental travels 1575–76. Similarity of plot and some Shakespearean word clusters raise the possibility that *Edmund Ironside* could be an earlier version of *Titus Andronicus*.

A black comedy listed in the Court Revels for 1579 as *Murderous*

Michael could have referred to *Arden of Faversham*. This play was based on the real life murder of the London merchant Thomas Arden in 1551. Issued anonymously, the play has a Shakespeare link in the character of the victim's wife, Alice Arden. She conspired with her lover to arrange for her husband's murder and by washing the blood from her hands forces comparison with Lady Macbeth. Both murderous wives have been considered as inspired by Catherine de Medici (mother of Charles IX of France) who gave the order to unleash the St Bartholomew's Day massacre of French Protestants. The two bungling assassins in the play are named Black Will and George Shakebag. William Shakespeare and Thomas Kyd have both been touted as possible authors for this domestic tragedy set in the small market town of Faversham in Kent. Unusually for the period this was a play with no tie-in to classical literature or ancient history.

Several of the canonical plays were preceded by anonymous plays with sufficient similarity of plot or title to be considered as stemming from the same source, and possibly from the same pen. The anonymous *The Troublesome Raigne of King John* is sufficiently close to Shakespeare's *King John* to have been by the same hand. Question, was *The Chronicle of King Leir* an early version of *King Lear* or a separate play on the same theme by another writer? We shall never know. The early play *The Taming of a Shrew* predated *The Taming of the Shrew*. The early play *Edward III* was once considered only borderline Shakespeare but is now included in the Oxford Complete Works. Also included is the manuscript play *Sir Thomas More*,[7] the main contributor being Edward de Vere's former secretary Anthony Munday.

The Famous Victories of Henry the Fifth was registered in 1594 and published in 1598, on both occasions without an author's name. This was a beginner's play. If by Edward de Vere it had no Italian or legal content and so could have been written before he enrolled at Gray's Inn to study law at the age of seventeen. This short play was later expanded into the two parts of *Henry IV,* and *Henry V*, three much admired plays in the Shakespeare repertoire.

A short play known as *Thomas of Woodstock* was possibly intended as the first part of *Richard II*, which opens in the manner of a sequel. *Nobody and Somebody* had similarities connecting it to *Antony and Cleopatra*. A play *The Spanish Maze* could be an earlier version of *The Tempest*, written at a time when anti-Spanish feeling was intensifying. Quarrels between the ducal families of Naples and Milan, both Spanish possessions at the time, were used on the English stage as examples of Spanish cruelty and treachery.

In 1619 the printer William Jaggard, in collaboration with Thomas Pavier, published a collection of ten Shakespeare plays. These included *A Yorkshire Tragedy* and *Sir John Oldcastle* neither of which have found acceptance in the Oxford Complete Works. Sir John Oldcastle was a Lollard and actively promoted this early but extreme form of anticlericalism, for which he was hanged and his body burned in 1417. In *The Famous Victories of Henry V* the 'fat knight' is shown as a drinking companion of the king and appears under his own name of Oldcastle. Only when rewritten as the two parts of Henry IV does he morph into Sir John Falstaff.

In March 1573 a murder arising from a domestic dispute took place on Shooters Hill near Greenwich.[8] The victim was a London merchant named George Saunders and the murderer was an Irishman named George Brown. Because Brown had once been employed by Edward de Vere as a servant, the case received more publicity than it might have done otherwise. De Vere's uncle Arthur Golding and the historian Raphael Holinshed both issued statements exonerating him from any involvement in the Shooters Hill murder. That the young playwright, and the historian whose *Chronicles* would make both their names famous, were known to one another is a direct link to the plays. As fellow residents at Cecil House they would have had equal access to Sir William's large library which provided much of the common source material for Holinshed's *Chronicles* as well as the History plays of Shakespeare.

Five of de Vere's servants were involved in another serious incident which Lord Burghley recorded in his diary for 21st May 1573. Three of the servants were still employed by the earl, the other two, William Faunt and John Wotton, now worked for his father-in-law, Lord Burghley. Faunt and Wotton were forced out of London by the other three and chased on to the road between Rochester and Gravesend. Here they were overtaken by the three pursuers, bullets being discharged from calivers, an early form of musket. Faunt and Wotton fought them off and the three attackers rode back to London 'with all possible speed'. William Faunt reported the incident to Lord Burghley in a letter written from Gravesend and countersigned by John Wotton. The letter named the three attackers as Danny Wilkins, John Hannon and Denny the Frenchman (Maurice Dennis), and referred to them as 'Lord Oxford's Men'. The letter explained that the three men had hidden in a ditch 'with full intent to murder us'.

This highway ambush incident is closely paralleled in Act 2 Scene 2 of *King Henry IV, Part 1*. Falstaff and three drinking companions lie in wait to rob travellers carrying the King's taxes on the same Rochester to Gravesend road where de Vere's servants waylaid two of Lord Burghley's servants, identified in the play as Gadshill, a local landmark. The difference being that the original assault was in earnest and ended badly whereas this comedic interlude in a grim regime-change drama is intended to relieve tension. This is a distinguishing Shakespearean stagecraft device, inherited from the medieval Miracle and Mystery plays, and later from Italian *commedia dell'arte*. Falstaff's recounting of his exploits established his braggadocio character in one of the most famous scenes in world literature. It also cements the link with an incident in Edward de Vere's life which resurfaces in a Shakespeare play.

Presumably aware and proud of his military ancestry, de Vere volunteered several times for active service but met with little encouragement from the Queen, even less from his father-in-law. In a letter to Burghley dated 22nd September 1572 he makes another appeal to be allowed to serve his country abroad, with a preference for the navy, 'If there be any setting forth to sea, to which service I bear most affection'. The letter continues, 'If there be no such intention then I shall be most willing to be employed on the sea coasts to be in readiness with my countrymen against any invasion'. The discovery of the American continents north and south, and the opportunity for enrichment and adventure, made ships and sailing a strong attraction for active young men, even a seventeenth earl. But this entreaty to Lord Burghley was also turned down.

As a young man Edward de Vere was physically vigorous and a tiltyard champion, competing on level terms against older men with military experience. In a tournament held at Whitehall in early May 1571 he prevailed in the tilt, tourney and barrier competitions against contestants including Christopher Hatton who was Captain of the Guard at the time, the courtier Thomas Knyvet, later appointed Master at Arms, and Sir Henry Lee the Queen's Champion. Historically the Veres had provided the country with some of its best soldiers but in spite of his success at the tourney Edward's interests lay elsewhere and he never fully committed himself to a career in the military. Nevertheless his skill in the martial arts, and his early fascination with armies and soldiering, have relevance to the authorship debate. Foreign wars, internecine conflict and violent death. The core and substance of many Shakespeare plays.

De Vere continued to petition for a licence to travel abroad, if not to fight for queen and country then at least to embrace the intellectual Renaissance which was peaking in Italy at about this time. Having turned his back on the court as an occupation, with no interest in managing his estates, and denied the right to fight or make a continental tour, Edward de Vere was badly in need of an outlet for his creative energies.

The universities were producing a steady trickle of young men with literary aspirations, and most were in need of a wealthy patron. Also resident at the Savoy where Edward de Vere still lived after separating from his wife were the writer John Lyly and the Cambridge scholar Gabriel Harvey. These formed the nucleus of a coterie of authors, actors and musicians who would soon gather round the earl and create a congenial milieu in which to fulfil his own talent. The opportunity to write and produce for the stage would provide him with an absorbing interest for the rest of his life.

Edward de Vere's penchant for louche company and a propensity for violence may not have endeared him to his Cecil in-laws but they strengthen his credentials as the author of plays featuring low life in London and elsewhere. The theatrical lifestyle he embraced was very different from that of the strict conventions imposed on those permanently at court. Familiarity with the men and women who spent their days drinking in taverns was something which had to be learned on the other side of the palace gates.

In July 1574, apparently on impulse, de Vere slipped the Burghley leash and with Lord Edward Seymour and others sailed to Bruges with the apparent intention of journeying on to Brussels. The fugitive earl of Westmorland was resident in Brussels so this was a cause for alarm in London, fearing that de Vere might have defected and joined other exiled English Catholics. He never reached Brussels and may not have intended to do so, wishing only to find some military action in which he could distinguish himself by fighting. He was not allowed much time to perform any great deeds as the Queen immediately despatched a search party with orders to bring him back to London. This was headed by his literary friend (and possible tutor) Thomas Bedingfield, who returned him unharmed before the end of the month. His fellow escapee Lord Edward Seymour, the third surviving son of Lord Protector Somerset, fared less well. He made his way to Italy but died the same year aged twenty-six, possibly from malaria.

This desperate act by de Vere may have convinced the Queen and Lord Burghley that it was better to grant the restless earl a licence to travel so that they could monitor his progress abroad. Burghley and Walsingham had an efficient security network of agents and informers who would indeed report on his whereabouts and activities on the continent. De Vere had already endured nine years of close supervision and lecturing by William Cecil as his guardian, and by marrying his daughter had consigned himself to many more years of the same. In Burghley's capacity as Lord Treasurer he drew the family purse-strings tight, determined to protect his daughter from the consequences of her husband's rapidly dwindling resources.

Oxfordian scholars who identify autobiographical references in the plays point to the character of Bertram in *All's Well That Ends Well*. Bertram inherited the title of Count of Roussillon after the death of his father and was immediately made a ward of the King of France. The young count's first speech in the play is a bitter complaint to his mother the Dowager Countess (1.1.5) that he will be kept 'evermore in subjection'. A telling phrase if written by Edward de Vere who was himself kept 'evermore in subjection'.

The question 'Who Wrote Shakespeare?' could be shortened to 'Who Wrote *Hamlet*?' For William Cecil and daughter Anne read Polonius and daughter Ophelia, with Edward de Vere as the permanently frustrated and embittered Hamlet railing against the establishment. His revenge came later, in print, with Lord Burghley skewered on stage for all time as the senile windbag Polonius.

5

Continental Travels

Full many a glorious morning have I seen
Flatter the mountain tops with sovereign eye
from Sonnet 33

Edward de Vere having been authorised by Queen Elizabeth to travel to Italy early in 1575, a Schedule of Debts was drawn up as an indemnity against his failure to return. He sold his properties in Cornwall, Staffordshire and Wiltshire to pledge the £6,000 required.[1] No English was spoken anywhere abroad at this time so a working knowledge of Italian was essential, in addition to Latin and French.

On the way to Italy he represented Queen Elizabeth at the coronation and wedding of King Henri III of France at Reims, staying on for a month afterwards. The King gave him letters of recommendation for his travels, as did the Venetian Ambassador, another guest at the wedding, who provided letters of introduction to his friends in Venice. Italian street theatre known as *commedia dell'arte* had featured in the royal wedding celebrations and was again witnessed by de Vere in Venice and other northern towns along the route. This form of entertainment migrated swiftly into the Shakespeare plays, in *Love's Labour's Lost, The Comedy of Errors* and *The Tempest*, as examples.

En route to Italy de Vere visited the German humanist and scholar Johan Sturmius[2] in Strasbourg, where Sturmius had founded a Protestant college. It is believed they conversed in Latin, a language in which they were both proficient. Continuing his journey de Vere took the southern Swiss Alps spring-thaw route down the Rhine valley and through the St Gotthard Pass, bypassing Milan to enter the Lombardy high plains.

Edward de Vere's sixteen months on the continent of Europe provided the inspiration for many plays. These plays, now world famous, or earlier versions of them, began to appear in the 1580s and accelerated the surge in literary excellence which has become associated with Queen Elizabeth's reign. In a remarkably short space of time the English language had evolved into a powerful and infinitely flexible medium of expression, for which much of the credit can be directly attributed to the author of Shakespeare. It would not be exaggerating to claim that de Vere's continental travels represent one of the most influential journeys ever made by any writer. Thirty Shakespeare plays are set partly or wholly outside the British Isles, many of them in Italy and other countries bordering the Mediterranean.

All's Well That Ends Well	Roussillon near Lyons; Paris, Florence, Marseilles
Anthony and Cleopatra	Rome in Italy and Alexandria in Egypt
As You Like It	The Ardennes area of north-eastern France
The Comedy of Errors	Ephesus, ancient city on the west coast of Turkey
Coriolanus	Rome
Cymbeline	Partly in Rome
Edward III	Partly in France
Hamlet	Elsinore Castle, Denmark
Henry V	Partly in France
Henry VI Part 1	Partly in France
Henry VI Part 3	Partly in France
Julius Caesar	Rome
King John	Partly in France
Love's Labour's Lost	Navarre, Northern Eastern Spain
Measure for Measure	Vienna (but with associations to Paris in the 1580s)
The Merchant of Venice	Venice
A Midsummer Night's Dream	'A wood near Athens' but Italian in character
Much Ado about Nothing	Messina, Sicily
Othello	Venice and Cyprus
Pericles	Antioch, Syria ; Tyre, Lebanon
Romeo and Juliet	Verona, Italy
The Taming of the Shrew	Padua, Italy
The Tempest	A volcanic island in the Mediterranean
Timon of Athens	Athens
Titus Andronicus	Rome
Troilus and Cressida	Troy, legendary city in North West Turkey
Twelfth Night	Illyria, an ancient Balkan region
Two Gentlemen of Verona	Verona and Milan
Two Noble Kinsmen	Athens
The Winter's Tale	Bohemia, modern day Czech Republic, once extending to the Adriatic coast near Venice.

Thirteen plays are set in Italy. Of these *Antony and Cleopatra, Coriolanus* and *Julius Caesar* are drawn from the classics. *Titus Andronicus* is set in Rome, the sources include Plutarch but otherwise remain vague. Other plays are set in the Italy of the period. Those from northern Italy are *Romeo and Juliet*, set in Verona, *Two Gentlemen of Verona* set partly in Verona and partly in Milan, *The Taming of the Shrew* in Padua, *The Merchant of Venice* in Venice, and *Othello*, subtitled *The Moor of Venice* partly in Venice and partly in Cyprus. *Much Ado About Nothing* is set in Messina in north eastern Sicily. *All's Well That Ends Well* is set partly in Florence.

A Midsummer's Night's Dream has the direction 'a wood near Athens' but is Italian in character. Richard Roe in his book *The Shakespeare Guide to Italy*[3] argues for the small walled city of Sabbioneta as the setting for the play. Sabbioneta is some twenty-five miles southwest of Mantua and is described in the tourist brochure as *La Picola Atena*, 'Little Athens'. Richard Roe also identifies the island Vulcano as the location for *The Tempest*. This island is situated in the Tyrrhenian Sea about twenty miles north of Sicily and contains geographic features such as the sulphurous lakes and other evidence of ongoing volcanic activity mentioned in the play.

The texts of these plays contain references from books written in Italian for which no translations existed at that time. Boccaccio's novella *Tito and Gisippo* is one example, cited by Geoffrey Bullough in his *Narrative and Dramatic Sources of Shakespeare* as a main source for *Two Gentlemen of Verona*. This text was not translated into English until 1620. Italian literary influence extends to the more serious plays, not just the comedies. Italian authors whose *commedia erudita* is considered by experts to have provided source material for Shakespeare, but which were not available in translation at the time, included Ludovico Ariosto (*The Tempest* and *The Taming of the Shrew*), Matteo Bandello (*Romeo and Juliet* and *Twelfth Night*), Giraldi Cinthio (*Othello* and *Measure for Measure*) and Ser Giovanni Fiorentino (*The Merchant of Venice* and *The Merry Wives of Windsor*).

De Vere's young Italian attendant Orazio Cuoco testified to the Venetian Inquisition in 1577 that the earl was a fluent speaker of Italian and Latin.[4] Cuoco was employed by de Vere as a singer from 1575 until he returned to Venice in 1577. Venetian citizens who had worked abroad were routinely interrogated on their return. During his absence both Cuoco's parents had died of the plague which was rife at the time, peaking in 1576.

De Vere rented a house in Venice, from mid-May in 1575 to early March 1576, using it as the base for his journeys to other parts of Italy. From clues in his letters home, and Cuoco's evidence that he attended mass at the Greek Church (*San Giorgio dei Greci*), this is believed to have been in the Frezzaria, a narrow street close to St Mark's Square. This street contained the Sagittary identified by Iago as the house where Othello and Desdemona were making love. (*Othello* 1.1.117–18). Sagittarius, the ninth sign of the Zodiac is represented by an archer. The name of the street derives from *frezze* the Venetian/Italian word for arrows.[5]

Because of its relevance to the authorship debate de Vere's knowledge of Italian geography, history, literature and customs has been intensively researched. His journeys took him from the north right down to the toe of Italy and on into Sicily. Sailing trips along the Adriatic shoreline extended his geographical knowledge of the region. His familiarity with Venice and the surrounding area exceeded that of any of the other Italian states he visited. Portia's villa at Belmont in *The Merchant of Venice*, for example, can be accurately identified as the Palladio designed Villa Foscari, situated along the Brenta river ten miles from Venice and two miles from a monastery. Portia refers to *'the traject, the common ferry / which trades to Venice'*. (3.4. 53–54). The 'traject' (*traghetto*), linked two of the many waterways of the region, enabling Portia's hurried journey to a wharf outside the ducal palace. In the trial scene Shylock's insistence on the single bond arrangement being referred to a notary would suggest that the author had some familiarity with the Italian legal system, as there was no parallel procedure in English law at the time.

On 3rd January 1576 de Vere wrote a letter to his father-in-law Lord Burghley from Siena. In the cathedral, dedicated to Santa Maria Assunta, there is a mosaic depicting the seven ages of man. *In As You Like It* (2.7.139–166) the famous speech by Jaques, 'All the world's a stage,' delivers the same bleak information that the mewling and puking infant will end his life in much the same condition that he entered it.

Using Venice as his base de Vere made four tours and there is sufficient evidence to believe that he visited or passed through Florence, Genoa, Mantua, Milan, Naples, Padua, Rome, Siena, Venice and Verona. Firsthand knowledge of northern Italy is implicit in the plays, for example the writer knew of the existence of the network of canals on the Lombardy Plain, and that it was possible to be shipwrecked on the Adige, the river which runs through Verona. And that it was also possible, as in *The Two Gentlemen of Verona*, to make the journey from Verona to Milan, two inland cities, entirely by boat using the canals which linked the Po and Adige rivers.

In the first act of *Romeo and Juliet* ('In fair Verona, where we lay our scene'), Romeo's mother asks his friend Benvolio if she has seen her son and receives the reply (1.1.118–120)

> Where, underneath the grove of sycamore
> That westward rooteth from this city side
> So early walking did I see your son.

Sycamore trees still grow outside the western walls of the city. Richard Roe includes a photograph of them in his book *The Shakespeare Guide to Italy* published in 2011.

That de Vere visited Mantua could be supported by the mention of Giulio Romano in *The Winter's Tale*. When needing to describe the lifelike statue of Hermione (act 5 scene 2) the speaker declares it to be worthy of Romano, 'that rare Italian master'. Giulio Romano (1499-1546) spent his adult life at the court of the Gonzago family in Mantua where he was given free rein and ample resources to rival Michelangelo in Rome. As architect, painter, sculptor and interior designer Romano's reputation would hardly have escaped the notice of a travelling nobleman. That his name uniquely figured in a Shakespeare play implies that his many masterpieces in Mantua had made a lasting impression on the visiting author. *The Winter's Tale* and *Twelfth Night* are set on the Adriatic coast, in the Byzantine state of Illyria. This was ruled for several centuries by the Orsini dynasty, Duke Orsino presiding at the time when the play would have been written. Duke (or Count) Orsino in *Twelfth Night* thus has a historical basis for the main story line in the play.

Palermo in Sicily may be added to the list[6] (and also possibly Messina, the setting for *Much Ado About Nothing*) but the other island states of Corsica and Sardinia were not visited and are not mentioned. Nor are the Italian towns of Bologna, Livorno, Parma, Ravenna, Rimini or Turin. These towns and cities were not included in de Vere's itinerary and no plays are set in them, nor are they mentioned in any of them. Vincentio in *The Taming of the Shrew* mentions the Lombardy town of Bergamo (5.1.71), and 'bergomask,' a rustic dance originating in Bergamo, occurs in *A Midsummer Night's Dream.* (5.1.347).

In reply to a letter from his father-in-law dated 24th September 1575 de Vere wrote from Venice, 'I have been grieved with a fever but with the help of God I have recovered the same and am past the danger thereof although brought very weak thereby.' A particularly virulent strain of plague had devastated Venice between 1575 and 1577, with sixty thousand recorded deaths. Because of de Vere's swift recovery the possibility exists that instead of the plague he had suffered a bout of malaria, a disease which historically had caused great loss of life in Italy. Recovery but not cure. Malaria is a recurrent condition and could have been the origin of de Vere's poor health in later life.

The peak year for the plague was 1576. One of the casualties, on 27th August that year aged eighty-eight, was the artist Tizianio Vecellio, anglicised as Titian. He painted a series of Ovidian myths, including *Venus and Adonis*. This has resonance for the authorship debate since there is a strong possibility that de Vere had seen a version of this famous painting on view in Titian's studio, in his house in the northern Venetian suburb of Biri Grande. The acknowledged original of the Titian art work *Venus and Adonis* is held in the Museo del Prado in Madrid. It depicts Adonis without his red hunter's cap and was painted in 1553 for Philip II of Spain to mark the occasion of his marriage to Mary Tudor, and sent ahead to London. When Philip left London in 1555 the painting went with his other possessions to the Low Countries, then under the control of the Spanish Habsburgs. A year later it reached the Prado where it has remained ever since.

Titian made five autograph replicas of Venus and Adonis (as distinct from copies made by students). Only one of these, the fifth, showed Adonis wearing the peaked cap. It was painted for the Holy Roman Emperor Charles V to hang in his picture gallery in Prague. It then passed into the ownership of Queen Christina of Sweden who brought it with her to Rome after her abdication in 1654. Successive royal owners took it to Paris and St Petersburg after which it was returned to Venice. As an item in the Torlonia collection it finally ended up in 1892 at the Palazzo Barberini in Rome, where it is currently still on view.

Shakespeare's long narrative poem *Venus and Adonis* has remained in print since its first publication in 1593 and continues to be admired for the intense mood of sensuality it conveys to the reader. The familiar Shakespearean anguish over unrequited love, as most famously expressed in the sonnets, is here reversed, since it is the woman and not the man who is rejected. For anyone who has studied the poem, and then viewed the Barberini painting in Rome, or seen a full-length print of it, the correlation between the two is so remarkable that the only explanation which serves is for the author of the poem to have seen the painting for himself.

Since Edward de Vere spent most of his sixteen-month tour of the continent in Italy, for much of that time in Venice, this was certainly possible. The contents of Titian's studio were not dispersed until after his death in August 1576 by which time the earl had returned to London. He would have had many opportunities to visit the artist's studio but whether or not he did so is one of many Oxfordian theories without hope of proof. But since the purpose of his visit in the first place had been to see as many of the art treasures of Renaissance Italy as possible in the limited time available it would strain credulity to believe that he spent so long in and around Venice without once bothering to visit Titian's studio. Titian's great fame as an artist, and the high social status of so many of his noble and royal patrons, would surely have put this at the top of any must-see list for a rich young man on a continental tour.

The poem accurately describes the lovely Venus with her imploring outstretched arms, and the awkwardly seated Adonis leaning away from her. In refusing to lay aside his boar-hunting spear, or release the leashes from his dogs, he signals an implacable resistance to her sexual advances, something not easy to understand. After his death, gored by a boar, Venus tearfully laments that Adonis will no longer need the cap which protected his beautiful face from the wind and sun. The bright sun can be seen breaking through clouds in the top right corner of the painting and in lines 1087–88 she describes the peaked cap

> And therefore would he put his bonnet on,
> Under whose brim the gaudy sun would peep.

Running out of money, and concerned at reports of his wife's infidelity, de Vere cut short his continental travels and headed for home. On his return journey he stayed at the town of Tournon-sur-Rhône, home of the wealthy aristocratic family of Roussillon. Living in the family chateau at the time was Hélène de Tournon and her mother the dowager countess of Roussillon. In the preface to his play *The Dark Lady of the Sonnets*, Bernard Shaw made his often quoted assessment that the Countess of Roussillon in *All's Well That Ends Well* was 'the most charming of all Shakespear's[7] women.'

6

Marriage to Anne Cecil

My sonne, my Gold, my Nightingale, and Rose
is gone
*From a sonnet attributed to Anne, Countess of Oxford
on the death of her newborn son.*

Anne Cecil, born 5th December 1556, was still only five years old when
Edward de Vere joined the Cecil family on 3rd September 1562 at the age
of twelve. She was the elder of Sir William's two surviving daughters,
both by his second wife Mildred Cooke.[1] At the age of thirteen Anne had
been pledged to Philip Sidney but the recently ennobled Lord Burghley
negotiated a better match for his young daughter with the wealthy young
earl of Oxford, a much more eligible bachelor. De Vere was twenty-one,
his bride a fortnight past her fifteenth birthday at the time of their
marriage on Wednesday 19th December 1571 with Queen Elizabeth and
the whole court attending.

Anne's father, William Cecil Lord Burghley, was the leading statesman of the age. His strong conduct of affairs at home and abroad established Britain as a trading and seagoing nation with increasingly global
interests. Ann's brother Robert Cecil, and her elder half-brother Thomas
Cecil, founded a political dynasty that has lasted until the present day.
Even for a seventeenth earl this was a very good marriage. For a
chronicler of history it was even better. No other writer in English has
lived so closely and for so long among those who controlled the affairs of
state and had the power to change the course of history.

The new young countess of Oxford had been well educated and was
also accomplished. From the Cecil archive a letter dated 4th December
1577 written to Lord Burghley from Strasbourg by the classical scholar
Johan Sturmius indicated that Anne Cecil as well as her husband was a
speaker of Latin. The French-born harpist John Southern credited six
sonnets to Anne in his small anthology *Pandora* published in 1584. Her
husband had attended his maiden debate in the House of Lords so it
seemed that a bright future beckoned for this gilded couple. Surely they
would live happily ever after? What could possibly go wrong? But go
wrong it did, spectacularly and horribly wrong, with bride and groom
soon living apart and with no indication that the marriage had been
consummated. The brutal execution of de Vere's cousin the duke of
Norfolk was one possible explanation for his disenchantment with the
Cecil family, his father-in-law being the main architect of the duke's

downfall and death. The hope of speedy relief from his financial difficulties had not materialised either so the marriage was beset with extraneous troubles from the start.

At twenty-one the earl was an adult man, six years older than his child bride, and in the normal course of events would have been the dominant and protective partner. Why this did not happen can only be conjecture but Anne's formidable parents may have been the grit in the oyster. Marriage of a ward to a guardian's daughter often carried with it the seeds of destruction, as in this case. Although Edward and Anne had shared a privileged upbringing in Cecil House they were no match for her domineering parents, the authoritarian William and his equally daunting wife Mildred. Edward tried to break free but never entirely succeeded and for the rest of his life was under the thumb of one or other of the Cecils, including later Anne's younger brother Robert.

As a teenage bride Anne seems to have been unprepared for marriage, running home in tears to her mother when faced with an approach from her husband. Edward may himself have been a maladroit lover, equally inhibited and inexperienced after many years of close surveillance in the sternly Protestant households of firstly Sir Thomas Smith and then Sir William and Lady Cecil. The verdict of history has condemned him as the partner entirely responsible for the dysfunctional marriage. This continues to tarnish his reputation and still makes him unattractive to the wider public as a candidate for the authorship. It certainly has not helped his cause and even at an academic level the Oxfordian case continues to encounter staunch resistance. A more fair-minded analysis of the events before and after the wedding leads to the suspicion that he was not wholly to blame for the marriage problems, and deserves at least some residual sympathy since he too was deprived of a happy married life as a young man.

In the year following the wedding Burghley was promoted to the post of Lord High Treasurer. This appointment directly affected de Vere's attempts to reclaim his estates after the end of his wardship. His personal and family affairs had now became inextricably entwined with his debts to the crown. These were overseen by his father-in-law in whose hands all the levers of political power and financial control now resided. Much as he may have resented it, and from the bitter tone of his many letters to William Cecil (and later to Robert Cecil) he obviously did, de Vere spent the rest of his life as a supplicant reduced to pleading with his in-laws for loans or favours. For a seventeenth earl this made it a less good marriage.

Almost three years later a pivotal moment arrived. In September 1574 Edward de Vere finally secured from the Queen the promise of a twelve-month licence to travel to Italy via France and Germany early in the new year of 1575. Countess Anne was still not pregnant, hardly surprising as she and her husband lived apart, and it would soon be their third wedding anniversary. With her husband about to go abroad and disappear for at least another year it was a now-or-never situation for their concerned families. The Queen would soon be returning to London from her progress to Bristol, breaking her journey at Hampton Court, and it was here in early October 1574 it is believed that the earl and countess of Oxford were obliged by court protocol and family persuasion to spend time together.

The long hoped for pregnancy was the happy result, with morning sickness as evidence to the court that a significant sequence of events had been set in motion. Anne's mother, Lady Burghley, asked Sir Thomas Smith, her son-in-law's early tutor and mentor, for his help in sustaining the pregnancy. Sir Thomas was a student of horticulture, a keen gardener and a herbalist, all of which he practised at his home at Theydon Mount in Essex. He was one of the first to employ Paracelsian methods of distillation to prescribe medication for specific conditions. He provided some medicine, to be administered 'a sponefull at a tyme' and assured Lady Burghley that it would prevent her daughter from miscarrying. In a letter to her dated 7th November 1574 he mentions fennel and angelica as two of the ingredients. The potion must have worked as a baby girl was safely born on 2nd July the following year. Named Elizabeth she was the earl and countess of Oxford's first child.

In a letter to Lord Burghley dated 17th March 1575 from Paris the earl wrote that having been informed of his wife's pregnancy he was 'a glad man' and looked forward to the birth of a son and heir 'to leave behind me one to supply my duty and service either to my prince or else my country'. Lord Burghley recorded in his diary that de Vere had written to his wife and sent her as presents a portrait of himself and two coach horses. At this stage there was nothing to suggest that he would later deny paternity of his wife's child.

Burghley must have written to de Vere in Italy informing him of the birth of his daughter on 2nd July, although this letter has not survived. Responding to Burghley in a long letter from Venice dated 24th September 1575, mostly about his financial difficulties, the earl spares ten words at the end of the letter to acknowledge the birth of his daughter, 'thanking your Lordship for good news of my wife's delivery'. Perhaps he was disappointed in having a baby girl rather than a son but even so this lack of enthusiasm or any hint of concern for his eighteen-year-old wife's welfare and happiness after the birth was an ominous portent of the unpleasantness to come.

On 20th April 1576 Edward de Vere arrived back in London by sea at Gravesend but in coming ashore refused to be greeted either by his wife or his sister Lady Mary Vere who had gone together to meet him. This was because he had been persuaded while abroad that he was not the father of his baby daughter Elizabeth. Exactly who had convinced him of his wife's infidelity in conceiving the child is not known for certain. Lord Henry Howard, younger brother of the executed Thomas Howard duke of Norfolk would be the nearest suspect as a close relative but his friend Roland York, in whose house he stayed on arrival to avoid meeting his wife, is another possible Iago who had poisoned his mind against her.

That all members of the Cecil family were distressed by this shocking development can be well imagined. Lord Burghley was in poor health at the time and received a comforting letter from his friend Sir Thomas Smith hoping that he would soon recover. In the letter, which was dated 25th April 1576, Smith also commiserates with Burghley for the 'undutiful and unkind dealing of my Lord of Oxford toward your Lordship which I am sure must very much grieve your honour'. He goes on to speak of his affection for de Vere and sorrow at his mistreatment of his wife, '... it grieveth me for the love I bear him, because he was brought up in my house'.

De Vere's implacable refusal either to forgive his wife for her alleged adultery, or to admit that he had been wrongly advised, is hard to understand or treat with sympathy. His letter written 27th April 1576 from his lodgings at Charing Cross to his father-in-law justifying his actions is cold and formal, believing himself to be the offended party. He spelled out to Burghley that he considered himself well rid of his wife and that her mother was welcome to her. '... as your daughter or her mother's more than my wife, you may take comfort of her, and I, rid of the cumber thereby, shall remain well eased of many griefs'. Three months later in a letter written on 13th July 1575 he brusquely rejects Burghley's attempt at a reconciliation, offering to bring Anne to meet him at court. Instead he reminds Burghley of his earlier agreement not to do so and insists on continuing the separation, and on the same terms.

> I did agree that you might bring her to the Court, with condition that she should not come when I was present nor at any time to have speech with me, and further that your Lordship should not urge further in her cause.

Other attempts to bring about a reconciliation between husband and wife also failed. Lady Mary Vere, Edward's sister, was engaged to be married to Peregrine Bertie, son of Catherine Willoughby the duchess of Suffolk. In a letter to Lord Burghley dated 15th December 1577 the duchess outlined a plan whereby Edward and his infant daughter Elizabeth could be brought together as though by chance. The plan failed and in spite of increasing financial pressure de Vere held out for another four years, his daughter living with her grandparents at Burghley House in London, and at Theobalds House in rural Hertfordshire.

In 1580 Edward de Vere purchased a house in Bishopsgate while continuing to live apart from his wife Anne. Having a house of his own he took a mistress, Anne Vavasour, one of the Queen's attendant gentlewomen. On 21st March 1581 she gave birth to a son, baptised as Edward Vere. The Queen was not amused and all three were imprisoned in the Tower, the earl, the mistress and the new-born son. De Vere was released after fourteen weeks and later wrote to his father-in-law thanking him for the efforts he had made to secure his freedom. Both the Queen and Burghley had tried to make a reconciliation with his wife a precondition for his release, and also to accept Lady Elizabeth Vere as his daughter, but he refused. Nine months later, on 27th December 1581, he finally capitulated and resumed his marriage after seven years of separation, calculated from January 1575. His daughter Elizabeth was by then six years and five months old.

Perhaps De Vere had been moved by this desperate appeal from his wife in a letter dated 7th December 1581, three weeks before the reconciliation.

> My Lord. In what misery may I account myself to be, that neither can see any end thereof, nor yet any hope how to diminish it. And now of late having had some hope in my own conceit that your Lordship would have renewed some part of your favour that you began to show me this summer, when you made me assurance of your good meaning though you seemed fearful how to show it by open actions. Now after long silence of hearing anything from you, at the length, I am informed but how truly I know not, and yet how uncomfortably, I do feel it, that your Lordship is entered into some misliking of me without any cause in deed or thought. And therefore my good Lord, I beseech you in the name of that God, that knoweth all my thoughts and my love towards you notwithstanding your evil usage of me, let me know the truth of your meaning towards me, at what cause you are moved to continue me in this misery, and what you would have me do in my power to recover your constant favour, so as your Lordship may not be led still to detain me in calamity, without some probable cause, whereof I appeal to God I am utterly innocent. From my father's house in Westminster.

The marriage ran its course with three surviving daughters, Elizabeth, Bridget and Susan, who were mostly brought up and supported financially by their Cecil grandparents. The earl and countess also had two other children, an unnamed baby son who died in 1583 and an infant daughter, Lady Frances Vere who died in 1587. During the sixteenth year of this ill-fated marriage Anne was anxious to have financial settlements for her daughters before her husband was completely bankrupt. She appealed to her father to make the necessary arrangements, her husband refusing to do so. In a letter to Sir Francis Walsingham in May 1587 Lord Burghley wrote despairingly 'of my poor daughter's affliction ... she spent all the evening in dollor and weaping'. The reason being de Vere's continuing refusal to make financial provision for his three daughters, hence the misery 'of his children to whom he will not leave one farthing of land'.

Only Anne's death at the age of thirty-one in 1588 brought this desperately unhappy marriage to a close.

7

Literary Connections

O this learning, what a thing it is !
The Taming of the Shrew 1.2.157

Edward de Vere's known interests correspond closely with the wide-ranging erudition which informs the Shakespeare canon. A caucus of academics from several countries formed The Shakespeare Authorship Coalition in 2007 and issued a document with the title *Declaration of Reasonable Doubt About the Identity of William Shakespeare.* On the question of the author's remarkable general knowledge the Declaration states

> The works show extensive knowledge of law, philosophy, classical literature, ancient and modern history, mathematics, astronomy, art, music, medicine, horticulture, heraldry, naval and military terminology and tactics; etiquette and manners of the nobility; English, French and Italian court life; Italy; and aristocratic pastimes such as falconry; equestrian sports and royal tennis. The works are based on myriad ancient and modern sources, including works in French, Spanish, Italian, Latin and Greek not yet translated into English.

The poet Matthew Arnold[1] in his early sonnet with the title '*Shakespeare*' described him as 'Out-topping knowledge'. Thomas Carlyle[2] in his book '*On Heroes and Hero-Worship*' published in 1841, wrote 'Shakespeare is the greatest of intellects'. The subjects and intellectual pursuits featured in the plays have been extensively researched by experts in their individual fields, as outlined in the list above. The consensus of their opinions favours authenticity. Many specialists have testified over a long period of time that the knowledge about their subjects contained in the texts of the plays was genuine rather than superficial.

In addition to his learning Edward de Vere qualified in more specific ways as the author of plays featuring so many royal and ennobled characters. His own high social status, his long association with Queen Elizabeth and her chief ministers, with his father-in-law Lord Burghley in particular, provide an adequate explanation for the specialist knowledge of the inside workings of a royal court evident in so many plays. As a member of the court himself, with close connections to the highest echelons of power, he could hardly have avoided observing at firsthand how the affairs of state were conducted at the top level. In his succession of privileged homes from childhood onward he would have been assimilating the language of statecraft and political intrigue, both of which run constantly through the Shakespeare Histories and Tragedies.

The distinctive speech patterns in which the high-born main characters speak to one another, and the subtle adjustments of manners and deference they adopt when speaking with subordinates, reflect the rigid hierarchical social structure of the times. *Julius Caesar* would serve as the example of a play where all the main characters are members of a governing elite and speak to one another accordingly. The leisure pursuits of the nobility and gentry feature prominently in the plays. These include the indoor activities of dancing, playing musical instruments, singing and acting. De Vere was equally assured in the outdoor activities of falconry, martial arts, the tiltyard and the chase.

Travel and soldiering feature in many of the plays. De Vere visited Scotland and the Netherlands on military service, and France, Germany and Italy on his continental tour. Using Venice as a base his sea voyages included the Adriatic and the Mediterranean around Sicily. Numerous nautical references indicate close acquaintance with ships and sailing. The author's reference to 'the giddy footing of the hatches' would be an example, drawn from Clarence's speech in *Richard III* (1.4.9–33), with its awful description of how it would feel to overbalance, fall into the sea and drown.

When he returned from his long visit to Italy in 1576 he found himself in the right place at the right time. With its expanding population and maritime wealth London was a good place in which to work, and a hundred years on from Caxton's printing press at Westminster the English language was ready and waiting for the arrival of its paramount exponent. The case for Edward de Vere as the writer of Shakespeare gathers pace at this point.

The first twenty years of Queen Elizabeth's reign, 1558–1578, did not yield much in the way of literary excellence, a situation which then changed for the better so rapidly that to refer to it as a cultural revolution would not be an exaggeration. Edmund Spenser, John Lyly, Philip Sidney and his sister Mary Sidney, and later Christopher Marlowe, were a flowering of talent that quickly established the English language as an uncluttered and surprisingly supple medium of expression, capable of adaptation to any literary requirement.

There were others, among them Francis Bacon, Richard Barnfield, Francis Beaumont, George Chapman, Henry Chettle, Samuel Daniel, Thomas Dekker, John Donne, Michael Drayton, Edward Dyer, John Fletcher, George Gascoigne, Robert Greene, Gabriel Harvey, Thomas Heywood, Ben Jonson, Thomas Kyd, Thomas Lodge, John Marston, Thomas Middleton, Anthony Munday, Thomas Nashe, George Peele, Walter Raleigh, Thomas Sackville, Thomas Watson, John Webster and George Wilkins. All of them produced work worthy of a note in the corpus of Elizabethan and early Jacobean literature, as did the translators Abraham Fleming, Arthur Golding, Thomas Hoby and Thomas North.

The missing name from this gallery of literary talent is the one which has transcended all others. The primacy of the works of William Shakespeare has not been disputed in modern times, so why does his name not appear and why do we know so little about him? How was it possible, in the full glare of Elizabethan public life, for his identity to remain concealed? London's bustling new world of information technology, namely the printers, publishers and bookshop owners who were disseminating knowledge at a tremendous rate, would surely have been curious and wanted to know. What of all the courtiers who liked to pen a poem? The scholars at Oxford and Cambridge? The theatre-loving lawyers in the Inns of Court? The landed gentry who liked a good read? The identity of William Shakespeare if deliberately concealed was most certainly a well kept secret.

Edward de Vere had separated from his wife Anne on returning in 1576 from his continental travels. Not nice for her or her baby daughter, but abandoning his family responsibilities allowed de Vere unlimited time for writing. Having already been absent for sixteen months the estrangement from his wife continued the process of distancing himself from the influence and control of the court. In 1580, at the age of thirty, he purchased from the London alderman Jasper Fisher a large house and garden in Bishopsgate. The cost of building the house had bankrupted the alderman, causing it to be known locally as Fisher's Folly. It was close to two new theatres in nearby Shoreditch, the Theatre and the Curtain. The Theatre is generally acknowledged to be the first successful custom-built premises for the performing arts in London, completed in 1576. The second theatre was built a year later, some two hundred yards further north in Curtain Close, and was known as The Curtain from its location.

Also in 1580, de Vere took over the earl of Warwick's Men and renamed them as Lord Oxford's Men, reviving his father's (and his grandfather's) acting company after an interval of sixteen years. Together with the Queen's Men, Leicester's Men and the Lord Admiral's Men, these were the four principal acting companies in London at that time. In the summer months the newly renamed company toured the provinces throughout the 1580s. De Vere also maintained a smaller troupe of young actors and singers known as Oxford's Boys, drawn from The Children of the Chapel Royal and Paul's Boys, (from St Paul's Cathedral). These boys were in demand to play female roles and many graduated to employment in the adult companies.

The European Renaissance which originated in northern Italy before migrating westward was based on architecture, painting and sculpture. The social and civic stability sustained by the strong Tudor dynasty in England provided an environment where these ideas could be well received. They found their expression through literature and music. The English composers William Byrd and John Dowland had transnational reputations during their lifetimes. They are still highly rated and their music is still regularly performed. References to music occur throughout the Shakespeare canon, including in the stage directions. Songs (almost a hundred) are a feature of the plays, as are dances and dancing, tavern and domestic music, the appreciation and instruction of music, and descriptions of musical instruments.

Early poems published in anthologies under Edward de Vere's own formal name (Earl of Oxenford), were mostly song lyrics. Some lute, keyboard and ensemble pieces bear his name, for instance *My Lord of Oxenforde's Maske* from Thomas Morley's *First Book of Consort Lessons* (1599). The madrigalist John Farmer dedicated two books of compositions to him. In the second of these, *First Book of English Madrigals* (1599), he thanks the earl for his generous patronage in a surprisingly candid tribute. To tell your noble patron that he could have made his living as a musician was bold indeed. Perhaps he knew that the earl would take it as a compliment rather than an insult

> ... without flattery be it spoken, those that know your Lordship know this, that using this science (music) as a recreation your Lordship have overgone most of them that make it a profession.

Edward de Vere was a patron to the composer William Byrd, seven years his senior. Among Byrd's 470 listed compositions appears the keyboard work *My Lord of Oxford's March*, also known as *The March before the Battle*. This was included in a compilation of forty-two keyboard pieces published as *My Ladye Nevells Booke*. The march is military in character with passages imitating trumpet calls or drum beats. Battle music has a long history, being mentioned in Homer. The ancient Greek Phrygian Mode was so warlike that Alexander reached for his weapons every time he heard it, or he did according to Machiavelli. (One of many similar anecdotes in *The Prince*, 1513). The custom at all Renaissance courts was to announce the entrance of high-ranking persons by playing a brief flourish on the trumpet and drums, known as a 'tucket'. These feature in the texts and stage directions of several Shakespeare plays. It is not known whether Byrd wrote the march mentioned above to commemorate an actual military incident in de Vere's life, or as a general tribute to his prowess in martial arts, which included staging mock battles for court entertainment.

William Byrd is widely accepted as the most accomplished of Elizabethan musicians and the equal of his French and Italian contemporaries, even quoted as 'The Father of British Music' in *The Grove Dictionary of Music*.[3] Byrd's fame as a musician protected him from the consequences of his Roman Catholicism and he composed openly for the Roman Church. Perhaps he was shielded also by having a powerful friend in Edward de Vere, a man suspected for most of his life as being a dormant Catholic sympathiser. Byrd had numerous residences, one of which, Battles Hall, Manuden, on the boundary separating Essex and Hertfordshire, was leased from Edward de Vere's estate.[4] This arrangement foundered when one of de Vere's agents assumed occupation of the property and Byrd was dispossessed. It was later sold to his brother John Byrd, a merchant but also a former chorister at St Paul's Cathedral. There is a possible reference to this incident in *All's Well That Ends Well*. The Countess of Roussillon's servant Lavatch says, 'I knew a man that ... sold a goodly manor for a song'. (3.2.8–9).

Edward de Vere's involvement with professional musicians began at an early age and demonstrates an interest in all aspects of music, including composition. In addition to Byrd and Farmer his protégés included the composer Henry Lichfield. Thomas Morley (1557–1602), a composer of madrigals, also lived at Bishopsgate. Morley's setting of the song 'It was a lover and his lass' from *As You Like It* (Act 5, Scene 2) has remained in print ever since.

The house known as Fisher's Folly became de Vere's literary salon and writers' workshop. From 1578 he had employed the author John Lyly as his private secretary, also as his stage manager when he took over the lease of the Blackfriars theatre in 1583. Lyly dedicated his prose romance *Euphues and his England* to his employer and patron, the earl of Oxford. This was the sequel to *Euphues : The Anatomy of Wit*, two books which made Lyly famous and founded a style of affected and pretentious writing, much parodied once it ceased to be fashionable. If Cinthia the Moon Goddess in Lyly's court comedy *Endymion* represents Queen Elizabeth so does Titania in *A Midsummer Night's Dream*. Edward de Vere or John Lyly? Patron, dedicatee, secretary, writer, collaborator? Theirs was an overlap and mingling of talents still not easy to disentangle.[5]

Bullough cites Lyly's two Euphues novels and his play *Endymion*, as possible source material for another Shakespeare play, *Much Ado About Nothing*. The prickly quickfire banter between Beatrice and Benedick is certainly Euphuistic in nature, as is the character Osric in *Hamlet*. The Lyly play *Endymion* contains (Act 4 Scene 2) a group of argumentative watchmen much given to incomprehensible logic, an obvious link to Dogberry and his equally inept watchmen in *Much Ado*. This play is set in Messina, Sicily. As mentioned in the previous chapter there is a recorded sighting of de Vere in Palermo the capital of Sicily during his Italian journeys, made by the travel writer Edward Webbe.

Anthony Munday, Robert Greene, Thomas Watson and Edmund Spenser were among the authors mentored by de Vere, and all gratefully dedicated books or verses to their generous patron. Munday and the clergyman Abraham Fleming also assisted Lyly in his secretarial capacity. Fleming was a prolific translator. A translation he made from the writings in Latin of the Danish theologian Niels Hemmingsen (1513–1600) he dedicated to Anne, Countess of Oxford. Listed among the papers in Fleming's large archive after his death was a manuscript described as, 'a pleasant conceit of Vere, Earl of Oxford'.[6] This is believed to have been an early draft of *Twelfth Night* but the manuscript was never published and has since vanished without trace.

Together with Christopher Marlowe, George Peele, Thomas Lodge and Thomas Nashe, (loosely known as the University Wits), this diverse and talented association of young men helped to raise the level of prose, poetry and theatrical writing in Elizabethan literature. The actual recipient of the 'Rival Poet' sequence of sonnets (78–86) is unknown but Marlowe and George Chapman have received most support in recent years, with Robert Devereux the earl of Essex, Michael Drayton and the soldier–poet Gervase Markham as outside candidates. De Vere also supported Thomas Churchyard, another soldier–poet and lodged him at the Savoy. Churchyard was much older than the others, born around 1520 and living on into his eighties. He was an old family retainer having served in the household of the poet and sonneteer Henry Howard, earl of Surrey, de Vere's uncle by marriage to his aunt Frances Vere. The satirist Gabriel Harvey was another resident at the Savoy. As a Cambridge scholar he was on friendly terms with de Vere but failing to secure employment with him took revenge by mocking the earl in verse as an Italianate fop under the title *Speculum Tuscanismi*. Holofernes, the tiresome pedant in *Love's Labour's Lost*, could be a retaliatory caricature of Gabriel Harvey.

It is likely that all these workshop writers knew one another, or knew of one another, and their daily conversation would have revolved around their individual work in progress. But among this bookish company there is one person missing, 'the elephant in the room', to use a modern phrase. The pre-eminence of the Shakespeare canon transcends and overshadows all the rest, yet during this decade, the 1580s, the name 'Shakespeare' is as yet unknown, and only a few oblique references to a possible incognito author can be gleaned from contemporary texts. Shakespeare as a living entity remains as elusive as ever. It is a matter of curiosity and regret.

One of the writers mentioned above, Thomas Watson, dedicated a collection of eighteen-line sonnets to de Vere. This was his *Hekatompathia*, subtitled *Passionate Century of Love*. Each of the hundred sonnets, or passions, was preceded by a short explanatory critique which Oxfordians believe were written by de Vere as the dedicatee. Long before he was put forward as the main authorship contender the literary critic Edward Arber,[7] emeritus professor of English literature at University College, London, proposed de Vere as the person most likely to have provided these deftly written and percipient introductions. Whoever was responsible possessed a formidable knowledge of literary texts in French, Greek and Latin and could quote freely from numerous sources.

The note for Sonnet 87 reads, 'The author of this Sonnet expresseth how Love first went beyond him, by persuading him that all was gold which glistered'. The disappointed Prince of Morocco in *The Merchant of Venice* reads aloud from the scroll in the wrong box, 'All that glisters is not gold'. (2.7.65). There is a closer Shakespeare link to Sonnet 47 in the *Hekatompathia,*, the first line being 'In time the Bull is brought to wear the yoake.' In *Much Ado About Nothing* Don Pedro speaks the line, 'In time the savage bull doth bear the yoke.' (1.1.243–44). The literary critic J Dover Wilson identified the Shakespeare Sonnet 130 (My mistress' eyes are nothing like the sun), as a parody of Watson's convoluted poetic style.

De Vere had just turned thirty when a succession of plays, later known to have Shakespeare connections, began to appear anonymously in the early 1580s, coinciding with the period during which he presided over his literary commune based at Fisher's Folly. Having exchanged the restrictions of the court for this coterie of poets, lyricists, dramatists, theatre folk and aspiring literati he had passed the point of no return. He had gathered around himself his own court, his own circle of admirers and helpers. He would never have more congenial surroundings, a more supportive milieu, or a better opportunity to consolidate his literary talent.

This had been achieved at a cost. By the mid-1580s de Vere had taken alarmingly large amounts of money from his inheritance, selling off his estates one by one, firstly to fund his continental travels and then to support his theatre and writing interests. In *As You Like It* the leading lady Rosalind spells it out to the alienated and permanently dejected courtier Jaques, (4.1. 20–22)

> ... you have great reason to be sad. I fear you have sold your own lands to see other men's.

A feature of Shakespeare's plays is the relief of dramatic tension by interludes in which a different set of characters take over. Until rendered obsolete by the rise of the professional theatre this use of comedic interludes would have been familiar to audiences of the medieval Mystery plays. The high-born characters briefly quit the stage and are replaced by a picaresque gallery of jesters, comic servants and engaging lowlifes. Falstaff and his cronies would be examples known to most. Launce and his dog Crab in *Two Gentlemen of Verona*, and Autolycus in *The Winter's Tale*, also come to mind. All these are good parts to play, popular with actors as well as audiences. Whoever wrote the Shakespeare plays seems to have been possessed with a lively sense of the ridiculous. Audience laughter punctuates the comedies. Flashes of humour relieve even the grimmest of tragedies.

The English polemicist Philip Stubbs published *The Anatomie of Abuses* in 1583. Now valued for its information on the social history of the time it railed against the low standards of conduct in public life. The author recoiled in horror from the licentiousness he saw around him in Elizabethan London, attacking the customs, manners, fashions and amusements of the rich. From which it may be deduced that de Vere did not need to venture far from the safety of the palace walls to become acquainted with London's bustling underclass.

This esoteric knowledge, added to his long formal education, his courtly upbringing, his foreign and military travels, his fractured domestic life and his close association with theatre people, would be sufficient to qualify him as a multi-talented contender for the authorship. If so he had through his own efforts, and over a period of years, made himself supremely well qualified and well prepared to be a versatile writer and a competent dramatist.

Fisher's Folly also provided Edward de Vere with the secluded accommodation in which to conduct an intimate relationship with Anne Vavasour, one of the Queen's young gentlewomen. The birth of their illegitimate son in 1581, also named Edward, resulted in fourteen weeks of imprisonment, served in the Tower. With this grim experience added to his bohemian way of life in the theatre district of London it should not be a surprise that the plays on the whole deliver a tolerant and sympathetic verdict on the human race, and on those who err. One reason among many for their continuing relevance and popularity.

8

Family Connections

A little more than kin and less than kind.
Hamlet (1.2.65)

The case for Edward de Vere as the author of Shakespeare is brought closer by his connection to the three other earls named in the dedications. For the two long poems the dedications to Henry Wriothesley the earl of Southampton would have been made during the lifetime of the author. For the First Folio published after the author's death the dedication is attributed jointly to the brothers William Herbert the earl of Pembroke and Philip Herbert the earl of Montgomery.

Edward de Vere was not much better as a father than he had been as a husband and after his wife's death in 1588 his three daughters, Elizabeth, Bridget and Susan were cared for by their grandparents, Lord and Lady Burghley. The young earl of Southampton was another royal ward boarded with the Cecil family and in 1590, when he was seventeen, Burghley proposed him as a suitor for his fifteen-year-old granddaughter Elizabeth Vere, Edward de Vere's eldest daughter. Southampton refused and Burghley as Master of the Court of Wards imposed a heavy fine for his disobedience in declining the match.

Three years later, in 1593, Southampton received the dedication of a long poem, *Venus and Adonis*, based on passages from Ovid's *Metamorphoses*. A year later he received the dedication to another long poem, *Lucrece*, soon reissued as *The Rape of Lucrece*. These dedications are the first appearances of the name William Shakespeare. Of significance is the jaunty nature of the prose. No humble deference here, instead a note of breezy, almost jocular, condescension marks the debut of the famous name. The two poems have remained in print to the present day. These are their dedications, the first for *Venus and Adonis*, the second for *Lucrece*.

To the
Right Honourable Henry Wriothesley
Earl of Southampton and Baron of Tichfield
Right Honourable,

I know not how I shall offend in dedicating my unpolished lines to your lordship, nor how the world will censure me for choosing so strong a prop to support so weak a burden: Only, if your honour

seem but pleased, I account myself highly praised, and vow to take advantage of all idle hours, till I have honoured you with some graver labour. But if the first heir of my invention prove deformed, I shall be sorry it had so noble a god-father, and never after ear so barren a land, for fear it yield me still so bad a harvest. I leave it to your honourable survey, and your honour to your heart's content: which I wish may always answer your wish, and the world's hopeful expectation.
Your honour's in all duty
William Shakespeare

To the
Right Honourable Henry Wriothesley
Earl of Southampton and Baron of Tichfield
The love I dedicate to your lordship is without end; whereof this pamphlet, without beginning, is but a superfluous moiety. The warrant I have of your honourable disposition, not the worth of my untutored lines, makes it assured of acceptance. What I have done is yours; what I have to do is yours; being part in all I have, devoted yours. Were my worth greater, my duty would show greater; meantime, as it is, it is bound to your lordship, to whom I wish long life, still lengthened with all happiness,
Your lordship's in all duty
William Shakespeare

A less happy connection between the two earls came in 1601 when Southampton and Robert Devereux the earl of Essex (yet another royal ward) were sentenced to death for their failed palace coup. Edward de Vere was the senior nobleman on the jury of peers which passed the death sentences at a trial held in Westminster Hall on 19th February. Essex was executed but Southampton was later reprieved. Robert Devereux has been considered, among others, as the so-called Rival Poet competing for the affections of the elusive Dark Lady (Sonnets 78–86) . Southampton and de Vere's son Henry, the 18th earl of Oxford, were friends and died as Protestant heroes in the long-running Dutch War of Independence against Spain.

The twenty-three year age gap between de Vere and Southampton has to be considered as part of the authorship mystery when discussing the sonnets. If judged by his 1603 portrait painted in the Tower of London the younger earl was very good looking and so could have been the 'Fair Youth' addressed so affectionately in the main part of the sonnets, first published in 1609. The identity of the recipient youth in the sonnets has never been established with certainty, nor for that matter the identity of the person who wrote them.

Although not a royal ward the future soldier and poet Philip Sidney (nephew of the earl of Leicester) had been boarded as a scholar in Cecil

House. He had been pledged in marriage to Anne Cecil when she was aged thirteen but this match never materialised. Instead Sir William Cecil brokered a better deal with Edward de Vere the wealthy young earl of Oxford and he was married to Anne Cecil two years later in 1571. Never on friendly terms, de Vere and Philip Sidney as adult men famously quarrelled over the use of a tennis court, and had to be separated by Walter Raleigh, another courtier poet.

The two brothers William Herbert and Philip Herbert of Wilton House near Salisbury were the Shakespeare First Folio dedicatees, fulsomely addressed as *The Most Noble and Incomparable Pair of Brethren.* William Herbert was 3rd earl of Pembroke and had been a suitor for de Vere's middle daughter Bridget. The marriage plans fell through and she later married Francis Norris the earl of Berkshire.[1] De Vere's youngest daughter Susan married Philip Herbert and became the countess of Montgomery when he was ennobled after the marriage. The case for Edward de Vere as the author of Shakespeare is not harmed by having his son-in-law's name in the front of the First Folio.

Lady Susan's husband (Philip Herbert) was the son of Mary Sidney Herbert, countess of Pembroke, and the nephew of Mary's brother Philip Sidney, mentioned above over the tennis court squabble. Mary's name will always be associated with the *Arcadia*, a long prose work which her brother Philip wrote originally to entertain her. Mary Sidney has been proposed as an outside candidate for the Shakespeare authorship but is more likely to have been an editor or reviser for some of the plays. There is a Mary Sidney Society based at Santa Fe in New Mexico. It publishes a newsletter, *The Cygnet*, the name alluding to swans on the Wiltshire River Avon. A biography of Mary Sidney by the American author Robin B. Williams has the title *Sweet Swan of Avon*.

Edward de Vere's biographer B. M. Ward in his 1928 *The Seventeenth Earl of Oxford* devotes a whole chapter to the earl's close friendship with his other son-in-law William Stanley, 6th earl of Derby. He married de Vere's eldest daughter Elizabeth on 26th January 1595 at Greenwich Palace in the presence of Queen Elizabeth and the court. He was thirty-four, his bride twenty, and although this is not authenticated, the play *A Midsummer Night's Dream* may have been performed as part of the feasting and revelry. When registered with the Stationers' Company in 1600 the title page stated that it had been 'sundry times publicly acted'. Such plays were often performed at aristocratic weddings and the Stanley–Vere wedding would have fitted into the time frame. Edward de Vere was forty-five years old on the occasion of his daughter's marriage, the daughter he had taken so long to acknowledge as his own.

William Stanley was immensely wealthy with estates and property in Cheshire, Cumberland, Lancashire, Yorkshire, and Wales as well as London. The Stanley family also owned the Isle of Man, and he held the title of Lord of Mann. He was also the owner of a playing company, Lord Derby's Men. He had inherited this in 1593 along with his title from his brother Ferdinando, the 5th earl of Derby, for most of life known as Lord Strange. Lord Strange's Men had been an active company from the late 1580s but were split up when Ferdinando died, some staying on as Lord Derby's Men, others joining a troupe led by Lord Hunsdon the Lord Chamberlain. These became famous as the Lord Chamberlain's men with Richard Burbage as their leading actor and by tradition were associated with the dramatist known as William Shakespeare.

Bernard Ward carefully avoids endorsing de Vere as Shakespeare but mentions the existence of a theory 'that the Earls of Oxford and Derby are in some way connected with the authorship of Shakespeare's plays'. He writes at length of their mutual love of music and the arts, points out that de Vere also had his own acting company plus a troupe of singers known as Lord Oxford's Boys. He lists the number of times that they stayed in one another's houses, in Stanley's house in Cannon Row in London and later in de Vere's house known as King's Place in Hackney. The possibility therefore exists that the earl of Derby could have been instrumental in preserving his father-in-law's Shakespeare manuscripts, in helping with their revision and editing, and in bearing or sharing the cost of the First Folio printing and distribution.

There are several elliptical references to both men as writers of plays. The merchant and spy George Fenner (1540–1618) wrote in a letter sent abroad, 'Our Earl of Derby is busy penning plays for the common players'. Francis Meres in his *Palladis Tamia* writes, 'the best for comedy among us be Edward Earl of Oxford'. The American *Encyclopedia of Shakespeare* states, 'Oxford's own plays are lost'. Orthodox scholarship allows Oxford credit as a collaborator, for example with his secretary John Lyly in his six court comedies, of which *Endymion* is the best known.

Wronged or badly treated young female characters feature in several Shakespeare plays. These include Hero in *Much Ado About Nothing*, Hermione in *The Winter's Tale,* Innogen in *Cymbeline* and Desdemona in *Othello*, who are all falsely accused of adultery or sexual misconduct. Helena in *All's Well that Ends Well* is brusquely rejected by Bertram her favoured suitor, Juliet in *Romeo and Juliet* and Hermia in *A Midsummer Night's Dream* are both bullied by their fathers to accept an arranged marriage. In *Measure for Measure* there are two more wronged female characters, Juliet and Mariana. Their wrongs are righted by Vincentio the duke of Vienna, a nobleman who conceals his identity for most of the play. (As, Oxfordians maintain, the earl of Oxford concealed his identity). These young women could all be linked to the earl's unfortunate wife Countess Anne, although she is more usually associated by Shakespeare commentators with Ophelia in *Hamlet*.

The main theme of *The Winter's Tale* is estrangement between a husband and wife (Leontes and Hermione) and Leontes' rejection of their baby daughter Perdita as being adulterously conceived. The parents are eventually reconciled and reunited with their daughter. This sequence of events mirrors that of Edward and Anne de Vere whose years of separation ended with reconciliation and an acceptance of paternity by the earl for his daughter Elizabeth. In the play a strong female character named Paulina tries unsuccessfully to soften the harsh treatment of Hermione by showing Leontes his baby daughter, an appeal he rejects. This recalls a similarly unsuccessful attempt made by Catherine Willoughby the duchess of Suffolk to engineer a situation where de Vere and his infant daughter Elizabeth could be brought together as if by chance.

The irrational and cruel treatment of his wife by Leontes in *The Winter's Tale* has been compared with the brutal way in which King Henry VIII disposed of his second wife Anne Boleyn, the mother of Queen Elizabeth. Hermione's speeches in her own defence (Act 3 Scene 2) are similar to Anne Boleyn's protestations of innocence at her trial. If Anne Boleyn was Hermione then her banished daughter Perdita could be viewed as based on the experiences of Queen Elizabeth herself, since she suffered similar childhood rejection and endured a precarious survival in adolescence.

During the years when she was separated from her husband Countess Anne lived with her parents, Lord and Lady Burghley, at their palatial residences of Theobalds House near Cheshunt in Hertfordshire and Burghley House in London. Her situation was not an enviable one, trapped between an authoritarian father and an absentee husband who had falsely accused her of adultery. Ophelia in *Hamlet* is driven crazy when her lover (Hamlet) kills her father (Polonius). As a result she dies young and her returning brother Laertes now has two deaths to avenge, those of his father and his sister. This makes it very much a family affair and if Burghley was indeed the role model for Polonius, and de Vere the author, then he had his revenge in print by portraying his loquacious father-in-law as a 'foolish prating knave'. (3.4.189).

The first recorded identification of William Cecil as the prototype for Polonius in *Hamlet* appeared in a book with the title *Shakespeareana Genealogica*, published by MacMillan & Co in 1869 (pp. 299–310). It was written by the Stratfordian biographer and historian George Russell French[2] who made the logical next step of linking brother and sister Anne and Thomas Cecil with Ophelia and her brother Laertes in the play. Subsequent Shakespeare analysts have concurred with Cecil as Polonius while simultaneously maintaining the orthodox Stratfordian authorship attribution, among them Sir Israel Gollancz,[3] Leslie Rowse and J Dover Wilson. The corrupt and deceitful character Pandarus in *Troilus and Cressida* has also been suggested as a portrayal of Lord Burghley.

Earlier, on 29th May 1561, Sir William Cecil's eldest son Thomas set out for Paris, carrying with him a travel document from his father. This took the form of a stern Puritan sermon listing the prayers Thomas should say night and morning and the confessions he should make if led astray in Paris by the pleasures of the flesh. These sententious precepts included advice on how to dress and conduct himself.

A Memorial for Thomas Cecil, my son, to peruse and put in use from time to time concerning divers things given to him in charge by me, Wm Cecil, his father. Anno Domini 1561. After morning prayer … you shall make you ready in your apparel of cleanly sort, doing that for civility and health and not for pride.

Suspecting that his nineteen-year-old son might be seduced by the temptations available to him in Paris he arranged for his secretary, Thomas Windebank, to spy on him and report back. A full account can be found in Conyers Read's biography of Sir William Cecil, *Mr Secretary Cecil and Queen Elizabeth*. This extends the family connection to Laertes, Ophelia's brother in the play. He was the recipient of similar tendentious advice from Polonius when he too set off for Paris. (*Hamlet* 1.3.55–81).

> Costly thy habit as thy purse can buy,
> But not expressed in fancy, rich not gaudy:
> For the apparel oft proclaims the man.

Later in the play Polonius briefs his servant Reynaldo to spy on his son in Paris (Act 2 Scene 1). How the author of *Hamlet* was made aware of the advice the humourless Cecil inflicted on his son Thomas will never be known. If written by Edward de Vere, his brother-in-law and fellow sufferer, the close family connection might provide an answer. Thomas Cecil lived on at Burghley House after the death of his father, later becoming the earl of Exeter. His younger half-brother Robert built a house next door on the western side. This was later known as Salisbury House when he became the earl of Salisbury.

These family connections between Edward de Vere and other members of the court, many of them associated with the theatre or actively engaged in creative writing, if added to the workshop writers mentioned in the previous chapter, make up an impressive roll-call of Elizabethan literary talent. Among them somewhere there must have lurked the elusive and incognito William Shakespeare. The early front-runner for the Shakespeare authorship was Francis Bacon, later viscount St Alban, and the author of many learned essays on a wide variety of subjects. He was a first cousin of de Vere by marriage and still has some supporters, as do Roger Manners the earl of Rutland, Sir Henry Neville, Mary Sidney the Countess of Pembroke and Edward de Vere's son-in-law William Stanley the earl of Derby.

But if Edward de Vere himself was the dramatist known as William Shakespeare, and did indeed write *Hamlet* and the other plays mentioned above, all of which contain a wronged female character, then a hypothesis could be advanced that he was working out some kind of penance in print. It would be a truism to say that authors draw on their own life experiences as plot material but his tragically unhappy marriage and his wife's early death could have been the subject of remorse in later life, and thus the wellspring for great drama.

Attachment and loss affects people in different ways. Delayed mourning after a bereavement can take many forms and have unexpected consequences. The character of Ophelia in *Hamlet*, if created by her husband, could be an example of great literature created from a profound personal tragedy.

9

A Reader of Books

How well he's read, to reason against reading !
Love's Labour's Lost 1.1.94

Edward de Vere's voracious reading habit became evident during a convalescent stay of several months at Windsor when aged nineteen. The nature of his illness is unknown. Letters written to Robert Cecil towards the end of his life indicate that he suffered from bouts of depression, a condition then referred to as melancholia. A major depressive episode has to be considered a possibility for a retreat of this length.

The young de Vere, still not yet twenty, remained at Windsor for the winter months of 1569 and into the spring of 1570, and is known to have purchased many books during this time.[1] The printer and bookseller William Seres held a licence from Lord Burghley to sell religious books from a stall in St Paul's churchyard and from him de Vere obtained his 1569 edition of the Geneva Bible. This was so called because it had been produced abroad by Protestant exiles during the reign of Mary Tudor. It was the first Bible to be printed in a Roman font, and to have numbered verses. It was also the world's first mechanically printed mass-produced Bible, containing maps, illustrations, indexes and scriptural study guides.

De Vere's Geneva Bible was bound in crimson velvet with the Oxford heraldic symbols of coronet, boar, crest and coat of arms fixed to the cover as silver medallions and badges. It has survived, complete with his marginalia, and now resides in the Folger Library[2] in Washington. There are approximately 1,064 annotations, marked verses which independent forensic analysis believes to be in de Vere's handwriting, over half of them from the Old Testament, and including some from the Apocrypha. In his PhD dissertation Roger Stritmatter[3] identified 295 marked verses with documentable influence in Shakespeare.

Other books that de Vere is known to have purchased at this time are a Cicero and a Plato, two unnamed Italian books and a Chaucer. Also a copy of Plutarch's Lives in the 1559 French translation by Jacques Amyot. This French version was rendered into English by Sir Thomas North[4] but there is sufficient difference between them to suggest that de Vere drew his allusions from the original French translation. Professor Geoffrey Bullough in his *Narrative and Dramatic Sources of Shakespeare* cites Plutarch's *Lives* as providing primary source material for the Shakespeare classical plays of *Antony and Cleopatra, Coriolanus, Julius Caesar* and *Timon of Athens*. Names taken from Plutarch appear in *Antony and Cleopatra* (Alexas), *The Winter's Tale* (Antigonus, Camillo, Cleomenes and Dion) and also in *A Midsummer Night's Dream* (Demetrius, Hippolyta and Theseus).

The small town of Windsor on the River Thames was not far from Sir Thomas Smith's house of Ankerwicke, a former priory, where Edward de Vere lived as a boy scholar. In *The Merry Wives of Windsor* (4.4.53) Mistress Page when organising the ambush of Falstaff by children speaks the words, 'Let them from forth a saw-pit rush at once'. Windsor Castle Great Park contained a saw-mill and timber-yard, marked on the map of the Windsor Estate made by Johannes Norden in 1607, and now kept in the Surrey History Centre Archive. His two long stays at Windsor could have provided Edward de Vere with this local knowledge.

An earlier American researcher, Professor Naseeb Shaheen[5] of the University of Memphis, in his 800 page book *Biblical References in Shakespeare's Plays,* demonstrates how important the Scriptures were as a literary source for the author, second only to classical mythology in the number of allusions drawn on for the narrative poems and the plays. The Geneva Bible differs sufficiently from other editions to be identifiable in many of these biblical references. This applies to some sixty allusions Shaheen recorded for *The Merchant of Venice*, most but not all from the Old Testament. Shylock, although Jewish, quotes from the New Testament with a reference to the Gadarene swine (1.3.31–2). In trading Biblical references Antonio remarks to Bassanio, 'The devil can cite Scripture for his purpose.' (1.3.97).

Another American biblical scholar, Richmond Noble, drew attention to the number of allusions drawn from the Psaltery, the 150 Psalms which form part of the Anglican Book of Common Prayer. In his 1935 book *Shakespeare's Biblical Knowledge* he extends this knowledge to the Latin titles of the psalms, which are still printed in modern versions of the Prayer Book. Noble speculated that Shakespeare might have acquired his excellent grasp of Latin more readily as a chorister than as a pupil at the Stratford grammar school. Noble differentiates quotations which can be matched to the individual translations of the Bible available to Shakespeare but expresses surprise that these do not include either the Douai Bible of 1609 or the Authorised Version of 1611. Edward de Vere's death in 1604 could provide a valid reason for these omissions. The Douai Bible was printed abroad (in Reims) by English Catholics in support of the Counter-Reformation. Noble also identified *Measure for Measure* as the only Shakespeare play with a title drawn from the Bible. This is from Matthew 7.2. 'With what measure ye mete, it shall be measured to you again'.

Geoffrey Bullough's eight-volume *Narrative and Dramatic Sources of Shakespeare,* published by the University of Columbia Press, remains a comprehensive guide to the texts, although it does not cover *The Two Noble Kinsmen* or *King Edward III.* Bullough identifies the classical authors Plautus, Seneca and Plutarch as exerting influence throughout the canon. He evaluates sources as 'possible', 'probable' or simply as a 'similar text', drawing no conclusions. Kenneth Muir, Professor of English at Liverpool University from 1951 until 1974 published *The Sources of Shakespeare's Plays* in 1977. Between them these great scholars list some three hundred books as likely sources for Shakespeare.

This breadth of book knowledge would have required years of background reading as a young man. Books were expensive but could be purchased from numerous bookshops in London, and as mentioned above Edward de Vere had begun his own collection as a teenager. The familiarity with untranslated texts in foreign languages (French, Italian, Latin, Spanish) evident in the works of Shakespeare, and the ability to quote so freely from the Scriptures, the classics, ancient history and philosophy, strongly suggest that the author must also have enjoyed privileged access to libraries in his youth. Libraries were few and far between in Elizabethan England. It is worth repeating that in Sir Thomas Smith's house as a student, in Sir William Cecil's house as a royal ward of court, at Cambridge University and at Gray's Inn in London, de Vere could have studied in some of the most exclusive privately owned libraries in the country.

In his monograph *Shakespeare as Literary Dramatist*, Lukas Erne writes on page 18, 'Anyone who is aware of T. W. Baldwin's[6] *Smalle Latine and Lesse Greeke* and Geoffrey Bullough's *Narrative and Dramatic Sources of Shakespeare,* knows that Shakespeare must have been an avid reader of books.' Indeed so.

10

A Writer of Letters

Sir, he hath never fed of the dainties that are bred in a book.
He hath not eat paper, as it were, he hath not drunk ink.
Love's Labour's Lost 4.2.24–25

Sixty-seven letters survive in Edward de Vere's distinctive italic handwriting, in all some fifty thousand words. Eighteen of these letters are about financial matters associated with the monopoly of the tin mines in Cornwall and Devon. There are nine other handwritten documents in addition to the letters, these being either legal depositions or short business memoranda connected with the stannaries.

Of authorship interest are forty-nine letters of a personal nature, all but two written to his Cecil in-laws. The earliest is dated 19th August 1563, written in French by the young earl at the age of thirteen and addressed to his guardian Sir William Cecil. After Cecil's death (as Lord Burghley) in 1598 fourteen letters are addressed to his son Sir Robert, later Baron Cecil. The last of the personal letters is dated 30th January 1604 and was written by de Vere directly to King James. It is worth noting that the king was more favourably disposed towards de Vere than Queen Elizabeth in her final years. King James not only restored Waltham (Epping) Forest and the keepership of Havering House to his custody but also renewed his £1,000 annuity. Whether or not he also appointed de Vere to the Privy Council, as some claim, is less clear. Only four letters survive from de Vere's continental tour 1575–76, these coming from Paris, Venice, Padua and Siena.

A selection of these personal letters has been recorded in a compilation on disc by Stephanie Hopkins Hughes,[1] with de Vere's words spoken by the English actor Derek Jacobi. When read aloud the prose is harmoniously cadenced, as well as cogent and courteous in tone. There is no striving for literary effect, or any indication that anyone other than the intended recipient would have been expected to read them. As private correspondence, written spontaneously in the manner of most letters, the language is sufficiently varied, lively and erudite to be worthy of the author of Shakespeare.

Consider these nicely turned lines, the first from the September 1572 letter in which de Vere urges Burghley to guard against an assassination attempt on his life following the St Bartholomew Day massacres in France

... the world is so full of treasons and vile instruments

and the second from the July 1581 letter in which he thanks Burghley for helping to negotiate his release from the Tower

> ... the world is so cunning, as of a shadow they can make a substance, and of a likelihood a truth.

Since letter writing seems to have come easily to Edward de Vere it must be possible, even very likely, that he wrote many more letters but which regrettably were never preserved. Those who have seen the original letters in the Cecil Papers at Hatfield House, or facsimiles of them, know that his handwriting is pleasingly elegant and flowing, with the characters well formed and easy to read. Only eighteen of the surviving letters were written before 1590 when he reached the age of forty, but sixteen are from the last five years of his life. Even with this bias it is possible to discern a transition from youth through middle age to death. While he still had his health the tone was confident and authoritative but as he began to age and suffer they became increasingly pathetic, lamenting his various disabilities and pleading for favours or money. Nothing of a literary or artistic nature is mentioned in any of the letters, nor any other allusion which would link him incontrovertibly to the plays.

In a postscript to the letter written to his father-in-law dated 30th October 1584, de Vere defiantly asserts his independence by writing 'I am that I am, and by alliance near to your lordship, but free'. In the Geneva Bible (*Exodus* 3:14) 'I am that I am' are God's words to Moses. As mentioned in the previous chapter de Vere owned a Geneva Bible. It was purchased from the London stationer William Seres who held a patent from Sir William Cecil for supplying religious books. De Vere's annotated copy of this Bible is now held in the Folger Library. Roger Strittmatter's thesis mentioned earlier links the marginalia in the Bible to works by Shakespeare. The phrase 'I am that I am' occurs in line 9 of Sonnet 121. Shakespeare's characters Iago and Viola both speak the antithetical phrase, 'I am not what I am'. Iago does so in *Othello* (1.1.65), Viola when disguised as Cesario in *Twelfth Night* (3.1.141).[2]

Five of the letters written to de Vere's brother-in-law Sir Robert Cecil were on the subject of the vacant Danvers estates. The landowner Sir Charles Danvers (1568–1601) was implicated in the failed Essex coup against Queen Elizabeth and was beheaded at Tower Hill on 18th March 1601 aged thirty-three. His Wiltshire estates were forfeited and by the legal process of escheat reverted to the Crown. De Vere's five letters to his brother-in-law in his capacity as Secretary of State were appeals to implement the Queen's promise that they be granted to him. His entreaties although patiently and courteously expressed were not successful and the lands were eventually restored to Sir Henry Danvers, younger brother of the executed Charles Danvers.

Professor Alan Nelson in his book *Monstrous Adversary* publishes all the personal letters but retains de Vere's original spelling. Although of historical interest and authenticity this inhibits the eye and makes them difficult to assess for their literary content. An earlier American commentator on the de Vere letters was William Plumer Fowler. In his 870 page book *Shakespeare Revealed In Oxford's Letters* published in 1986 he modernised the spelling 'to accord with that in current editions of Shakespeare'. This makes it easier to study the letters and evaluate them for their relevance to the authorship debate. Using a concordance Fowler matches words and phrases in the letters to parallel usages in the plays. More contentiously he also draws attention to the number of iambic pentameter lines which occur naturally in de Vere's letters, as though the writer had an inherent tendency to order his thought processes in this way. Fowler was a retired lawyer and a poet so his observations merit consideration.

Apart from the letters there is not much to offer as examples of de Vere's prose style apart from the prefaces to works by his literary associates Bartholomew Clerke and Thomas Bedingfield, mentioned earlier. The Shakespeare play *The Merry Wives of Windsor* is written almost entirely in prose. (By contrast *King John* and *Richard II* contain almost no prose lines). Various attempts were made in the twentieth century to establish an order of chronology for the Shakespeare plays based on the proportions of verse, rhyme and prose. None of these nor other stylometric experiments produced a reliable guide and the method is considered of limited use by most modern scholars. Many years earlier Edmond Malone came to recognise before his death in 1812 that the scarcity of documentary evidence, and the extensive textual revision which had taken place, were always going to make such dating attempts difficult.

The eighteen tin-mining letters, mostly addressed to Lord Burghley as the Lord Treasurer, make up forty percent of de Vere's prose writings, and so warrant scrutiny. The tin was mined under licence, purchased in bulk and by the business practice of 'preemption' licensed for sale at a controlled price. The first letter in the sequence is dated 20th March 1595 and takes the form of a long appeal from de Vere to his father-in-law to put him in the way of making some money by acting as the crown agent for the supply of tin. Neither Burghley nor the Queen responded favourably to this or any of his subsequent entreaties. De Vere writes

> I most earnestly and heartily desire your Lordship to have a feeling of mine unfortunate estate, which, although it be far unfit to endure delays, yet have consumed four or five years in a flattering hope of idle words.

He was still writing in the same way in 1599, which added to the 'four or five years' mentioned in the letter implies that almost the whole decade was spent in the hopeless pursuit of a business income. Although ultimately unsuccessful in convincing either the Queen or Burghley that he should receive the tin franchise he does appear to have mastered his brief. In a long memorandum written directly to Queen Elizabeth the depth of knowledge and grasp of financial detail are remarkable, particularly so considering de Vere's reputation for lack of business acumen.

Tin mining does not lend itself to great literature and in contrast to the correspondence on personal matters the lacklustre prose in the business letters is suitably uninspired. But why these applications should have been so repeatedly turned down by Burghley and the Queen, as were his attempts to secure the vacant Danvers estates after being promised them, is open to interpretation. Suspicion that he was still insufficiently loyal to the Protestant cause could be one reason, the unwillingness of the Cecil family to overlook the misery inflicted on his first wife Anne Cecil could be another, or that the mismanagement of his own finances as a young man rendered him as simply not creditworthy.

If he did indeed write Shakespeare then de Vere's cumulative bitterness and frustration could be seen as worked out in the plays, where the lives and ambitions of so many noble characters also end in dismal failure.

11

As an Actor

All the world's a stage
As You Like It, 2.7.139

No stigma would have attached to Edward de Vere as either a poet or a writer of plays, still less as a theatrical producer. The Queen and the court had an insatiable demand for entertainment and rewarded handsomely those who could provide it. From Revels Office accounts de Vere was included in lists of courtiers involved in providing entertainments for the royal palaces, including the staging of plays. With singers from the royal chapels to call on, and several acting companies to choose from, their main problem was to find scriptwriters and composers to keep them supplied with a constant flow of new material.

At Queen Elizabeth's court short dramatic pieces known as Interludes, in the style of morality plays, alternated with the more elaborate Masques. These were expanded into lavish extravaganzas with disguised players representing mythological or allegorical characters. The Queen and her circle of courtiers were sufficiently well educated in Latin and classical literature to understand and appreciate what they were witnessing. Those taking part would be the lords and ladies of the court, masked and costumed, accompanied by musicians and dancers, with verse spoken individually and in chorus.

For a big occasion such as a court wedding these would be spectacular events with sumptuous costumes and the very best and newest in poetry, drama, dance and song. The earl of Oxford is known to have collaborated in staging these productions and presumably to have participated in them as well, with other courtiers. When these masques were later developed into dramatic form and acted in the royal palaces, or at the Inns of Court and the universities, no eyebrows would have been raised if the young earl took the stage occasionally. It was only when these upper-class forms of entertainment transferred out into the public theatres that the social standing of an aristocrat would have been compromised by treading the boards himself.

The acting profession had been changed by the play *Gorboduc*, performed before Queen Elizabeth in 1561 by the Gentlemen of the Inner Temple. Collaboratively written by Thomas Norton and Thomas Sackville it showed Gorboduc, King of Britain, dividing his kingdom between his two sons. The younger son promptly killed his elder brother and was then in turn killed by his mother, triggering a civil war. Having in the recent past recovered from a long civil war where the leading participants were mostly close relatives, and which had arisen because the childless Richard II had no designated heir, those present at a performance of *Gorboduc* would have been reminded that their own childless monarch Queen Elizabeth, (their third in a row) was likely to die in similar circumstances.

The Shakespeare plays *Titus Andronicus* and *King Lear* perpetuate the inheritance theme, and from a literary viewpoint also emphasise the distance travelled in a comparatively short space of time from Senecan tragedy and morality plays to full scale Elizabethan drama. Speaking blank verse, however turgid, in *Gorboduc* had led directly to a more natural style of stage action, one which required the accurate delivery of lines. When the lumbering fourteeners (seven iambic heptameter feet) were replaced by taut Shakespearean pentameters the speeches became even more exacting for actors to deliver with the necessary flair and élan. The ability to express a wide range of emotions, to react to other characters, to recreate historical situations with insight and sensitivity, required a new level of professionalism.

From 1580 when de Vere revived his father's acting company, Lord Oxford's Men, he could have been the casting director as well as the producer and given himself good parts to play. The turnover of plays became so rapid that producing them was almost an industry. From 1576 onwards the Theatre and the Curtain in Shoreditch brought the latest plays to the public gaze, and were followed by other large theatres including Newington Butts and the old and new Blackfriars. The transpontine Rose and Swan theatres on the south bank of the Thames were joined by the Globe in 1599.

In the early 1580s the calibre of writing in English suddenly escalated. Oxfordians maintain that it was Edward de Vere as Shakespeare who led the literary revolution, changing forever the way that drama was written, produced and performed. The emergence of English as an infinitely resourceful vehicle for dramatic art inspired other writers, among them John Lyly and Christopher Marlowe. They swiftly raised the standard of writing to a height that required the actors of the day to lift their levels of performance commensurate with the range and vigour of the language they were required to memorise and speak.

Orthodox Stratfordian opinion has always been on safe ground by asserting that the author of Shakespeare must also at some point in his career have been an actor. Theatrical imagery is abundant throughout the plays and is used with such telling authenticity that it would be perverse to deny that the author was writing from anything other than first-hand stage experience. De Vere's entire adult life was spent in London devoted to writing and producing for the stage. To advance the proposition that he may at some point have wished to speak his own lines, or those of other dramatists, should not be unduly controversial. As a writer he may have done so specifically to gain first-hand experience of what works on the stage and what does not, and no one disputes that the Shakespeare plays are well crafted. Also adaptable, capable of being successfully staged in widely varying forms of production, in time, location and costume.

Any aristocrat who fancied to 'strut and fret' his hour upon the open stage, even for one with his own company of actors, would arouse comment. Society was not very forgiving for those who violated its norms and appearing in public performance under his own name, with 'My Lord of Oxenford' featured prominently on the playbills, would have been unthinkable. Scholars have been unable to agree on why the name 'William Shakespeare' was chosen as the earl's stage name, and later for the pseudonymous authorship of the plays. An unexpected and ultimately unwelcome complication arose when the man with a similar name turned up in London. Literary analysts still find it impossible to disentangle one from the other but the possibility exists that the few references to William Shakespeare as an actor could have been for Oxford using this as his stage name.

No other writer has lauded the profession of acting so forcefully, or championed its ability to re-interpret the great deeds of history. In *Hamlet* the prince effusively welcomes the touring company of players (Act 2, Scene 2) and himself declaims part of a speech from their repertoire. Hamlet then instructs Polonius, Denmark's chief minister, to treat the actors with the dignity that he considers their due. 'Do ye hear? – Let them be well used, for they are the abstracts and brief chronicles of the time. After your death you were better have a bad epitaph than their ill report while you live'. (2.2.526–29). 'Use them after your own honour and dignity.' (2.2. 534). In the next act, when they are about to perform *The Murder of Gonzago* to a court audience, Hamlet directs how he wishes them, in exact detail, to present their play and deliver their lines. (3.2.1–35).

Consider also these words spoken by Cassius after the violent assassination of Julius Caesar. (*Julius Caesar* 3.1.112–14) .

> How many ages hence
> Shall this our lofty scene be acted over,
> In states unborn and accents yet unknown!

In other words the ability to retell history, to make great men live again, to glorify their noble deeds and high aspirations, are skills greatly to be admired and actors therefore worthy of respect. The author of the plays seems to have been acutely aware that the written words on their own were not enough. They had to be spoken, and here a direct comparison with notes of music may be drawn. A piano sonata by Beethoven or a soliloquy by Shakespeare are just squiggles of ink on a page until they are transmuted into sound by a performer. The more skilful the performer the better the music or the speech will seem to the listener. Which means that the composer and the writer as primary creators are dependent on secondary agents, the re-creators, to convey and interpret what they have written. However admirable the words or the notes of music may look on the page, if they are imperfectly delivered by a mumbling actor or a banana-fingered pianist, they fail. As Bottom exhorts his fellow actors in *A Midsummer Night's Dream* as they go off to learn their lines – 'Take pains; be perfect.' (1.2.101).

The tradesmen characters led by Bottom the weaver put on their bumbling version of *Pyramus and Thisbe* as a court entertainment for a noble wedding. Pyramus and Thisbe are drawn from Roman mythology but the plot follows closely the version of the story recounted by Ovid in the translation by de Vere's uncle Arthur Golding. Some scholars believe that the *Dream* was first performed at the real life marriage of Sir Thomas Heneage and Mary Wriothesley, the earl of Southampton's mother, on 2nd May 1594. Another possibility is the marriage of Edward de Vere's eldest daughter Elizabeth to William Stanley the earl of Derby on 25th January 1595.

There is another 'play within a play' in *Love's Labour's Lost* where the below-stairs characters put on a masque, the *Nine Worthies*, to entertain the nobles and are mocked for their efforts. Weddings, three of them, conclude *The Taming of the Shrew* which begins with a play staged by a troupe of actors at the house of a nobleman. This Induction featuring Christopher Sly is sometimes omitted from performance.

The fragmentary play *Sir Thomas More*, a collaboration by de Vere's former secretary Anthony Munday and others, has over fifty speaking parts and so is difficult to stage. The small contribution supposedly from Shakespeare has led to the play being included in the Oxford Shakespeare complete works. *Sir Thomas More* consists of a series of short plays, some serious, some comic, illustrating aspects of Sir Thomas More's life.

The glumly cynical character Jaques in *As You Like It* is a world-weary aristocrat who failed to find advancement at court and left it in self-imposed exile. His famous speech in the second act sums up how he sees the tragi-comedy of existence (2.7.139–142)

> All the world's a stage,
> And all the men and women merely players.
> They have their exits and their entrances,
> And one man in his time plays many parts.

How does it feel actually to stand on a stage and see the audience gaping back at you? Or the dread of forgetting your lines? The agony of being hissed? The ecstasy of being applauded? To counterfeit emotions which the audience must see as real? These are some examples drawn from the plays and sonnets.

Richard Gloucester in *Richard III* enquires of the Duke of Buckingham (3.5.1–4)

> Come, cousin, canst thou quake and change thy colour?
> Murder thy breath in middle of a word?
> And then again begin, and stop again,
> As if thou were distraught and mad with terror?'

to which Buckingham replies (3.5.5–9)

> True, I can counterfeit the deep tragedian,
> Tremble and start at wagging of a straw,
> Speak, and look back, and pry on every side,
> Intending deep suspicion; ghastly looks
> are at my service, like enforcèd smiles.

From *King John* (2.1.375–76) the writer appears to be viewing the audience as from a stage

> As in a theatre, whence they gape and point
> At your industrious scenes and acts of death.

and similarly from *Richard II* (5.2.23–26)

> As in a theatre the eyes of men,
> When a well graced actor leaves the stage,
> Are idly bent on him that enters next,
> Thinking his prattle to be tedious.

From *Coriolanus* (5.3.40–41)

> Like a dull actor now
> I have forgot my part

and from Sonnet 23, the first two lines

> As an imperfect actor on the stage
> Who with his fear is put beside his part

In *The Winter's Tale* the actions of Leontes in falsely accusing his wife of adultery and disowning the paternity of his daughter Perdita recall de Vere's similar rejection of his daughter Elizabeth for the same reason. Leontes rails against his wife in front of their young son Mamillius. (1.2.188–190)

> Go play, boy, play. Thy mother plays, and I
> Play too; but so disgraced a part, whose issue
> Will hiss me to my grave.

The self-assured and talkative character Touchstone in *As You Like It* pokes fun at a rustic character named William. Whether or not these and similar exchanges with bumpkins refer to the Warwickshire man will never be established beyond reasonable doubt. Autolycus in *The Winter's Tale* mocks the dimwitted Clown and Ben Jonson's *Everyman Out of His Humour* (1599) contains a gormless character named Sogliardo with pretensions to gentility. These connections are tenuous at best, as are other oblique contemporary references supposedly to the man from Stratford-upon-Avon.

There does seem to have been a hardening of attitude towards the theatre at the end of de Vere's life when he realised that the honours and sinecures he coveted, and to which his rank should have entitled him, would always be withheld, and that his acting on the public stage was one possible explanation. The Elizabethans took their orders of chivalry seriously and those who had received the supreme accolade of a Garter Knighthood were unlikely to admit to their ranks one who had thrown in his lot with the common players. Even so, many great actors since that time, having achieved fame by performing in Shakespeare plays, have been honoured with titles. Justly have they been considered as great men and women in their own right. But there were no honours for the 17th earl of Oxford in his long self-imposed exile from the court. These are the bitter opening lines of Sonnet 110.

> Alas, 'tis true, I have gone here and there
> And made myself a motley to the view

We cannot sorrow on his behalf because it was his all-embracing knowledge and experience of the actor's craft that helped to fashion the plays of Shakespeare. In 1602 Oxford's Men merged with another playing company, Worcester's Men. They performed at the Boar's Head Theatre, sited in the yard of the Boar's Head Tavern in Aldgate, London. These buildings disappeared but the adjacent Blue Boar Inn lasted until the coming of the underground railways in the late nineteenth century.

A blue boar was the cognizance (heraldic badge) of the Vere family and although Edward de Vere owned property in Aldgate, (the Great Garden of Christchurch) there is no record that he owned the Blue Boar Inn. In 1604 Worcester's Men became the Queen's Men. Anne of Denmark, the wife and queen of King James I, was a generous patron of the arts until her death in 1619.

The amalgamation with Worcester's Men in 1602 finally severed de Vere's links with the theatre. Gwynneth Bowen, in an article published in the Summer 1973 edition of the *Shakespearean Authorship Review*, wrote that the earls of Oxford had maintained acting companies since 1492. If so, Edward de Vere, as Shakespeare, would have been a worthy last custodian of a long and proud family tradition.

12

Why the Pen Name?

My name be buried where my body is
from Sonnet 72

Writing under an assumed name has been a common practice for centuries. It allows the writer greater freedom of expression and countless thousands of books (and poems, songs and plays) have been published under a name other than the writer's own. Fear of reprisal for calumnies uttered or reputations tarnished is a compelling reason for a writer wishing to conceal his or her identity. When the offended party may have been a crowned head, either prince or pontiff, the penalty could be extreme.

In Reformation Europe translating the Bible was a dangerous occupation, viewed with suspicion by the state as well as the church. A notable casualty was William Tyndale, whose printed translation into English spread unwelcome ideas of social change across Europe, incurring the wrath of King Henry VIII in the process. Tyndale fled to the continent but was hunted down, imprisoned near Brussels, tried for heresy, then strangled and his body burned. Another translator, Miles Coverdale, spent much of his life in exile and so escaped the fate of Robert Barnes and Thomas Cranmer who were burned and Thomas Cromwell who was beheaded. The so-called *Matthew Bible* was named after the translator Thomas Matthew and published in 1537. No such person existed, the real translator John Rogers prudently using Thomas Matthew as a pseudonym. This did not save him and he was 'tested by fire' at Smithfield on 4th February 1555, the first of Mary Tudor's many Protestant Martyrs.

Historians risked the same fate as Biblical translators if failing to support the winning regime with sufficient enthusiasm. The Welsh scholar William Thomas, whose *Historie of Italie* published in 1549 provided plot material for *The Tempest*, including the names Prospero and Ferdinand, was a Protestant openly opposed to the marriage of Queen Mary Tudor to Philip II of Spain. He was tried in the Guildhall on 8th May 1554, found guilty of treason and hanged at Tyburn. He was quartered the next day and his severed head was set up on London Bridge.

Edward Hall was the historian most closely associated with promoting a benevolent image of the Tudor regime. His masterwork *The Union of the Two Noble and Illustre Famelies of Lancastre and Yorke* inspired the Shakespeare double tetralogy, eight history plays in sequence from *Richard II* (succeeded to the throne 1377) through to *Richard III* (died 1485). Hall's work was prohibited under Queen Mary and his books were publicly burned. Richard Grafton, whose *A Chronicle at Large and Meere History of the Affayres of Englande*, supplied the Simon Simpcox comic diversion in Henry VI Part 2 (Act 2, Scene 1) was twice imprisoned in a chequered career of printing Bibles and issuing seditious ballads.

Raphael Holinshed remains a shadowy figure even though his name was used to front the famous *Chronicles,* the principal source of detailed material in Shakespeare's British history plays. Contributing writers to the *Chronicles* included Edmund Campion, William Harrison, Richard Stanyhurst and John Hooker. As a non-recanting Jesuit the forty-one year old Edmund Campion became another high profile victim of Queen Elizabeth's displeasure, racked before being hanged, drawn and quartered on 1st December 1581.

Edward de Vere could hardly have failed to be aware of the perils awaiting the chronicler who published under his own name. Writing was a dangerous business in an age of religious and political paranoia. It is possible that William Shakespeare was not his first pen-name, although scholars have been unable to link him with any certainty to minor works by little known authors which could have been his earliest literary efforts. It should always be kept in mind how far back in time the Shakespeare plays were written. If de Vere (born in the reign of King Edward VI) began to write the first drafts in 1576 soon after his return from Italy it would have been only a hundred years since Caxton's printing press was set up at Westminster. Even if the lack of evidence is frustrating, at least the great works of Shakespeare survived the vicissitudes of time and chance, when they could easily have been lost.

The penalties for 'seditious writing' under the strict censorship enforced by Lord Burghley were severe. The politician John Stubbs[1] together with his publisher and printer were all sentenced to death in 1579 for issuing a pamphlet opposing Queen Elizabeth's marriage negotiations with François Valois, duke of Anjou. The death sentences on Stubbs and his publisher William Page were rescinded as an act of clemency and replaced by the more lenient punishment of amputation. Both men had their right hands hacked off on a butcher's block, a meat cleaver smashed down by a mallet being the method of dismemberment. The printer was pardoned.

Few escaped the censor. Ben Jonson was twice imprisoned and roughly treated, a branding iron being applied to his left thumb. Edmund Spenser was exiled to Ireland, Thomas Nashe imprisoned, as later were George Chapman and John Marston for derogatory references to the Scots in their satire *Eastward Ho*. Reportedly they were also sentenced to have their ears and noses cut off but these punishments were never carried out. Less fortunate were four men accused of slandering Lord Burghley. John Stow's *Annales* of 1601 record a Star Chamber judgement that they be whipped and lose their ears, punishments duly carried out on the Cheapside pillory.

Although as an aristocrat de Vere could have hoped to be spared a similar fate, it can hardly come as a surprise if he chose to publish anonymously for almost twenty years and then sought the protection of a pseudonym. Oxfordian research tends towards the belief that his serious writing career began soon after his return to England in 1576 when the intellectual stimulus of continental travel would have been fresh in his mind. He freed himself from the restrictions of the court by setting up his own household in Bishopsgate at a time when the apparatus for writing, printing, theatrical production and commercial publication were becoming readily available.

Two long narrative poems were the first publications in which the famous name appeared. These were *Venus and Adonis* in 1593 followed by *The Rape of Lucrece* a year later, and both carried the name of William Shakespeare in their dedications. The sensuous language and bittersweet eroticism of *Venus and Adonis* ensured its commercial success. By comparison the tone of *Lucrece* is unrelievedly serious but both poems have remained in print to the present day. If, as some scholars have proposed, Edward de Vere was already using the stage name William Shakespeare for his acting performances, then extending its use as a pseudonym for his writing activities should not come as a surprise. For whatever reason the choice of 'William Shakespeare' seems to have been coincidental rather than borrowed from the businessman with a similar name.

But did Edward de Vere come to know, or know of, the man from Stratford-upon-Avon? It is possible that his marriage into the Trentham family provides an affirmative answer. Thomas Trentham of Rocester Abbey was a wealthy landowner in Staffordshire. His daughter Elizabeth was one of the young gentlewomen attending on Queen Elizabeth in London. Plots against the queen were believed to originate from Mary Stuart, a prisoner in Sheffield Castle for many years. The first moves to bring her to trial began in 1586 when she was moved to Chartley Manor House in Staffordshire. The Privy Council appointed Thomas Trentham to escort her from there to Fotheringhay Castle in Northamptonshire for her trial. Edward de Vere was one of the peers who recommended her death to Queen Elizabeth.

In 1591 de Vere sold his property known as the Great Garden of Christchurch in London to Francis Trentham, son of Thomas Trentham. Early in 1592, the exact date is unknown, he married Elizabeth Trentham, a capable woman who with her brother took over the management of the Vere estates. The Trenthams were descendants of the Throckmorton family. Arthur Throckmorton (brother-in-law of Walter Raleigh) was on friendly terms with Edward de Vere and was present at the tennis court quarrel between the earl and Philip Sidney. The intermarried Midland families of Trussel, Throckmorton, Arden and Trentham extended to the moderately prosperous Shaksperes of Stratford-upon-Avon. As an enterprising provincial businessman with interests in London (a shareholder in the Globe Theatre) it is possible that William Shakspere's path crossed at some point with the earl of Oxford, whose circle of acquaintances was not confined to the court.

Not wishing to share the fate of other translators, historians and satirists would have been reason enough to write under a pseudonym. It is also possible that the decision was forced on the forty-three year old earl by others. The exact date of the publication of *Venus and Adonis* in May 1593 could have been the key issue. When his first wife Anne Cecil died in 1588 his family life collapsed, he was out of favour and down on his luck, with his health beginning to fail. He may have been a seventeenth earl but he was a seventeenth earl with no son and not much of a future. By all accounts his second marriage was more successful than the first, and it got better. On 24th February 1593 his son and heir Henry de Vere was born, a boy child destined to become the eighteenth Earl of Oxford.

By this time Countess Elizabeth and her equally competent brother Francis Trentham were collaborating with Lord Burghley over financial provision for his granddaughters. The eldest of these, Lady Elizabeth Vere, was now seventeen and Lord Burghley was actively promoting her as a bride for his latest ward, the young earl of Southampton. Lady Bridget and Lady Susan would soon be in the queue for husbands of suitable rank and these family considerations may have influenced the publishing decision. Estates and titles were in the gift of the sovereign. They could be given but they could also be taken away, and often were. It worked out successfully for the three daughters because all three became countesses, having netted the earls of Derby, Berkshire and Montgomery respectively.

Would this desired end have been accomplished so readily if salacious poetry and a string of highly charged and politically sensitive publications by '*My Lord of Oxenford*' were on sale at every London bookstall? Probably not, because violation of caste was the one unforgivable sin for a nobleman. Not the act of writing as such, because penning a poem was considered an appropriate accomplishment for a courtier. No, the risk would have been in the contentious subject matter of plays featuring rebellion, regime change and violent overthrow. Exposing the political chicanery of the governing elite if made by one of their own would have been to court martyrdom.

Although his earldom had given him a good start at court de Vere was soon overtaken by ambitious young men in his own age group. They may not have had his advantages of wealth and close connection to the throne but they made up for it with diligence and loyalty. In Elizabeth's meritocracy none rose faster or finished higher than Christopher Hatton. He was a career courtier, entering the royal service straight from St Mary Hall, Oxford, and rose steadily through the ranks, as successful at court as de Vere had been unsuccessful. At thirty-two he was Captain of the Bodyguard, then promoted to Vice Chamberlain, next a Privy Councillor, knighted at thirty-eight and Lord Chancellor at forty-seven. He was dependable, even-tempered, unswervingly loyal, a zealous Protestant and a good dancer, which also recommended him to the Queen. She rewarded him handsomely with estates and privileges, appointing him Lord Lieutenant of Northamptonshire, his home county, as well as making him a Garter Knight and Chancellor of the University of Oxford.[2]

The disgraced and insolvent earl of Oxford had not endeared himself to this hardworking minister who had eclipsed him at court and received the Grace and Favour awards he coveted himself. It was inevitable that he and Hatton would be enemies, and they were, implacably so. But de Vere as Shakespeare took his revenge in print, as authors always can, by casting Hatton as the cruelly humiliated Malvolio in *Twelfth Night*. The steward Malvolio receives a prank letter signed *The Fortunate-Unhappy* and believing it to be a declaration of love from Olivia, and thinking to please her, behaves and dresses foolishly. Hatton was another courtier with literary pretensions and used *Felix Infortunatus* as the Latin pen-name for his poetry, or *'Master F.I.'* in the anthology *An Hundreth Sundrie Flowers*. The letter written to Malvolio also includes the jibe, 'Some are born great, some achieve greatness, and some have greatness thrust upon them'. (2.5.140–41). The Queen's pet name for Hatton was 'mouton', the French word for sheep. In the play (2.5.5) Sir Toby Belch refers to Malvolio as the 'rascally sheep biter'. Earlier Malvolio is described three times as a puritan. The unbending Hatton tended towards this extreme form of Protestantism.

Another of de Vere's enemies, the soldier–poet Sir Philip Sidney, could be identified as the cowardly duellist Sir Andrew Aguecheek in the same play, *Twelfth Night*, so named, it is believed, from smallpox scars on Sidney's face. As younger men de Vere and Sidney had themselves come close to a swordfight, needing to be separated after a tennis court quarrel at Greenwich. Oxfordians also see Sidney as the inept and feeble Abraham Slender in *The Merry Wives of Windsor*, this time as a suitor for the spirited Anne Page. It should be remembered that Sidney had been a rival suitor for the teenage Anne Cecil but lost out to the dashing young earl of Oxford. In the play Slender also fails to win the bride, Anne Page much preferring to marry the dashing young aristocrat known only as Fenton. A parallel could be drawn with de Vere's real life marriage.

Philip Sidney's uncle, the earl of Leicester, and the Queen's long-time favourite courtier, was another enemy with whom de Vere had a legitimate cause for grievance over the loss of income from some of his wardship estates. Leicester's closeness to Queen Elizabeth, and the perceived influence he had over her, made him many enemies. An anti-Protestant tract supporting the dynastic claims of Mary Stuart vilified Leicester, and among other accusations cited him as a serial murderer who disposed of his enemies by poisoning them. First circulated in 1584 it became known as *Leicester's Commonwealth*.

With the possible exception of Prospero, the title role in *Coriolanus* features Shakespeare's least likeable protagonist. Caius Marcius Corio-lanus is a successful commander promoted to the rank of Consul but is too haughty and uncompromising when seeking the necessary endorsement from the common people. This leads rapidly to his downfall, and after changing sides in the war between the Romans and the Volscians, Coriolanus ends up killed by his rival Aufidius and a group of conspirators.

If a contemporary link has worth it must lie with Robert Devereux earl of Essex who was sent to subdue the rebellious Irish but changed sides, was summoned back to London and imprisoned. Released, he launched a futile attack on the Queen with a few desperate followers, was captured, tried, convicted and finally beheaded on 25th February 1601. Edward de Vere was the senior peer in a jury that sentenced Essex, a fellow royal ward, to death.

Shortly after the execution took place on Tower Green in the Tower of London, one of the divines later engaged on a new translation for the *King James Bible*, Dr William Barlow, preached a sermon at St Paul's Cross. In the sermon he compared Essex with Coriolanus, saying he 'might make a fit parallel for the late Earle, if you read his life'.[3] Coriolanus was one of the Romans featured in Lord North's translation from the French of Plutarch's *Lives*, published in 1579.

De Vere's brother-in-law, Robert Cecil, had the misfortune to be born with a deformed spine, a condition known as scoliosis, and which gave him a humped back. Even if not exactly an enemy Robert was certainly no friend of the hard-up earl and refused all his requests to be helped out of his financial difficulties. He would be a good model for the villainous Richard Crookback as demonised in *Richard III*.

The 'fishmonger' taunt in *Hamlet* (2.2.176) is a reference to Robert's father Lord Burghley and his unsuccessful attempts to promote fish-eating on Wednesdays as well as on Fridays. As a Lincolnshire man, Burghley was trying to revive the fortunes of the declining east coast fishing industry. As Polonius in *Hamlet* he is comprehensively trashed as an interfering dotard. Did Edward de Vere hate his father-in-law enough to want to kill him? Whatever his true feelings, and whether he wished it to happen or not, he wrote Burghley's death into the script and assuaged a lifetime of irritated despair with a violent sword thrust. Since then not once but countless thousands of times Burghley has been run through behind the arras, his death destined to be re-enacted in every performance of *Hamlet* until the end of time. Vengeance or catharsis? Only the author would know.

Poking fun at his Cecil in-laws, at the earl of Leicester's nephew or Sir Christopher Hatton, would have been flirting with disaster under his own name but was just about survivable under that of the nebulous William Shakespeare. Exposing the Queen to ridicule would have been a jest too far. In *A Midsummer Night's Dream* even school text books make the connection between Queen Elizabeth and Titania the queen of the fairies. The poetry may be sublime but the idea of the queen having enjoyable sex with a donkey makes a persuasive argument in favour of the nom de plume. The obscure and elusive William Shakespeare on the title page got away with this act of lese-majesty. It would be hard to see an out-of-favour courtier being equally fortunate. In a violent age it would have been prudent to avoid upsetting as few easily-provoked noble personages as possible.

It could be the reason why we have the Shakespeare authorship mystery. The Cecils, the Trenthams, and other branches of the extended Vere family, might have disapproved, and strongly, if he had insisted on publishing under his own name. The Queen's displeasure would have been almost certain. With all these people ganging up on him, an impoverished author in failing health may well have capitulated and agreed to publish under a pseudonym rather than not at all.

There exists a convincing alternative, namely that de Vere at the age of forty-three having finally acquired the precious heir, might himself have been anxious not to do anything that would compromise his son Henry's inheritance of the title. It is reasonable to suppose that Countess Elizabeth would be equally protective of her new-born son's rights and just as concerned to avoid any notoriety arising from her husband's literary exploits. Either way, on 18th May 1593, *Venus and Adonis* was entered in the government's pre-publication registry the *Hall Book of the Worshipful Company of Stationers*, complete with its dedication to the twenty-year-old Right Honourable Henry Wriothesley by William Shakespeare. Thus began the authorship mystery.

With Lord Burghley safely dead on 4th August 1598, plays finally bearing the name William Shakespeare began to leave the printing presses, *Love's Labour's Lost* the first. No one could possibly have known at that time, well over four hundred years ago, how illustrious this name would later become, or anticipated the mystery that would surround it for evermore. Contemporary evidence is scarce, hence the mystery, but there is an explicit reference to Oxford as a writer in George Puttenham's *The Arte of English Poesie* published in 1589.

> Now of such among the Nobility or Gentry as be very well seen in the making of poesie, it is come to pass that they loath to be known of their skill. So, many that have written commendably have suppressed it, or suffered it to be published without their names: as it were a discredit for a gentleman to seem learned. And in Her Majesty's Time that now is, are sprung another crew of courtly makers [writers], Nobles and Gentlemen of Her Majesty's own servants, who have written excellently well as it would appear if their doings could be found out and made public with the rest, of which the first is that noble gentleman the Earl of Oxford.

A parallel situation between Copernicus and the Vatican over the heliocentric nature of the solar system could be drawn with the Oxfordian authorship claim.[4] Not so much 'It isn't true', as 'You can't prove it'. And we can't.

13

Dating the Plays

We do not know when the plays of Shakespeare were written,
or in what order.
Dating Shakespeare's Plays: A Critical Review of the Evidence,
edited by Kevin Gilvary

Dating and sequencing the plays of Shakespeare has exercised the minds of editors and literary scholars for very many years, and for a compelling reason, namely that with so few biographical details available there was no other way to plot the author's career trajectory and artistic development. Uniquely for a writer of Shakespeare's worldwide renown there are no surviving letters or diaries that would provide information of value to biographers. There are no childhood reminiscences, no notebooks, no first drafts, no books from his possession with revealing marginalia, no mention in memoirs written by any of his contemporaries, no personal anecdotes, no interviews or sightings that would place him at the scene. Not in theatre-land, nor anywhere else in Elizabethan literary London.

Researchers continue to grapple with a common problem. Not just that William Shakspere, the grain trader, maltster and property speculator from Stratford-upon-Avon, was an improbable incumbent for the title of 'world's greatest dramatist' but also because the dates of first performances or first publications of many of the plays were incompatible with his birth and death dates. Born in 1564 he was too young to have written the plays with Shakespeare connections which began appearing in the 1580s, nor can any new play be confidently dated between 1604 when Edward de Vere died, and 1616 when William Shakspere died. This left an awkward gap for which 'early retirement' was an unconvincing explanation.

There are three possible events for each play, the date of first writing, the date of first performance and the date of first publication. For first writing there is no contemporary evidence to date any play attributed to Shakespeare. Nor, apart from the eighteen plays appearing for the first time in the First Folio of 1623, can many performance or publication dates can be established with certainty. This lack of positive dating applies also to the other four plays now attributed in whole or part to Shakespeare, namely *The Two Noble Kinsmen, Edward III, The Famous Victories of Henry V* and *Pericles, Prince of Tyre.* The generally accepted poetry in the canon apart from the 154 *Sonnets* and the appended *A Lover's*

Complaint are *Venus & Adonis*, *The Rape of Lucrece* and *The Phoenix and the Turtle*. Not one page of original manuscript, of either drama or poetry, has survived.

This scarcity of dates continues to affect the study of comparative literature of the period, making it difficult to say for certainty which writer influenced which. The Irish barrister Edmond Malone (1741–1812) published in 1778 *An Attempt to Ascertain the Order in which the Plays of Shakspeare Were Written*. (Malone's spelling). This attempt was unsuccessful but the depth of research it necessitated exposed the unbridgeable disconnection between the calibre of the writing and the supposed author. Malone assembled as much detail as was then available for an intended biography of the poet and playwright known as William Shakespeare but never carried the project through to completion. The inference could be drawn that Malone's legal expertise and the insight he had gained as an editor of Shakespeare gave him reason to be cautious, even perhaps to have doubts, as an explanation for not proceeding with his plans to write a biography. His literary trustee James Boswell (son of the biographer of Samuel Johnson) had no such qualms and used Malone's papers to publish the biography in 1821, seven years after Malone's death.

Almost nothing is known about William Shakspere of Stratford-upon-Avon until he was approaching thirty, and not much even then, from which could be deduced that books about him would be short in length and few in number. Exactly the opposite has proved to be the case. Even if not entirely *carte blanche*, the scarcity of documentation has allowed countless scholars, editors, commentators, literary critics, historians, writers and journalists to write long and learned books about the Stratford man. Many thousands of pages of text crammed with dates and details about his life and works have found willing publishers. They have done so, and continue to do so, with little fear of challenge or contradiction.

The lack of dates for first composition has distorted the way in which the history of Elizabethan literature was taught, and continues to be taught. The fourteen-year discrepancy in age between Edward de Vere earl of Oxford born in 1550 and Shakspere of Stratford-upon-Avon born in 1564, although not insuperably large, still favours the older man within the time frame of the plays. The classically educated and widely travelled de Vere, a long-time resident in the capital city of London, had been active in literary pursuits from an early age and by 1580 (aged thirty) he had acquired his own acting companies, and presided over a salon of writers at his home in Bishopsgate. For a short period 1583–84 he held the lease of the Blackfriars Theatre together with his secretary, the writer John Lyly. All this before Shakspere had left his home town in Warwickshire for his first business trip to London.

The point is often made in study notes that Shakespeare was not an originator but took his starting point ideas from classical literature and books written in foreign languages. Of the canonical plays in a Complete Shakespeare only the main plots and story lines of *A Midsummer Night's*

Dream, The Tempest and *Love's Labour's Lost* have no obvious literary derivations and could be viewed as mostly original compositions. Of the rest not just ideas but plots, characters, settings, names and in many cases excerpts of text are seen as borrowed, for example the description of Cleopatra in her barge, lifted from Sir Thomas North's English translation of Plutarch's *Lives*.

Another writer inspired by the Antony and Cleopatra love story was the poet Samuel Daniel. In 1594 he published *The Tragedie of Cleopatra*, a Senecan style drama consisting of long formal speeches. Shakespeare's *Antony and Cleopatra* was recorded in the Stationers' Register in 1608 and so chronologically could have been influenced by the earlier Daniels play. But as with so many other Shakespeare plays there are no firm dates and since the plot was mostly taken from North's Plutarch translation of 1579 the direction of influence could have been reversed. North's translation was not from the original Greek but from the widely acclaimed version in French by Jacques Amyot published twenty years earlier in 1559. Edward de Vere was known to have purchased a copy of the Amyot translation while living in Windsor in the winter of 1569–70[1] and so could have been aware of the source material many years before.

Because Shakespeare drew so heavily on classical and foreign literary sources it was assumed *a priori* that he similarly plagiarised the works of his fellow writers. That he was in fact a serial plagiarist, borrowing in particular from Christopher Marlowe and John Lyly. This notion has taken root in text books and study notes but is not compatible with the case for Edward de Vere as the real author of Shakespeare. He was older than the cadre of young writers and University Wits who were pleased to have him as their generous patron and is more likely to have been the originator than the copier.

Marlowe's *Edward II*, registered in 1593, is said to have influenced Shakespeare's *Richard II* but this can be dated as early as 1587 when the second edition of Holinshed was available. In 1580 when de Vere moved into Fisher's Folly, the young Marlowe born in February 1564, would have been only sixteen. John Lyly was de Vere's secretary for some ten years in the 1570s and 1580s and dedicated his novel *Euphues and His England* to his employer. Their working relationship may have been of a literary nature but there can be no doubt that de Vere was the master and Lyly the servant.

Professor Kenneth Muir in his *The Sources of Shakespeare's Plays* reasserts the orthodox Stratfordian position. He expresses strongly his belief that the author of Shakespeare learned his craft from Christopher Marlowe and John Lyly, from the two Euphues novels most of all.[2]

> Shakespeare learned from Lyly how to write prose. He remained to the end of his career profoundly affected by it … It sharpened the edges of his wit and gave his dialogue more bite and sparkle. But, as everyone recognises, his debt to Marlowe was more profound.

His own blank verse was developed from Marlowe's 'mighty line' and his own conception of tragedy was evolved from Marlowe's. Shakespeare learned a good deal from the other University Wits, and their pioneering work reduced the period of his apprenticeship.

While this type of orthodoxy persists Shakespeare will remain a provincial arriviste dependent on filching ideas and inspiration from his university-educated betters. Nor is there a good case for collegiate authorship. Revising or completing unfinished work on behalf of another writer is not the same as collaboration. Plays which are believed to be co-authored would include *Henry VIII* and *Two Noble Kinsmen* (with John Fletcher), *Pericles* (George Wilkins), *Timon of Athens* (Thomas Middleton) and *Titus Andronicus* (George Peele). Several hands were responsible for the collaborative play *Sir Thomas More*[3] which survives in manuscript form. Writing under the Tudors was a dangerous business so spreading the risk made good sense, either by publishing anonymously, by using a pseudonym, or by collaboration as in *Sir Thomas More*.

Any discussion on Shakespeare profits from a reminder of how far back in time the plays were written. Whether by Edward de Vere born 1550, or by William Shakspere of Stratford-upon-Avon, born 1564, or by anyone else of that period, the plays came at a time when the printing and publishing industries were at an early stage of development and the spelling of words in English lacked consistency. The newly formed public theatres began keeping records of performances but for plays performed in the privacy of the royal courts, the universities or the chambers of the law societies, any form of records is scarce. Editors have mostly opted for the latest possible dates of first performance or first publication of individual plays, moving them forward to the late 1590s and into the first decade of the seventeenth century, as more compatible with Shakspere's 1564 date of birth.

Works by Edmund Spenser, Philip Sidney and Edward de Vere as the anonymously published Shakespeare began to appear in the 1580s. This was made possible by the availability of source material widely used in the Shakespeare plays, notably the Golding translation of Ovid's *Metamorphoses* in 1567, the first edition of Holinshed's *Chronicles* in 1577 and in 1579 North's translation of Plutarch's *Lives* which he retitled as *Lives of the Noble Romans and Grecians Compared Together*. There are persuasive arguments by Oxfordian scholars that contemporary allusions and topicality in *Hamlet*, the most famous of the plays, allow it to have been written as early as 1587. It would be hard to argue that the author of *Hamlet* was a young man in his early twenties newly arrived in London from the Warwickshire countryside.

A hundred years after Malone came Edward Dowden,[4] Professor of Oratory and English Literature at Trinity College, Dublin. He sought to classify the plays by style and content in another attempt to trace the playwright's intellectual development. In his *Shakspere:* [sic] *A Critical*

Study of his Mind and Art first published in 1874 he subdivided the plays into four groups but without much success beyond outlining a progression that would apply to the practitioner of any art form, namely first attempts, growing mastery, full maturity and a valedictory final phase. Dowden called these respectively, 'In the workshop', 'In the world', 'Out of the depths', and 'On the heights'. By the third edition of his book in 1881 he had extended these groups from four to twelve, but with no more success. However, Malone and Dowden's efforts to find a chronology for the plays had a lasting influence on the way in which later researchers approached the problem.

The best known and most influential of these was the widely respected Shakespeare scholar E.K. Chambers[5] who consolidated the work of Malone and Dowden. His two volume *William Shakespeare : A Study of Facts and Problems* published in 1930, although subscribing to the orthodox Stratfordian position, tacitly concedes that there are problems about the authorship which needed to be more closely investigated. Chambers refers to a cluster of plays as a 'lyrical' period in Shakespeare, believed to be composed in the mid-1590s, among them *Romeo and Juliet, Love's Labour's Lost, A Midsummer Night's Dream* and *Richard II*. Professors Stanley Wells and Gary Taylor in their monumental and indispensable *William Shakespeare : A Textual Companion* staunchly maintain the orthodox chronology, and the Warwickshire authorship.

All attempts at classifying and sequencing the plays have foundered on the same problem, namely that extensive revision has smoothed out textual differences and levelled up their psychological content and impact, the inference being that while he was alive the author constantly drafted, reworked and refined his material. It is not possible to apply a date of composition to any Shakespeare play, nor by the same lack of proof is it possible to say when revision was made, or by whom. Wells and Taylor in their *Textual Companion* write on page 17, 'Editors and critics have long resisted the obvious conclusion, that Shakespeare occasionally, perhaps habitually, revised his work'.

The lapse of time between the author's death and the publication of the First Folio in 1623, nineteen years in the case of the earl of Oxford, makes it certain that at least one other person continued the editing and revising process during this period. Although some of the less frequently performed plays are mostly considered on grounds of style and content to be earlier than the more famous plays it is still difficult to tell early from late with any degree of certainty, or to distinguish where the darker comedies, and the downfall of great men in the histories, differ greatly from the plays classified as tragedies.

Lacking in the Shakespeare canon are plays that can be confidently classified as juvenilia, although *Cymbeline, Pericles* and *The Two Noble Kinsmen* are less well crafted than the other plays and might fall within this category. The two narrative poems, *Venus and Adonis* and *The Rape of Lucrece*, can be accurately dated to 1593 and 1594. These long poems are sufficiently polished and sophisticated to provide a benchmark in considering whether plays, or sections of plays, less well constructed, can be dated stylistically earlier or later than 1593. *The Oxfordian* journal in America produced *Shakespeare's Dates: Their Effects upon Stylistic Analysis* (1999) edited by W. Ron Hess, in an attempt to grapple with this difficulty.

Dowden bracketed together *Cymbeline, Pericles, The Tempest* and *The Winter's Tale*, classifying them as 'romances'. Rightly or wrongly this description has remained entrenched, and modern productions often treat these plays as fables and allegories of the supernatural. *The Tempest* is the opening play in the First Folio, *Cymbeline* the last. The opening part of *The Winter's Tale* is a grim portrayal of a man, Leontes, in the grip of a savage depression. He is paranoid and impervious to any form of appeal or reasoning. In a strange mood swing this dark psychological drama changes direction and is concluded with comic characters and a happy, if unconvincing, ending.

Orthodox dating makes *The Tempest* a late play to accommodate a famous 1609 shipwreck in the North Atlantic in an area off Bermuda noted for severe weather conditions. By a coincidence de Vere had previously owned a ship, the *Edward Bonaventure,* which was also wrecked off the American east coast but much earlier, in 1594. However all the source material for this play was available by 1580 and de Vere's association with the mathematician and astronomer John Dee (1527–1608)[6] could have provided him with a role model for Prospero in this strange play which has no obvious literary source for its main plot. Because of his side interest in astrology John Dee's scientific reputation has waned but as an expert in oceanic navigation, and the possessor of a large library of books on scientific interests, he was one of the best known characters attending Queen Elizabeth's court.

Prospero is one of Shakespeare's most idiosyncratic main characters. His opening exposition to Miranda acquainting her (and the audience), at length, with details of their family history could indicate that stylistically *The Tempest* was an early rather than a late play in which this kind of tedious background information would have been introduced in more subtle ways. Prospero's volcanic island is more likely to have been sited in the Mediterranean than the Atlantic. Richard Roe in his book *Shakespeare in Italy* makes a convincing case for the small island of Vulcano in the Tyrrhenian Sea.

In addition to *The Tempest*, Montaigne's *Essays* are cited in study notes as sources for *King Lear, Timon of Athens* and *Hamlet*. Professor Kenneth Muir in his *The Sources of Shakespeare's Plays*, commenting on the number of words borrowed from Montaigne, writes, '… it seems probable that he [Shakespeare] had been reading it not long before he wrote *King Lear* and several critics have argued that certain ideas in the play were derived from Montaigne, or at least that Shakespeare had discovered a kindred spirit.'[7] Montaigne's *Essays* were popular in many

European countries, with reprints in 1588 and 1595.

The character of Caliban (anagram, *canibal*) can be linked to Montaigne's essay '*On cannibals*'. Michel de Montaigne's collected essays were first published in French in 1580, with an English translation by John Florio following in 1603. The uncouth Caliban speaks some of the most movingly poetic lines in *The Tempest* (3.2.138–146)

> Be not afeard. The isle is full of noises,
> Sounds, and sweet airs, that give delight and hurt not.
> Sometimes a thousand twangling instruments
> Will hum about mine ears, and sometimes voices
> That if I then had waked after long sleep
> Will make me sleep again; and then in dreaming
> The clouds methought would open and show riches
> Ready to drop upon me, that when I waked
> I cried to dream again.

Hamlet's wry and cynical philosophising are seen as influenced by Montaigne's discursive style of essay writing, with some quotes, '... for there is nothing either good or bad but thinking makes it so'. (2.2.251–52), To get round the problem that John Florio's translation of Montaigne's *Essays* into English was not published until 1603, and *Hamlet* was entered in the Stationers' Register on 26th July 1602, Wells and Taylor in their *Textual Companion* explain that the author must therefore have seen Florio's translation in manuscript form. They write 'The play's indebtedness to John Florio's translation of Montaigne's *Essays* results from access to the translation in manuscript. Florio clearly existed in manuscript years before it was published.'[8] Edward de Vere's daily two hours of studying French while a ward in Cecil House would have allowed him to read Montaigne's essays in their original language.

The perceived 'other-worldly' element of this so-called 'romantic' group of plays has been compared with works by later authors including Sir Walter Scott, Lord Byron, Goethe, Hugo and Wordsworth, all writers at the heart of the Romantic literary movement in the nineteenth century. One of the most uncompromising Stratfordians, the historian A.L. Rowse[9] writes in his biography of Shakespeare (*William Shakespeare*, Macmillan, 1963) that these four plays contain '... a world of meanings and wonder withdrawn within itself like the late quartets of Beethoven'. Oxfordian dating puts all these 'romances' as more likely to be early rather than late plays, contrary to orthodox opinion.

Cymbeline has an interesting Oxfordian subplot. The character Posthumus Leonatus is the son-in-law of King Cymbeline, the most powerful man in Britain, but abandons his wife and travels to Italy, being sympathetic to imperial Rome. While there he is deceived into believing his wife's adultery and wishes her dead. On his return he is imprisoned but learning of his wife's innocence seeks her forgiveness, and that of his angered father-in-law. This sequence of events would apply equally well to Edward de Vere, his journey to Italy, his falsely accused wife Anne, and his politically dominant father-in-law Lord Burghley.[10]

Timon of Athens is another play which appears to mirror closely the trajectory of Edward de Vere's rise and fall. Timon in Athens and de Vere in London both maintained a lavish lifestyle but were soon ruined by their reckless extravagance and refusal to heed warnings from their advisers. The young George Chapman wrote a poem in which he recalls encountering the earl in Italy in 1575 and describes him 'as liberal as the sun'. Generous patronage of the performing arts could be viewed as laudable philanthropy but all too soon the coffers were emptied and the distribution of largesse came to a precipitate and bankrupt end. The fictional Timon and the all too real Edward de Vere were shocked by the equally swift desertion of their friends when news of this reversal of fortune became known. Both realised too late that they had been cheated by those they had trusted, even more so when they sold all their remaining lands and property but could still not reconcile their debts. Humiliated, they withdrew into embittered seclusion and neither died well. *Timon* is a disturbing play, and from an Oxfordian viewpoint, tragic.

Three so-called 'problem' plays[11] *All's Well That Ends Well*, *Measure for Measure* and *Troilus and Cressida* contain distasteful material and have proved difficult to categorise as either comedies, histories or tragedies. Dowden's grouping together of the great tragic plays *Hamlet, King Lear, Macbeth* and *Othello* has obvious merit, as these are the epic works of literature which established Shakespeare's worldwide reputation. Whether written early, middle or late they are impressively intellectual in nature, the work of a dramatist at the height of his powers. They are also profoundly troubled, steeped in anguish and despair. In *Shakespeare By Another Name* Mark Anderson writes on page 379, 'Late Shake-speare[12] is more like late Beethoven: angry and intransigent, alienated and disturbed'.

No work of literature can have received closer scrutiny or undergone more analysis than Shakespeare's *Hamlet*. There is some measure of agreement among scholars that the play as it is published in standard editions today is a composite of three versions of the same play, the longest in the canon at 3,929 lines. The first quarto edition known as Q1 was printed in 1603 but the text is considered inferior to the First Folio version of 1623, and is also shorter at 2,221 lines. This could be explained if it was partly compiled by memorial reconstruction. This is a process by which a group of actors remembering their own lines are able between them to reconstruct most of the other lines as well. Despite these shortcomings Q1 in performance is coherent and actable, having less rambling philosophising than the later versions.

The second quarto known as Q2 underwent substantial revision but still ended up lengthier than the F1 version at 4,056 lines. On the second page of this 1604 edition the royal coat of arms is printed at the head of the text. This is a unique honour for any work of literature in English and may be presumed as indicating royal approval from King James. All three versions are agreed by modern scholars to be by the same hand and all have textual authority. There exists a possibility that parts of the F1 text were drawn from an earlier Hamlet play, a so-called Ur-Hamlet, now lost and perhaps written by someone else. Margrethe Jolly in her monograph *The First Two Quartos of Hamlet* concludes that contemporary evidence does not indicate that anyone other than Shakespeare was associated with a Hamlet play.

Although it is skilfully blended together to conceal the joins, we have ended up with a play which does not unfold consistently. The scenes with the ghost and the graveyard episode do not fall neatly into place and Hamlet's age is never clearly established. As a student at Wittenberg University he could have been under twenty. If calculated from Yorick's disinterred skull, he was much older, in his middle or late twenties. The contradictions in his character, varying from scene to scene and switching between lucidity and the pretence of derangement, have always presented difficulties for actors and directors. Although there is little agreement among scholars on the relationship between the different versions, the play itself remains an endless source of fascination for playgoers and students of literature.

Hamlet is richly sourced as an Elizabethan revenge tragedy. Geoffrey Bullough lists numerous French, Italian and Latin books whose influence can be traced in the text, the longest in the canon. The Danish historian Saxo Grammaticus (1150–1220) was responsible for a Latin history of Denmark (*Historia Danica*) which contains the story of Amleth, a prince seeking revenge for his murdered father but disguising his intentions with foolish behaviour. The Amleth legend surfaces again in a rendering into French by the prolific author François de Belleforest (1530–1583), retold in Book V of his *Les Histoires Tragiques*. Although no mention is made of either the ghost of Hamlet's father, or the 'play within a play', Shakespeare's character of Hamlet (an anagram of Amleth) closely follows the same story line.

Saxo and Belleforest both feature the closet scene where Hamlet vilifies his mother and murders the concealed councillor. No remorse is shown, and in the Shakespeare version Hamlet's contempt for the dead man never softens. He says, 'I'll lug the guts into the neighbour room,' but what he does with the body afterwards although hinted at is not spelled out. Belleforest describes how Amleth cut the body into pieces and disposed of them 'downe through the privie' to feed the waiting worms. The translation of Book V into English by Thomas Pavier in 1608 was titled *The Hystorie of Hamblet*.[13] In Belleforest the prince does not die but relocates to England for further adventures. Hermetrude the Queen of Scotland falls in love with Hamlet, describing him as 'the Adonis of the North' and persuades him to marry her and become the greatest prince in Europe.

Publication of the First Folio in 1623 was soon overtaken by political events which resulted in the closure of places of assembly and entertainment, which included the public theatres. The civil war and the puritan regime which followed lasted from 1642 until 1660, an unhelpful hiatus breaking the continuity of performance. When the restrictions were lifted the period of repression was followed by a period of licence. Coarse and bawdy Restoration Comedy soon displaced the more poetic Elizabethan drama. Audiences responded with relish to female performers acting in plays with sexually frank dialogue, and in dramatic situations where immorality was openly flaunted.

The Shakespeare plays languished in comparative neglect for another hundred years until the actor and impresario David Garrick brought them to London theatre audiences in the next century. This lapse in time could be one explanation of why the authorship puzzle has proved so hard to unravel with any degree of certainty. Garrick's early performances in *Richard III* and *King Lear* revitalised the London theatre and drew these impressive large-scale works to the attention of a discerning and appreciative audience.

14

Printing the Plays

If Shakespeare were not inspired, one may well doubt
if any man ever was.
Lewis Carroll in the preface to his novel Sylvie and Bruno, *1889.*

The King James Version of the Bible appeared in 1611 and was followed twelve years later by the Shakespeare First Folio. As a global language English has continued to evolve but these two books set the standard and are still widely admired and quoted.

Considerably more is known about how the King James Bible was commissioned, translated, edited and compiled than how the 1623 First Folio came into existence. The Bible was an anthology of writings from many contributors over a long span of years, reaching far back into antiquity and filtered through many previous editors and translators. The Shakespeare Folio contained the original work of one man, written in one not very long lifetime. His command of the English language and the continuing relevance of his plays to the human condition in all its many forms, still enjoy worldwide acclaim. Reprinted editions of the Folio followed in 1632, 1663 and 1685.

There were some minor Shakespeare collaborators but these were few in number and do not alter the widely held perception that from *The Tempest* through to *Cymbeline*, the first and last plays in the Folio, a single dominant intellect was guiding the pen. The people who assisted in the production of the Folio were likewise few in number. Whether for commercial reasons (and to obtain the Shakespeare franchise was a great coup for the Jaggard printing family and needed to be protected), or to maintain the authorship secrecy, nothing leaked out prior to publication. The Folio contained thirty-six plays, eighteen of them never before published or known to have been performed. Eighteen new plays by William Shakespeare suddenly appearing must rank as a publishing event of the first magnitude. Who had been guarding the missing manuscripts, and who oversaw the preparation of the First Folio, are intriguing appendices to the Shakespeare authorship mystery.

Below are listed the thirty-six plays in Folio order. They were in three sequences separately numbered as Comedies, Histories and Tragedies. *Troilus and Cressida* was included in the Folio although omitted from the Catalogue of contents. In the Folio it is positioned at the end of the Histories but is described on the title page as a Tragedy. In the preface to its quarto edition registered with the Stationers' Company on 7th February

1603, prior to publication in 1609, it is referred to as a Comedy.

The Comedies
The Tempest
The Two Gentlemen of Verona
The Merry Wives of Windsor
Measure for Measure
The Comedy of Errors
Much Ado About Nothing
Love's Labour's Lost
A Midsummer Night's Dream
The Merchant of Venice
As You Like It
The Taming of the Shrew
All's Well That Ends Well
Twelfth Night, or What You Will
The Winter's Tale

The Histories
The Life and Death of King John
The Life and Death of Richard the Second
The First part of King Henry the Fourth
The Second part of King Henry the Fourth
The Life of King Henry the Fifth
The First part of King Henry the Sixth
The Second part of King Henry the Sixth
The Third part of King Henry the Sixth
The Life and Death of Richard the Third
The Life of King Henry the Eighth
(The Tragedy of Troilus and Cressida)

The Tragedies
The Tragedy of Coriolanus
Titus Andronicus
Romeo and Juliet
Timon of Athens
The Life and Death of Julius Caesar
The Tragedy of Macbeth
The Tragedy of Hamlet
King Lear
Othello, the Moore of Venice
Antony and Cleopatra
Cymbeline, King of Britain

Pericles, Prince of Tyre was published as by William Shakespeare in a quarto edition of 1609 but was not included in the First Folio. George

Wilkins is credited with co-authorship and *Pericles* was included in the Third Folio issued in 1663.

Plays not included in the First Folio
Pericles, Prince of Tyre
The Two Noble Kinsmen
The Reign of King Edward the Third
The Famous Victories of Henry the Fifth

First edition plays that appeared in quarto prior to the First Folio in 1623

Titus Andronicus	1594
Henry VI Part 2	1594
Henry VI Part 3	1595
Edward III	1596
Richard II	1597
Richard III	1597
Romeo and Juliet	1597
Love's Labour's Lost	1598
Henry IV Part 1	1598
Much Ado About Nothing	1600
A Midsummer Night's Dream	1600
The Merchant of Venice	1600
Henry IV Part 2	1600
Henry V	1600
The Merry Wives of Windsor	1602
Hamlet	1603
King Lear	1608
Troilus and Cressida	1609
Othello	1622

No efforts were made to suppress these plays in the eleven years between 1594 and Edward de Vere's death in 1604 so we may presume that in the last decade of his life he approved of their publication, or even that he was himself actively engaged in the process of revising and issuing them one by one. The three quarto editions that appeared between 1604 and 1623 had been previously registered or performed and so were not new plays. No play can be definitively dated after 1604. On five quartos the title pages state that the texts had been edited, 'corrected and augmented', by the author but no further revisions occurred after 1604. The updated versions were for *Love's Labour's Lost, 1 Henry IV, Romeo and Juliet, Richard III* and *Hamlet.*

Edward de Vere's death in 1604 brought this publishing sequence to an end. Whether he had made any arrangements about publication in advance of this event will possibly never be known but as he appears to have died suddenly, probably not. A great debt of gratitude is therefore owed to those who preserved his manuscripts and began the task of compiling them into a single volume. Who were the prime movers with sufficient faith in the importance of these plays to set the task in motion? Who oversaw the editing and the corrections? And more pertinently, who paid the bills? Someone had to authorise the expenditure, facilitate the work and underwrite the project through to completion.

The quarto edition of the Shakespeare play *Troilus and Cressida*, mentioned above, contained an address to the reader, headed 'A never writer, to an ever reader'. For those who seek cryptic clues embedded in texts this oddly worded construction may suggest that the name E Vere is indicated, one of several ways in which the earl signed himself. (In his letter to Lord Burghley dated 18th May 1591 he concludes, 'Your Lordship's eVer to command, Edward Oxenford). The purpose of the *Troilus and Cressida* address to the reader is an affirmation that it had not yet been publicly performed. It contains two enigmatic references, firstly to 'those grand censors' and secondly to 'the grand possessors'. Neither has been identified with any degree of certainty and remains part of the authorship mystery

Edward de Vere died on the 24th June 1604. Six months later, on 27th December, his youngest daughter Susan aged seventeen married the twenty-year-old Philip Herbert, the younger brother of William Herbert the earl of Pembroke. These brothers were the sons of Mary Sidney, a literary figure in her own right, and sister of the soldier and poet Philip Sidney. Philip Herbert's entry in the *Dictionary of National Biography* states that he was named after Philip Sidney, his uncle. These two brothers were the 'incomparable pair' who achieved lasting fame as the dedicatees of the Shakespeare First Folio. William Herbert together with Henry Wriothesley the earl of Southampton are also generally considered as the most likely candidates for the 'fair youth' featured in the main sequence the Shakespeare sonnets

In 1615 William Herbert was appointed as Lord Chamberlain and remained in that position until 1625 when he was promoted to Lord Steward. If the prefatory epistle to *Troilus and Cressida* has relevance he would qualify as a 'grand censor', deciding the fate of what could or could not be published in print or performed on the London stage. His remit was to oversee the printing and publishing industries, with the intention of suppressing anything of a seditious nature. Also as Lord Chamberlain he held the archive material of the King's Men, formerly the 'Lord Chamberlain's Men', the acting company which had performed many of the Shakespeare plays. By virtue of office he could have facilitated the transfer of copyright for play manuscripts privately held, a legal process which may explain why compiling the Folio had been so long delayed. Since no play written entirely by Shakespeare escaped the trawl, and no wrongful play was included, those responsible for assembling the various handwritten manuscripts and quarto editions were obviously familiar with the material and aware of which plays were eligible for inclusion, and which not.

The DNB also quotes from the writings of the diarist John Aubrey, and from the historian the earl of Clarendon, which explain that King James was physically attracted to Philip Herbert and remained so until the end of his life. The King played a prominent part in Philip's elaborate wedding ceremony and lavished gifts on him and his new wife Lady Susan Vere. A knighthood (Order of the Bath) was followed in quick order by a barony (Shurland) and in 1605 by an earldom (Montgomery), all bestowed on the handsome young man whose skill at hunting with horse and hounds delighted the king.

Although not scholarly, Philip Herbert was active as a literary patron with fifty dedications, mostly on his own but some jointly with his brother or his wife. He supported the dramatist Philip Massinger (1583–1640) and also his relative George Herbert (1593–1633), a religious poet and priest born in Montgomery but resident in Wiltshire. In 1619 an English version of the medieval romance *The Ancient, Famous and Honourable History of Amadis de Gaule* was published as a folio volume and dedicated jointly to Philip Herbert and his wife Susan, the earl and countess of Montgomery. Printed by William Jaggard they are effusively saluted on the title page, 'To the Most Noble and Twin-like Paire'.

Four years later, published by Edward Blount and from the same Jaggard workshop, came the Shakespeare First Folio with its famous dedication to the brothers William and Philip Herbert, the earls of Pembroke and Montgomery respectively, addressed on the title page as 'To the Most Noble and Incomparable Paire of Brethren.' These three members of the Herbert family, William, Philip and his wife Susan are strong candidates as the 'grand possessors' who between them ensured that Shakespeare's literary legacy would be preserved for all time. Although now universally referred to as the First Folio the result of their labours appeared at the end of November 1623 as *Mr. William Shakespeares Comedies, Histories & Tragedies.* This was the dedication

TO THE MOST NOBLE
AND
INCOMPARABLE PAIRE
OF BRETHREN
WILLIAM
**Earle of Pembroke, &c. Lord Chamberlaine to the
Kings most Excellent Majesty.**
AND
PHILIP
**Earle of Montgomery, &c. Gentleman of his Majesties
Bed-Chamber. Both Knights of the most Noble Order**
of the Garter, and our singular good
LORDS

Opinion varies as to the extent of Ben Jonson's involvement in the First Folio enterprise. As a Latinist and writer for the stage he could have provided valued practical assistance. The actors John Heminges (died 1630) and Henry Condell (died 1627) were also named in the First Folio and their memories could have provided valuable knowledge of the texts, how they had been abridged for touring companies, and how past performances of the plays had been staged. Ralph Crane, a professional scrivener formerly employed by the King's Men, is credited with preparing transcripts for several of the plays, others were typeset from the prompt books or from corrected copies of quarto editions.

Commendatory verses in praise of the author were contributed by Ben Jonson, Hugh Holland (died 1633), Leonard Digges (1588–1635) and James Mabbe (1572–1642), listed as I.M. None of these encomiums specifically refer to the identity of the playwright. A case could be made that they were of a promotional nature, praising the contents of the book to encourage its purchase.

The strangely named anonymous play *The Wisdom of Doctor Dodypoll* may have been considered as borderline for inclusion but never made it into the Folio. It was entered into the Stationers' Register on 7th October 1600 and published in quarto form. The character Doctor Dodypoll speaks with a thick French accent which forces a connection to Doctor Caius in *The Merry Wives of Windsor*. Other words and various ideas in *Dodypoll* find an echo in other Shakespeare plays, the concept of reason having fled to animals for example, in *Julius Caesar*. The direction of influence between contemporary writers in this period is of great interest to scholars but is never decisive for either side of the authorship debate.

Several of these plays had no documented performance dates until many years after their publication. Even *Hamlet* was not shown on the public stage until 1639 although there are some references to earlier versions performed for small private audiences in London, Oxford and Cambridge. In *The First Two Quartos of Hamlet* quoted earlier, Dr Jolly writes, p.186, 'At some point between its composition and its printing *Hamlet* is performed in the two universities of Oxford and Cambridge and in London and elsewhere'.

Troilus and Cressida has no performance history before 1668, *Coriolanus* before 1669 or *Timon of Athens* before 1674. Others had to wait until the following century for a first performance, *King John* in 1737, *All's Well That Ends Well* in 1741 and *Two Gentlemen of Verona* in 1762. The 1598 quarto version of *Love's Labour's Lost* claimed on the title page that it had been 'presented before her Highness this last Christmas', but the play languished and there is no record of a first performance until it was revived in 1839 at the Theatre Royal, Covent Garden. Although versions of *Antony and Cleopatra* had been performed it was not staged as a full text until 1849 and even then was not well received. Audience distaste for the flaunting of adultery in publicly performed drama lingered on well into the twentieth century.

Fear of seditious material being published meant that printing firms had to operate under strict constraints of guild and government control. A Star Chamber decree of 1586 limited the number of print shops to twenty-five in London and one each for Oxford and Cambridge. They were subject to search and seizure, with severe penalties for printing illegal books. Not only huge fines but also jail terms were imposed. Once a book was entered in the Stationers' Register the copyright was held in perpetuity by the printer. One ruse to bypass the censor was to claim on the title page of a newly printed play that it had already been performed, either in public or at court, implying that it had been previously sanctioned and so did not require further scrutiny.

Edward de Vere was associated with printers and publishers from an early age.[1] William Seres was the original printer of Arthur Golding's translations of Ovid's *Metamorphoses* in 1567, Golding being de Vere's maternal uncle. As a young man de Vere purchased books from William Seres, among them the Geneva Bible which still bears his marginalia. Cuthbert Burby, who published *Love's Labour's Lost* and *Romeo and Juliet*, also published *Palladis Tamia* which listed the earl of Oxford as an author of comedies. Burby also published Angel Daye's *The English Secretary* which contained a fulsome dedication to Edward de Vere, and displayed a woodcut block print of the Oxford coat of arms.

Even without *The Taming of a Shrew* and other apocryphal works there were almost as many printers and booksellers as there were plays. Of the eighteen authenticated Shakespeare plays that preceded the First Folio appearance in 1623 the bookseller-publishers included William Aspley, Cuthbert Burby, John Busby, Thomas Fisher, Thomas Heyes, Arthur Johnson, Nicholas Ling, Thomas Millington, Edward White and Andrew Wise. The first-edition printers from *Titus Andronicus* in 1594 to *Hamlet* in 1603 were Thomas Creede, John Danter, James Roberts, Peter Short and Valentine Simmes. So many names deepen the authorship mystery. It is hard to understand how, within this gallery of entrepreneur craftsmen, all of them active in the book publishing trade, no record was left behind that would positively identify the author whose works they were so busily occupied in immortalising.

Producing the First Folio cannot have been a project lightly undertaken. Thirty-six densely worded plays, nine hundred pages of small print to set up and proof-read, all constitute a prodigious labour. Paying for the printing was not enough on its own, although the cost in time, money and effort would have been considerable, even for a wealthy family. More critical would have been the level of competence required. Revising and collating thirty-six plays would have required years of dedicated and laborious work and should not be underestimated. Much sensitive interpretation of the original texts would have been necessary, some corrections needed, even the judicious insertion of amendments if the meaning of a line or phrase was unclear. Literary expertise of the first order would have been essential.

Edward de Vere's business-like widow Elizabeth was the immediate custodian of the manuscripts and she may well have been instrumental in ensuring that her husband's work was preserved, in the early stages at least. She died in 1612 so this may never be known, nor where the manuscripts were taken after King's Place was sold to Fulke Greville in 1609. Greville renamed the property as Brooke House after becoming Baron Brooke and it remained in his family for the next two hundred years. There has been persistent speculation that some Shakespeare manuscripts may have been left behind and absorbed into the Greville archive. It should always be remembered that the Shakespeare plays did not achieve their worldwide fame until many years later. Any surviving papers associated with them may have been treated less reverently then than they would be today.

Even if the 'grand possessors' referred to in the quarto edition preface of *Troilus and Cressida* were confirmed as the Herbert brothers and Lady Susan Vere, two other questions would still remain unanswered: Where were the manuscripts held prior to publication? And what became of them afterwards? Two possible locations were Baynard's Castle[2] in London, a former royal palace, and Wilton House near Salisbury, both owned by the Herbert family. It is worth mentioning that Baynard's Castle is referred to in *Richard III* (3.5.96). Although nothing of the castle remains today it can be seen in views of old London. It occupied a commanding military position on the bank of the Thames where the city walls came down to the river, by the River Fleet and the Fleet Tower, not far from the present day Blackfriars Station.

What finally became of the Shakespeare manuscripts no one knows, and almost certainly never will. Lathom Castle in Lancashire, home of the Stanley family and a Royalist stronghold, was besieged by Parliamentary forces during the civil war, from July until December 1645. The castle surrendered and was ransacked. If at some stage William Stanley, Edward de Vere's son-in-law, had removed the manuscripts from London to Lancashire for safe keeping in the family home it is unlikely they would have survived the pillage.

Destruction by fire is another possibility. In 1647 the south range of buildings comprising Wilton House was destroyed in this way. Baynard's Castle in London fared even worse. During London's great fire, on the evening of Monday, 3rd September 1666, this historic former royal palace was completely consumed, burning all night. Also destroyed by fire on the same night were the adjoining Royal Wardrobe, and the nearby church of St Andrew-by-the-Wardrobe, although this was later rebuilt.

For editing and revising the manuscripts prior to publication, William Stanley earl of Derby would be a candidate with strong credentials. He was a distinguished man of letters who would have been well qualified to carry out any necessary revision. He was married to de Vere's eldest daughter Elizabeth and he still receives limited support as a candidate for the Shakespeare authorship itself. This is based on his involvement in the theatre (with his own acting company, Lord Derby's Men, formerly Lord Strange's Men), his international travels, his intimacy with court life, and several poems authored as W.S. His father and his brother Ferdinando (Lord Strange) had also maintained acting companies.

Edward de Vere's biographer B. M. Ward devotes a whole chapter to the close friendship and shared interests that existed between the two earls, including their knowledge and love of music. As in-laws they stayed at one another's houses, Lord Oxford and his second wife Elizabeth living at King's Place in Hackney, Lord Derby and his wife Elizabeth at Cannon Row in London, The wealthy and highly cultured William Stanley having the advantage of family intimacy, and close association with his father-in-law, would have known his mind better than most if it came to interpreting unclear passages in the plays.

When Stanley retired from public life in 1628 he named the Herbert brothers as the trustees of his estate until his son James could inherit as the seventh earl of Derby. As a young man William Herbert was involved in negotiations with Lord Burghley to marry his granddaughter Bridget, the middle surviving daughter of Edward de Vere, but no financial agreement could be reached and so the marriage never took place. When William Herbert died in 1630 he had no legal heir so the Pembroke earldom and the large Wilton Estate (46,000 acres) passed to his brother Philip. His wife Susan Vere had died a year earlier, in 1629, and so missed out on being the Countess of Pembroke as well as Countess of Montgomery. John Aubrey assessed Philip's income at £30,000 a year. At his London home he employed eighty servants, at Wilton one hundred and fifty. He would certainly have had the means to subsidise the First Folio project.

Another possible helper in setting up the First Folio could have been Mary Sidney, the widowed mother of the two Herbert brothers, and the mother-in-law of Susan Vere. Mary was also the sister of Philip Sidney who had lived in the Cecil household with Edward de Vere. Mary Sidney Herbert, countess of Pembroke, was the first English woman to achieve a significant literary reputation. She was a poet and writer, a translator and a patron of other writers, among them Samuel Daniel whose epic poem *The First Fowre Bookes of the Civile Wars* provided source material for *Richard II*. In recent times Mary Sidney has had some support as a contender for the Shakespeare authorship and she may well have provided valuable editorial assistance in processing the First Folio manuscripts through to publication.

The countess will always be associated with her brother Philip's most enduring prose work *Arcadia*, which he wrote originally to entertain her. The second version was unfinished when he died in 1586 and she published another edition with revisions in 1593. The work has always been known as *The Countess of Pembroke's Arcadia* and there are some references from it in Shakespeare. Bullough cites it as a minor source for both *Hamlet* and *The Winter's Tale*. More significantly it provides the Gloucester subplot in *King Lear*. In the preface to his play *The Dark Lady of the Sonnets*, Bernard Shaw argues convincingly for Mary Sidney as the role model for the dowager Countess of Roussillon in *All's Well That Ends Well*.

De Vere's literary executors erred on the side of caution when publishing his manuscripts. Those responsible, and William Herbert as Lord Chamberlain would have possessed the casting vote, must have taken the view that to continue publishing under the pseudonym of William Shakespeare might spare the Cecil, Herbert, Howard, Norris, Stanley, Trentham and Vere families needless embarrassment, however slight. So it proved. The authorship mystery was launched simultaneously with the First Folio and remains stubbornly tenacious four hundred and more years later.

After a slow start, seventeen new editions of the plays were published in the eighteenth century.[3] In the late nineteenth and early twentieth centuries, when the Shakespeare authorship was coming under increasing scrutiny, the first alternative contender to receive a broad measure of support was Francis Bacon, viscount St Alban. Bacon was a prolific writer and a relative of Edward de Vere by marriage, being his first wife Anne Cecil's cousin, and Lord Burghley's nephew. Advocates for Bacon as the main author were on the wrong trail, although not by much, and his literary and kindred connections still put him close to the scene. Roger Manners the 5th earl of Rutland, nephew of de Vere's youthful friend Edward Manners the 3rd earl, and married to Sir Philip Sidney's daughter Elizabeth, has enjoyed some measure of support for the authorship, for the Sonnets in particular. Of these authorship candidates, Francis Bacon, William Stanley and Mary Sidney could have played some part in the First Folio compilation and issue.

Getting Shakespeare into print would have required a sustained collaborative effort, and in the event seems to have been very much a family affair. But no ordinary family. Theirs was a close-knit clan of soldiers, poets, scholars, courtiers, intellectuals and aristocrats, with Edward de Vere as their main man.

15

Families in Shakespeare

Mother, mother, mother!
Hamlet 3.4.6

Domestic bliss does not feature prominently in Shakespeare. Edward de Vere never saw much of his own mother, Countess Margery, because he was sent as a young child to be tutored at the home of Sir Thomas Smith. After Earl John's death in 1562 she remarried and moved away, dying six years later. Although Edward would most likely have attended her funeral at Earls Colne in Essex, where she was entombed with his father, there is no supporting evidence that he did so. Nor that there had been any contact between them during his six years in London. Edward was eighteen when his mother died, having lost his father when he was twelve.

As mentioned earlier in this study, Edward's elder half-sister Lady Katherine Vere unsuccessfully challenged his legitimacy, claiming that his mother Margery Golding had not been legally married to their father. As an adult Edward himself fathered an illegitimate son by his mistress Anne Vavasour. The birth of his eldest daughter Lady Elizabeth by his first wife Anne Cecil, born while he was absent in Italy in 1575, was also disputed. He was convinced that he had not fathered this child, perhaps because he had not been co-habiting with his wife at what he thought was the right time.

De Vere's rejection of his daughter and the accusation of adultery against his young wife, followed by years of separation, were not conducive to a happy family life. It was hard to believe that the teenage countess of Oxford, so strictly brought up and so closely protected by her controlling parents, would have had sexual relations with anyone other than her lawful husband. Financial pressure and the Queen's displeasure eventually forced a reconciliation with his wife, and the acceptance of his daughter Elizabeth's paternity, however reluctantly. The much put-upon Anne Cecil, daughter of William Cecil the country's senior statesman, possibly lives again on stage as Ophelia, the much put-upon daughter of Polonius, the senior statesman of Denmark.

Nor does a charge of bastardy ever quite go away and there is a parallel with the play *King Lear*. De Vere had one legitimate and one illegitimate son, as does the Earl of Gloucester in the play, where the illegitimate Edmund tries to supplant his legitimate half-brother Edgar. In an earlier play, *King John*, there is a good part for Philip the Bastard, the illegitimate son of Lady Falconbridge by King Richard I. He was later knighted as Sir Richard Plantagenet. Edward de Vere's illegitimate son, also called Edward, followed the family tradition by pursuing a career in the military and was knighted by King James I as Sir Edward Vere for his service in the Anglo-Spanish wars, a war in which he was later killed. Edward de Vere's legitimate son Henry the 18th earl also died in the same conflict.

Father and daughter relationships outnumber mother and son relationships in the Shakespeare plays but are seldom straightforward and most are troubled. King Lear is an obvious example, with three daughters in need of generous dowries. Goneril, Regan and Cordelia are the recipients but only the darkest tragedy follows for this unhappiest of all Shakespeare's families.

Egeus and Capulet are bullying fathers seeking to marry off their daughters Hermia and Juliet to rich men they don't love. Leontes and his rejected daughter Perdita replicate Edward de Vere and his rejected daughter Elizabeth. Baptista has two daughters to find husbands for: Katherine the Shrew and her more docile sister Bianca. Cymbeline and his daughter Innogen, Leonato and Hero, Brabantia and Desdemona, Pericles and Marina, Prospero and Miranda, Titus and Lavinia, Calchas and Cressida, the Duke of Milan and Silvia – all are fathers whose daughters find themselves in unfortunate situations from which they need to be extricated.

The shortage of happy families in Shakespeare should not come as a surprise when considering the numerous and often hasty and ill-assorted marriages which wind up the action in many of the plays, three apiece in *Measure for Measure* and *The Taming of the Shrew*, four in *As You Like It* and a postponed four in *Love's Labour's Lost* where the suitors have to wait a year for their weddings. The author's cynical attitude to marriage favours expedience over romance. What are the chances of Katherine and Petruchio living happily ever after? Not great, one would suspect. Would French-speaking Catherine fare any better with King Henry V? Bassanio and Portia? Bertram and Helena? Whoever wrote Shakespeare had a jaundiced view of love, fidelity and holy matrimony.

Although the plays have good parts for women of all ages not many of them are mothers. One of the best known, the Countess of Roussillon in *All's Well That Ends Wel*, is the mother of Bertram and the guardian of Helena. She acts in a tender and sympathetic way towards Helena and encourages her love for Bertram. The opening speeches in the play are spoken by Bertram and his mother, both dressed in black, and they strike a chord in the authorship debate. They are in mourning because the count of Roussillon has just died and the King of France promptly summoned the count's young son Bertram to court to be entered as a ward. Neither mother nor son is very happy with this state of affairs but they have no option except to obey.

> COUNTESS: In delivering my son from me I bury a second husband.
> BERTRAM: And I in going, madam, weep o'er my father's death anew; but I must attend his majesty's command, to whom I am now in ward, evermore in subjection.

If Edward de Vere wrote Shakespeare then this closely mirrors his own unhappy experience of being a royal ward, because in his case the subjection did indeed last for 'evermore'. The Queen exacted large sums of money from him to fund his nine years of wardship and appointed her favoured courtier Robert Dudley to oversee and manage as trustee a large proportion of the Vere estates. The money troubles which lasted until the end of his life began at this point. Marriage to his guardian's daughter Anne Cecil perpetuated the unhappiness.

A less gentle mother than the Countess of Roussillon is Volumnia, the mother of Coriolanus. He is the conquering general in *Coriolanus,* she is equally regimental. She proudly counts up his victories and his battle wounds and urges him on to further glories. Coriolanus fails to win public support, is banished and joins forces with the enemy. In a vengeful mood he returns from exile with an attacking army and refuses all entreaties to spare the city. Only when Volumnia begs him on her knees to be merciful does he relent, while knowing that it will destroy him. He sues for peace with Rome but this incurs the wrath of his Volscian allies, who have him killed. Unbending and arrogant, Coriolanus is hard to like but the poignant family scene with his mother, wife and young son redeem him in this austere and sombre play.

Equally distressed are the royal widows featured in Act 4 Scene 4 of *Richard III.* Queen Margaret (of Anjou) is the widow of King Henry VI and she appears as a strong character in all three parts of the *Henry VI* trilogy as well as in *Richard III.* Her only son, Edward Prince of Wales, was killed in battle by the Duke of Clarence. The ageing Duchess of York is the widow of Richard, Duke of York and the mother of four sons, two of whom become king. Her eldest son was crowned as King Edward IV and her youngest son followed as Richard III. Her second son the Earl of Rutland was killed at the Battle of Wakefield in 1460. Her third son George, Duke of Clarence was believed murdered on the instructions of his younger brother Richard in 1478 while imprisoned in the Tower of London. Richard is also suspected of murdering his two young nephews, the so-called 'Princes in the Tower'. The mother of the two young princes, named Edward and Richard, was Queen Elizabeth. Born Elizabeth Woodville, in the play she is the widow of King Edward IV.

Historically, Margaret of Anjou had actually returned to France by the time of the action in *Richard III.* However, the three women are portrayed by the author with great sympathy as the 'chorus of grieving queens', understandably so with many deaths to blame on their viciously treacherous menfolk, most of all on Richard Crookback, 'hell's black intelligencer'. (*Richard III*, 4.4.71). David Crystal and his son Ben Crystal in their book *Shakespeare's Words* interpret the word 'intelligencer' as 'agent' or 'spy'. Everyone spied on everyone else at a time of great tension and suspicion in a rapidly changing and dangerous world.

There are associations with Edward de Vere because two of the queens mentioned above founded Queens' College at Cambridge, these being Margaret of Anjou in 1448 and Elizabeth Woodville, Edward IV's queen, in 1465. When John de Vere the 12th earl of Oxford and his son Aubrey de Vere were executed by Edward IV in 1462 some of their lands were confiscated and made over to the college. When the Lancastrians under Henry VII reversed the advantage the lands were restored to John de Vere the thirteenth Earl.

King Richard III made over large grants of land to Queens' College during his brief reign 1483–85, and also proclaimed his wife Anne Neville as a founder and patroness of the college. Anne Neville was the younger daughter of the earl of Warwick and the widow of Edward of Westminster, the only son of Henry VI. Although she endowed the college with considerable generosity, Anne Neville is not now considered to be a founder. Edward de Vere attended Queens' College 1558–59 and so could have been aware of this association with his family.

Another mother is Queen Gertrude, the mother of Hamlet in *Hamlet*, and their fraught relationship has been the subject of much literary and psychiatric debate. When the play opens Gertrude's husband, old King Hamlet, has recently died and she has married his brother Claudius, now King Claudius. Danish kings, like Anglo-Saxon kings, were elected from among the ruling elite so sons did not necessarily succeed fathers. Hamlet would seem to have been the victim of an opportunistic palace coup while he was absent at university, being presented with a *fait accompli* on his return. At the reception for the new king and his bride, the second scene in the play, Claudius and Queen Gertrude make haste to placate Hamlet who remains in mourning for his father and to prove it is still dressed in black. Claudius reassures him that his position at court is secure. 'You are the most immediate to our throne' (1.2.109).

Hamlet's age if calibrated from the graveyard scene would be in his middle to late twenties since Yorick who bore him on his back 'a thousand times' has lain in the earth 'three-and-twenty years'. This is rather old for a university student who would more likely have been much younger. Either way, Hamlet was certainly old enough to have contested with his uncle for the succession, but given the lack of resolution in his nature, which becomes evident as the play unfolds, it seems that instead he tamely allowed the moment to pass. Hamlet had been studying at the German-speaking Wittenberg University, a Lutheran foundation in the forefront of the Protestant Reformation. King Claudius tries to dissuade Hamlet from returning to Wittenberg (1.2.113), as does his mother who implores him to stay.

Even though Claudius later emerges as the villain of the piece he is also portrayed as energetic and decisive, acting quickly to consolidate his position by marrying the widowed queen. From the opening lines of the play it is made plain that civil unrest exists, 'Something is rotten in the state of Denmark', as the soldier Marcellus observes. Members of the court readily accept Claudius as the new king and also approve his marriage, perhaps seeing it as a stabilising influence. Polonius, Denmark's chief minister, has adjusted quickly to the changed situation and also defers to the new king's authority. Only the returned Hamlet, defiantly wearing black at the wedding celebrations, signals his resentment at the regime change and with it his intention to spoil the party.

The play unfolds from Hamlet's viewpoint. The ghost of old King Hamlet is used as the device by which the author informs the audience of events in the recent past that will foreshadow the action to come. Everyone loves a ghost story so this gets *Hamlet* off to a flying start. The Ghost informs Hamlet that his death had been unnatural, that he had in fact been murdered, and that the murderer, 'Now wears his crown'. (1.5.35–45)

'Mine uncle?' Hamlet queries in surprise, apparently having no suspicion of foul play before that point. The Ghost replies, 'Ay, that incestuous, that adulterate beast.'

Other references to incest occur throughout the play. Hamlet accepts this calumny against his mother by his father, presumably on the grounds that marriage between in-laws breached the church's canon law at the time. In the same speech the Ghost, as a character in the play, also condemns the marriage between his widow Gertrude and his brother Claudius as adulterous. 'Our o'er-hasty marriage', as Gertrude describes it when trying to find a reason for her son Hamlet's disturbed behaviour (2.2.57). The Ghost implies that Gertrude had been skilfully seduced into adultery by Claudius '... won to his shameful lust / The will of my most seeming-virtuous queen'.

To describe his wife as only 'seeming-virtuous' is a damaging slur on her character which could have adversely hardened Hamlet's behaviour towards her in their agitated exchanges later in the play. Nothing in the text corroborates the Ghost's implication that the queen and her brother-in-law had been lovers in an illicit liaison prior to her husband's death. Nor is there anything in the text to suggest that Gertrude thought her husband's death was suspicious, thus exonerating her from complicity in a plot to murder him. In the later closet scene the queen admits to some past misdemeanours but whether this refers to an adulterous relationship with Claudius is too vague to be conclusive. (3.4.79–81).

> O Hamlet, speak no more!
> Thou turn'st mine eyes into my very soul.
> And there I see such black and grained spots
> As will not leave their tinct.

With all these revelations the Ghost has successfully set the plot in motion, providing Hamlet with a three-pronged imperative for wishing to kill King Claudius: for murdering old King Hamlet his father, for seducing and incestuously marrying his mother Queen Gertrude, and for denying him consideration for the throne of Denmark. Hamlet is deeply unsettled by these disclosures, most of all by his father's command that he should, 'Revenge his foul and most unnatural murder'.

Hamlet also has problems of his own. As a university student the opportunity existed for him to have gained some measure of sexual experience while living away from home but in view of his maladroit relationship with Ophelia, and to a lesser extent with his mother, this may not have happened. His palace courtship of Ophelia during the play is ineptly prosecuted and ends disastrously, perhaps because he lacked this basic experience of how to approach and treat women. Considered in tandem with his revulsion at his mother's remarriage, Hamlet emerges as a deeply disturbed young man unable to cope with adult life and sexuality. He is repressed and inhibited, he rails against his mother for having sexual feelings, feelings which he considers unseemly for a woman in middle age (3.4.67–8).

> You cannot call it love, for at your age
> The heyday in the blood is tame

The agitated exchanges between Hamlet and his mother Queen Gertrude in the closet scene must qualify as one of the most amazing cascade of words and images in the English language, a tour de force of dramatic script-writing.[1] Hamlet's fixation with his mother's sexuality, and his fantasising over intimate details of her lovemaking with her new husband, are expressed with equal levels of disgust and fascination, but always delivered on stage in a blaze of passion. (3.4.81–4).

> Nay, but to live
> In the rank sweat of an enseamèd bed
> Stewed in corruption, honeying and making love
> Over the nasty sty

If 'enseamèd' can be read as a bed 'soiled with semen' these are certainly strong words for a young man to speak in reproof to his mother. Modern productions of the play now routinely include a bed in the closet scene, thus implying an oedipal context. It was the Austrian neurologist Sigmund Freud (1856–1939) whose pioneer methods in psycho-analysis identified the Oedipus complex as the underlying cause of much mental disorder. Freud saw in *Hamlet*, this most famous of plays, a vindication of his theory that all men at some stage in their lives are jealous of their fathers and incestuously desire their mothers. In his important work *The Interpretation of Dreams* (in the translation by James Strachey) he postulates that this is the explanation for Hamlet's feverishly disordered state of mind, a condition which he can only assuage by murdering King Claudius.

The British neurologist Dr Ernest Jones (1879–1958) became closely associated with Freud and enthusiastically disseminated his methods of psycho-analysis across the English speaking world. His book *Hamlet and Oedipus* based on Freud's theories was published by Victor Gollancz in 1949. Although plausible as a theory there is nothing in the actual text to support a Freudian hypothesis that Hamlet is jealous of his mother's new lover, or that he incestuously desires her for himself. This simplistic view may have been triggered by mentions of incest in the text of the play, but they are made either by Hamlet or his ghostly father and clearly refer to Gertrude's remarriage with her husband's brother contrary to contemporary ecclesiastical law, not from Hamlet's suppressed desire to have sex with his mother.

The docile Ophelia and the sybaritic Gertrude are the two women in Hamlet's life, his lover and his mother. What of their characters, as revealed by the text? If they seem passive, childlike even, it could be because they lived in a patriarchal society and had been conditioned from birth to be obedient and submissive. Gertrude may have had little say in whether or not to marry Claudius but clearly there were advantages in her doing so, if only to retain her status and spending power as the Queen, and to afford some measure of protection to her son Hamlet. From the text Claudius and Gertrude seem genuinely fond of one another, although she never addresses him or refers to him as 'Claudius'. (Nor is this name used by anyone else in the play).

Ophelia's circumstances are pathetic throughout, a tragic heroine if ever there was one, meekly obeying her father's instructions to reject Hamlet's offers of love. She is also a recipient of similar advice from her brother Laertes, who is not only unduly possessive but as equally long-winded as her father. Ophelia's age is never established with certainty but she seems to have been a troubled adolescent overwhelmed by the malign forces resulting from the regime change, confused and hurt by Hamlet's rejection and finally maddened by her father's brutal death.

A case could be made that Hamlet as well as Ophelia was in awe of a stern overbearing father. Judging from his speeches as the Ghost, the recently deceased king was not possessed of a frivolous nature. A childhood spent in his bleak seashore castle could go some way to explaining Hamlet's social and sexual difficulties. Although no precise parallels can be drawn Edward de Vere's mother Countess Margery also remarried soon after the death of her husband John de Vere the 16th earl of Oxford. Whether Edward as an adolescent was troubled by this earlier example of an 'o'er hasty marriage' can only be a matter of speculation but the difficulties he experienced in consummating his own marriage with Anne Cecil point to an uneasy parallel with Prince Hamlet's bungled courtship of Ophelia.

Hamlet's derangement comes and goes as the play unfolds, when real or when feigned is hard to determine. When Polonius, concealed behind the draperies, was slain by Hamlet's rapier the king must have known that he was the intended victim and made haste to have the recalcitrant prince removed as far from his sight as possible. The journey to England and back again seemed to have stabilised Hamlet's mental turmoil but this is resurrected by his graveside grief when he sees the unburied Ophelia in her grave.

So who wrote Hamlet? And when? Topical allusions would support a date of writing as early as 1587–9. The soldier Barnardo's description of a bright star has been identified as a supernova observed in 1572 by the Danish astronomer Tycho Brahe. (1.1.34–36)

> When yon same star that's westward from the pole
> Had made his course t'illume that part of heaven
> Where now it burns ...

Edward de Vere's brother-in-law Peregrine Bertie, Baron Willoughby d'Eresby, journeyed to Denmark five times between 1582–85 on official government business. It is recorded in state papers that on one of these visits he called on Tycho Brahe at the observatory and research institute provided for him by the Danish government. In the course of his ambassadorial duties Bertie spent many months living in the castle of Elsinore, another intriguing link to de Vere as the author of *Hamlet*, which is set in this castle.

The execution of Mary Queen of Scots in February 1587 could provide another topical allusion. The grim example of Richard II and his untimely death in captivity amply demonstrated the dark forces that are unleashed when an anointed sovereign is deposed and murdered. Queen Elizabeth's long-sustained anguish about whether or not to kill her long-imprisoned cousin was eventually solved by allowing Lord Burghley to enforce the outcome and shoulder the blame. Hamlet is likewise superstitiously reluctant to be responsible for the death of a king and cannot screw himself up 'to the sticking place'. In both cases only a direct threat to their lives prompted the final drastic action. Queen Elizabeth allowed herself to be convinced that Mary Stuart was conspiring to bring about her death. Hamlet was finally motivated to act when discovering that King Claudius had conspired with Rosencrantz and Guildenstern to bring about his death in England. In his exchange with Horatio (Act 5, Scene 2) he makes clear his intention to kill the king and explains his reasons, which include being denied the throne of Denmark:

> Does it not, think'st thee, stand me now upon –
> He that hath killed my king and whored my mother,
> Popped in between th'election and my hopes,
> Thrown out his angle for my proper life,
> And with such cozenage – is't not perfect conscience
> To quit him with this arm?

Hamlet is not only the longest of the plays but also the most richly sourced. Although the Danish historian Saxo Grammaticus was the originator of the Amleth legend, and François Bellforest's *Les Histoires Tragiques* the closest model, a myriad of other writers have been identified by literary scholars as having an influence on the text of *Hamlet*. Geoffrey Bullough, Harold Jenkins and Kenneth Muir between them list many books in Latin, French or Italian for which no translations into English had been published. The French essayist Michel de Montaigne is agreed to have been widely quoted in *Hamlet* (and also in *King Lear*). His *Essais* were published in French between 1580–88, long before John Florio's English translation of 1603. Harold Jenkins identified *Cardanus Comforte* as a source for the 'To be, or not to be' speech. Edward de Vere commissioned Thomas Bedingfield to provide a translation of this book from the Italian. The vast range of texts drawn on for *Hamlet* would have been readily available to de Vere, a competent linguist and buyer of books, who also had access to Lord Burghley's extensive library.

The character of Polonius is generally agreed on all sides of the authorship debate to be an unflattering caricature of Lord Burghley, portraying him as senile and interfering. If so a comparison is forced with their respective daughters, Ophelia and Anne Cecil, Edward de Vere's wife. Could any other contemporary dramatist possess sufficient knowledge of Burghley's private life and mannerisms to write *Hamlet*? Or who would have dared to expose him to ridicule on the open stage? By the same reasoning it could offer an explanation why Edward de Vere prudently opted to write behind the shield of a pseudonym. This denial of authorship came with a price, the permanent forfeiture of his rights to the intellectual property contained in the plays, and the lack of worldly acknowledgement for his literary achievements, both of which continue to the present day.

As a dramatist of genius he had created Shakespeare's ultimate dysfunctional family, six cleverly differentiated characters (seven with old King Hamlet) whose fates are worked out within the stone walls of a medieval fortress. Ophelia had to cope with her possessive brother Laertes and her murdered father Polonius. Gertrude had to cope with her deeply disturbed son Hamlet and the machinations of her second husband Claudius. Shakespeare's widely acclaimed masterwork, so full of highly charged emotion, derives its energy and momentum from the interplay of these complex family relationships.

Hamlet merits its reputation as the most powerful drama in the English language, and its central character has independently achieved iconic status. Although stage interpretations of Hamlet's personality differ widely, from neurotic and obsessed to princely and thoughtful, a literary consensus has emerged against which other young male characters in life and fiction can be compared. A Hamlet figure would be melancholy, dignified and highly intellectual while at the same time vulnerable, misunderstood and ineffectual.

Does the text of the play actually support this? Could it be open to an alternative interpretation, namely that Hamlet and not Claudius is the villain of the piece? Consider this. Prince Hamlet returns home from university to find his father dead, his uncle occupying the throne he coveted for himself, and entered into a married sexual relationship with his mother. His fragile state of mind in the opening reception scene at court reveals him as angry and resentful. The Ghost does not speak to anyone other than Hamlet who hears only what he wants to hear and thus justified sets out self-righteously on a path of destruction, sustained with unrelenting malevolence and purpose. Hamlet's last words in the play take account of the vacancy he has created for the throne of Denmark, and how he would cast his vote (5.2.307–08).

> But I do prophesy th' election lights
> On Fortinbras. He has my dying voice.

The sequence of events resulting from Hamlet's mental derangement culminate in the annihilation of himself, his family and those nearest to him. This is revenge and self-destruction on an epic scale. The coinciding putsch by Fortinbras completes the rout with the overthrow of the royal family, the court and the state of Denmark. It is an awe-inspiring end to a stupendous drama.

16

Tudor Myths

Were I a king

Were I a king I could command content;
　Were I obscure, unknown should be my cares;
And were I dead, no thoughts should me torment,
　Nor words, nor wrongs, nor loves, nor hopes, nor fears.
A doubtful choice, of three things one to crave,
　A kingdom, or a cottage, or a grave.

Written by the Earl of Oxenford

Although much is known about the reign of Queen Elizabeth I there are also many gaps in the documentation. Novelists and film makers have filled these gaps with popular historical fiction, loosely based around real events involving the queen. Her flirtatious nature, her love of entertainment and her fondness for handsome courtiers, inevitably generated gossip of affairs.

One of the more persistent stories about Elizabeth is that she was made pregnant as a teenager by her guardian Thomas Seymour and gave birth to his child. This was then farmed out to a surrogate family of suitable rank and brought up as their own, with the wealthy and aristocratic Veres of Hedingham Castle a convenient choice, and Edward de Vere a baby at about the right time. Thus begins the 'Prince Tudor' hypothesis, ignoring the fact that such a child would have been illegitimate, and royal bastards are excluded from succession to the throne.

Thomas Seymour, Lord Sudely, had married Catherine Parr four months after the death of her husband King Henry VIII in 1547. It was her fourth marriage. Catherine had provided a home for Henry's three children, all future sovereigns, Mary, Elizabeth and Edward, but only Elizabeth stayed on with her when she moved to a house in Chelsea after her remarriage. Catherine was officially Elizabeth's guardian, but her husband Thomas Seymour acquired this automatically on marriage, and he was also the guardian of Lady Jane Grey. The fourteen-year-old Elizabeth soon became the object of the forty-year-old Seymour's affections, even obsession, since he refused to moderate his amorous behaviour even when his wife intervened and sent Elizabeth to the royal residence of Hatfield for her own safety. The former queen consort was herself pregnant and died in childbirth at the age of thirty-six, allowing Seymour to renew his pursuit of Elizabeth.

Thomas Seymour was a well-connected member of the ruling elite, a

Garter Knight and Lord High Admiral. His sister Jane Seymour had been King Henry's third wife which made him the uncle of the young King Edward VI. But Thomas was eclipsed by his elder brother Edward Seymour, Duke of Somerset, who was appointed Lord Protector as the de facto ruler of the country, since the new king was only ten years old. Things soon began to go wrong for Thomas, who was jealous of his brother's power and schemed to overthrow him. Suspected of plotting to marry Elizabeth and bid for the throne himself he was convicted of high treason by a Bill of Attainder and summarily executed after the briefest of trials. He was beheaded at the Tower on 20th March 1549.

Still only fifteen, Elizabeth had written a long letter dated 28th January 1549 to Lord Protector Somerset protesting her innocence. She denied the rumours that she was with child by the Lord Admiral and asked to be allowed to come to court and show herself as not pregnant. The Seymour affair had been very unsettling for Elizabeth whose position was increasingly precarious with her underage and sickly half-brother on the throne as King Edward VI. The strain on her nerves and delicate constitution precipitated a long period of illness, both physical and mental. Held in virtual captivity, and in constant danger and fear for her life in the ten years preceding her succession in 1558, Elizabeth's health never fully recovered.

Contrary to popular belief she was far from robust, subject to recurring illnesses and infections for the rest of her life. This makes all the more remarkable her grasp of affairs and ability to cope with the pressures of monarchy in turbulent times. She outlived most of her enemies, including the Duke of Somerset who suffered a similar fate to his brother. He was beheaded on 22nd January 1552, victim of a coup led by John Dudley earl of Warwick, the main complaint against him being his unsuccessful and financially draining wars against Scotland and France.

Scholars arguing the case for Edward de Vere as Shakespeare have always strenuously refuted any suggestion that he was the love child of Thomas Seymour and the teenage princess, not only viewing it as untrue but worse, a damaging irrelevance. The idea had vestiges of credibility because John de Vere the 16th earl of Oxford at the time in question was leading a complicated love life. Separated from his aristocratic first wife Dorothy Neville (daughter of the 4th earl of Westmorland), he had at least two mistresses and went through a bigamous marriage ceremony with one of them. Dorothy Neville died in 1548 and in the same year he married as his second wife Margery Golding.

As mentioned in an earlier chapter, when Earl John died twelve years later the legitimacy of this second marriage was challenged by his eldest daughter Lady Katherine Vere, the daughter of his first wife Dorothy Neville, on the grounds that her mother was still living when the second marriage took place. All the circumstances surrounding Edward's date of birth in 1550, his parentage and his right of inheritance were thus brought into question. Edward, by this time twelve years old, had been summoned to London as a royal ward and installed in the home of Sir William Cecil. Edward's maternal uncle Arthur Golding, a Cambridge graduate, was a member of Sir William Cecil's administrative staff and issued a strongly worded rebuttal document on behalf of his sister and his nephew. This was dated 28th June 1563 and resulted in Lady Katherine Vere and her husband Lord Edward Windsor not pursuing the matter further.

Although Edward de Vere's legitimacy and right of inheritance were not challenged again a charge of bastardy is never entirely lived down. Matters were not helped when Arthur Golding's written response gave Edward and his younger sister Mary Vere the same age, thus perpetuating the confusion over his exact date of birth. So if there had been a changeling baby boy needing to be smuggled away from Hatfield and accommodated elsewhere, the solid stone walls of Hedingham Castle could have offered all the concealment, confusion and subterfuge that such a plan would have required.

Edward de Vere married his guardian's daughter Anne Cecil nine years after his summons to London. From the start theirs was not a successful marriage. One of the many theories put forward to account for Edward's separation from his young wife so early is that as a member of the court he witnessed at first hand the efforts made to find the queen a suitable husband and realised too late that had he not been married he might have been an acceptable suitor himself. The possibility exists that he could have been thinking of annulment through non-consummation of his marriage, in which case he would have been free to marry the queen.

During the years 1572–73 de Vere was certainly high in the queen's favour and the court gossips suspected that he was in a sexual relationship with her. Gilbert Talbot, later the 7th earl of Shrewsbury, was a court insider who wrote candidly, indiscreetly and disparagingly about de Vere in letters to his father, including the information that the earl's neglected young wife Countess Anne was jealous because of his close association with the queen.[1] Both of de Vere's early twenty-first century biographers, Mark Anderson[2] and Alan Nelson,[3] quote from the letter Mary Stuart, imprisoned in Sheffield Castle, wrote to Queen Elizabeth '... the Earl of Oxford dared not reconcile himself with his wife for fear of losing the favour which he hoped to receive by becoming your lover'.

Queen Elizabeth's final suitor, in 1579, was the Duke of Anjou, heir to his brother King Henri III of France. He was twenty-four, the Queen was forty-six. Edward de Vere was twenty-nine so the age difference might not have been an insurmountable problem for him had circumstances permitted. François de Valois, Duke of Anjou and Alençon (1555–1584) was the youngest son of Henri II of France and Catherine de Medici. He became heir to the French throne in 1574 and in 1579 came to London as a suitor. Deformed and eccentric, and twenty-two years younger than the Queen, the suit failed, although on friendly terms. The Duke died prematurely at the age of twenty-nine and was replaced as heir by Henry of Navarre, a Huguenot, later King Henri IV of France.

The buffoon character of Bottom in *A Midsummer Night's Dream* could be seen as a parody of Alençon. In the exchanges with Titania and her fairies when transformed into an ass, he makes frequent use of the term 'Monsieur'. This is the title used to address the Dauphin, the French king's heir, a position held by Alençon at the time of his visit. Portraying the Queen as Titania making love to Alençon as a donkey would have been insensitive and provocative, one more reason perhaps why the author of this play wisely chose not to disclose his identity. Another member of the acting troupe, Quince, needs only one letter changed to be the French 'Quinze'. The French ambassador Bertrand de Salignac Fénélon, seigneur de la Mothe, later published anecdotes of his life at Queen Elizabeth's court, *Memoires touchant l'Angleterre*. One of Titania's fairy courtiers is given the name Moth, an allusion that would not have been lost on a courtly audience.

Oxfordians are equally unconvinced about an alternative version of events which suggests that Henry Wriothesley the third Earl of Southampton was the natural son of Edward de Vere, with Queen Elizabeth as his mother. Portraits of the earl and his real mother show such a remarkably close resemblance that the notion of an alternative royal mother is impossible to sustain. The portrait of the incarcerated earl in the Tower of London was painted by John de Critz in 1603 and hangs in Boughton House, Northamptonshire. The portrait of his mother Mary Browne, daughter of the 1st Viscount Montagu, painted in 1565, hangs in Welbeck Abbey, Nottinghamshire

Did de Vere believe any of these royalty stories himself? Did he have delusions of inheriting the throne? His flamboyant signature has been much studied for clues.

This gives his name underlined with a bar (for the numeral ten) with seven slashes to make seventeen, overtopped by his earl's coronet. Does this stake a claim to be King Edward VII, as some have supposed? Surely not. Throughout his life de Vere behaved with the innate sense of superiority consonant with high caste, and in his plays upheld respect for the old feudal structure which Tudor modernisation had superseded, but there is no evidence that he coveted the crown for himself, or even that he believed himself to have a realistic claim.

There is a considerable literature on variations of the Prince Tudor (or more accurately 'Royal Bastard') theme with Dorothy and Charlton

Ogburn's biography of de Vere, *This Star of England*, 1952, the first and most influential. Others include Paul Streitz, *Oxford: Son of Queen Elizabeth I*, 2001; Elizabeth Sears, *Shakespeare and the Tudor Rose*, 2002; Hank Whittemore, *The Monument*, 2005 and Helen Heightsman Gordon, *The Secret Love Story in Shakespeare's Sonnets*. The latest is *Shakespeare's Lost Kingdom* by Charles Beauclerk, published in 2010. A film, *Anonymous*, with even more lurid Prince Tudor action perpetuates this strange belief.

Speculation over the identity of the so-called 'Dark Lady of the Sonnets' (127–152) helped to stimulate popular interest in Shakespeare. The notion of an illicit love affair added a much needed frisson of danger and excitement to the Stratford man, in what would otherwise have been an uninspiring life story. It involved class, always of interest, as it was assumed that the dark lady in question occupied a higher social status than the humbly born playwright and so was beyond his reach. Hence the outpouring of frustration and anguish in poems of unrequited love. London was not only the capital city it was also the nation's largest port. A steady inflow of people from elsewhere, many of them wealthy merchants and their families, made London increasingly cosmopolitan. Rich migrant families established over several generations contributed to the racial mix with many beautiful women of Jewish, Italian and middle eastern origin. Could one of these have had a complexion meriting the 'dark lady' accolade?

Early sixteenth-century sonneteers adapted Italian and French models, translating from Petrarch and Ronsard. The English sonnet, which became known as the Shakespearean sonnet, was pioneered by Thomas Wyatt and developed by Henry Howard, the 5th earl of Surrey, who was Edward de Vere's uncle. He established the strict rhyming metre and the division into three quatrains concluded by a rhyming couplet. Later poets, Wordsworth most notably, criticised Shakespeare for not adhering closely enough to these classic structures.

The English obsession with class prompted Alfred Lord Tennyson to write a poem with the title *Lady Clara Vere de Vere*[4] It is about a lowly suitor who woos the aristocratic lady of the title, 'the daughter of a hundred earls'. It contrasts his solid proletarian worthiness against the disdain of a high-born snooty heiress. She has 'a coat of arms and lions on her gates' while he has a mother not quite up to the mark.

> Her manners had not that repose
> Which stamps the caste of Vere de Vere

So there was no happy ending for the lovelorn swain of the poem who consoled himself with the thought that

> Kind hearts are more than coronets
> And simple faith than Norman blood

If Tennyson's poem is remembered at all it is for these often quoted lines.

And if, as many believe, and seems likely, Shakespeare's sonnets carry an autobiographical subtext then the 'Dark Lady' sonnets certainly need explaining because some of them contain an astonishing parade of bitter misogyny. What kind of woman could have provoked such anguished desire and angry resentment? The last line of Sonnet 147 reads, '*Who art as black as hell, as dark as night*'. Does any woman deserve to be reproached in these terms? What unhappy state of mind caused such words to be written?

Bernard Shaw was so intrigued by these difficult poems that he wrote a short play with the title *The Dark Lady of the Sonnets*. It takes the form of a dialogue between Queen Elizabeth and Master Will Shakespear, with contributions from Mary Fitton.[5] As a dramatist Shaw had a high opinion of his own work, which he considered superior to that of Shakespeare.[6] He was a perceptive critic, of literature as well as of music, and singled out the jealousy scenes in *Othello* for special praise. He described Othello's cataract of wild abstract images as 'word-music'. This is contained in his *Dramatic Opinions and Essays* and includes his belief that Mary Sidney was the role model

> ... for the most charming of all Shakespear's old women, indeed the most charming of all his women, young or old, the Countess of Roussillon in *All's Well That Ends Well*.

This is a play in which links to the life of Edward de Vere can be advanced as part of the authorship debate. The two main characters are Helena the daughter of a physician, and Bertram the young Count of Roussillon. Helena has grown up in the same house as Bertram just as Edward de Vere had lived in the same house as his future wife Anne Cecil (Hamlet and Ophelia likewise). Helena and Anne are commoners while Edward and Bertram are noblemen. Apart from not being sufficiently attracted to the young ladies to want to marry them, Edward and Bertram share another mutual problem, namely that both are wards dominated by their authoritarian guardians, William Cecil and the King of France respectively. Both are eager for active military service, both had their applications refused, and both escaped the court in search of battlefield glory. Both become unhappy marriage partners. Bertram, a royal ward 'evermore in subjection', married Helena at the King's insistence but against his will. In a defiant letter to his mother he writes, 'I have wedded her, not bedded her.' Nor does he intend to, and flees the country. (3.2.19–27). But Helena is resourceful and determined. Having used her medical skills to cure the King of France of a fistula she is awarded Bertram as her fee, and when he rejects her, she makes use of the bed-trick to consummate her marriage, impregnate herself and force a reconciliation with her absentee husband.

The bed trick involves substitution, almost invariably one woman for another rather than a male substitute. Making the switch in a darkened bedroom is obviously difficult but not impossible. With the development of brighter methods of house lighting the bed trick as a literary device became rare. Until then it occurred regularly in theatrical and literary history, in the Arthurian legends among others. In *Genesis* Chapter 9 Jacob has served seven years for Laban's second daughter Rachel, but on their wedding night Laban substituted a veiled Leah, claiming in justification that the elder daughter should be married first. The plot of *All's Well That Ends Well* is based on Boccaccio (ninth story of the third day).

The American writer Marliss C. Desens cites over two hundred and fifty examples in her book *The Bed-Trick in English Renaissance Drama: Explorations in Gender, Sexuality and Power*, published by the University of Delaware in 1994. Substitute sex partners occur elsewhere in Shakespeare, Hero instead of her cousin in *Much Ado* and Palamon and the jailer's daughter in *The Two Noble Kinsmen*. In *Measure for Measure* the disguised Duke acting as facilitator for Angelo substitutes the rejected Mariana for the heroine Isabel in order to bring the play to a conclusion. Iachimo in *Cymbeline* infiltrates Innogen's bedroom while she is asleep.

J Thomas Looney in *Shakespeare Identified*, (page 234), quotes from a local history source that Anne Countess of Oxford used the bed-trick to be made pregnant by her husband, from whom she had been separated for three years. Her daughter Elizabeth was born on 2nd July 1575 which would have required conception to have occurred on or around the 9th of October 1574, at which time she was staying at Hampton Court. In *The History and Topography of the County of Essex* published in 1836 the author Thomas Wright claimed, 'He (the earl of Oxford) forsook his lady's bed but the father of Lady Anne by stratagem, contrived that her husband should unknowingly sleep with her, believing her to be another woman, and she bore a son to him as a consequence of this meeting'. (Volume 1 p. 517). The resulting baby was a daughter rather than a son, which casts doubt on the story, as does implicating Lord Burghley in the subterfuge, but it remains an interesting link between Edward de Vere and plays by Shakespeare.

The case for Edward de Vere as Shakespeare does not depend for its validity on any of the dynastic claims inherent in the Prince Tudor or other royalty theories involving his birth and ancestry. Although he received Queen Elizabeth's patronage as a young courtier he soon fell from grace and afterwards received little by way of favouritism. He was allotted only token military commands, was denied membership of the Privy Council, was regularly voted down for a Garter Knighthood, was refused the governorship of Jersey (awarded to Walter Raleigh), the presidency of Wales (awarded to his Hackney neighbour Baron Zouche), and the lucrative Cornish tin-mining franchise, all sinecures that he coveted.

If *Hamlet* is the most autobiographical of Shakespeare's plays, as many scholars on all sides of the authorship debate have considered it to be, then the prince's bitter reply to Rosencrantz (3.2.327), truthfully expresses his frustration and disappointment. 'Sir, I lack advancement'.

17

Unruly Servants

I scorn to think I am so weak of government as to be ruled by servants
From the postscript of a letter to Lord Burghley in 1584.

Edward de Vere's early letters to William Cecil as his guardian, and later as his father-in-law, were formal and courteous, and his references to the queen unfailingly respectful. As he reached his thirties, with his father-in-law still regulating his expenditure, a note of irritation can be detected in his letters. Until the end of his life he was never able to free himself from the Cecil grip over his financial and domestic affairs. The family overlap had led in the past to Burghley treating de Vere's servants as if they were his own, something that was always going to lead to friction.

Even before he came into his money at the age of twenty-one the young earl had done his best to slip the Cecil leash. He began aggregating around himself a company of unattached young men eager to prove themselves as loyal followers. One of these was Roland York, the ne'er-do-well son of a good family, blamed by de Vere's in-laws and others for leading him astray. Not that he needed much encouragement and his capricious nature and liking for low company began the process of disengaging himself from the conventional career development expected of an aristocrat with close connections to the court.

In January 1576, while on his continental travels, the journeying earl wrote a long letter to his father-in-law from Siena. He was rapidly running out of money and wanted Burghley to sell off more of his lands to raise some ready cash. He was determined to continue with his tour even though foreign travel with servants was draining his resources. Burghley had his daughter's future to consider and tried to slow down the rate at which de Vere was impoverishing himself.

On this occasion the earl had someone at home in England to blame for his present shortage. His man Edwin Hubbard was acting as a land agent, buying and selling properties on his behalf. They had worked out a scheme whereby Hubbard promised de Vere he would buy properties and then sell them back when asked but ended up with the money as well as the properties. De Vere was furious but all he could do from a distance was to ask Burghley to 'discharge him from all dealings of mine'. To explain this request he writes, '... he has taken more than I meant ... he deserveth very evil at my hands.'

In April 1576 de Vere's return from Italy marked the start of an acrimonious estrangement from his wife that lasted for six years. His false friend Roland York was suspected of poisoning de Vere's mind against his wife, convincing him that he had not fathered Anne's daughter Elizabeth, born while he was out of the country. De Vere's Catholic cousin Lord Henry Howard (younger brother of Thomas Howard the executed duke of Norfolk), has also been held responsible for the rumours of marital infidelity that blighted the marriage. In Shakespeare a case could be made for either York or Henry Howard as the duplicitous ensign Iago who turns Othello's mind against his wife Desdemona. Iachimo in *Cymbeline* is another character who spreads lies about a recently-married and innocent woman. On 27th April 1576, from Greenwich, de Vere wrote an angry letter to Lord Burghley, blaming him for making his domestic affairs public. Bitterly he writes, 'This might have been done with private conference and had not needed to have been the fable of the world'.

Another servant of de Vere's, William Sankey, was knifed by a man named William Weekes, and died from his wounds. Weekes was pursued, quickly captured, tried, convicted and hanged. The story which emerged later suggested that Weekes had killed the wrong man, Roland York being the intended target at the instigation of de Vere. Why the earl should have wanted to kill York no one knows: the accusation that he did came from his alienated cousin Henry Howard. When captured Weekes had a large sum of money on him. Howard claimed this was his assassin's fee and had come from de Vere. This may well have been another unproved Charles Arundel–Henry Howard accusation levelled against the earl in retaliation for his exposure of them as Catholic conspirators.

In a letter to Burghley in 1581, referring to the time he had spent imprisoned in the Tower after fathering a child with one of the queen's gentlewomen, de Vere complained about the behaviour of his servants during his absence. He told Burghley that during his incarceration the queen was aware that he 'had been hardly used' by some of his servants. This implied criticism of the queen, and less deference in his subsequent letters to Lord Burghley, are consistent with his steady detachment from the court as he moved into his thirties.

Edward de Vere employed the accomplished writer John Lyly as his Blackfriars stage manager, and also to carry out various secretarial duties which apparently involved keeping track of financial matters, the reason for their falling out. The earl's squabbles with his retainers were almost always about money, or rather the lack of it. In July 1582 Lyly wrote to Burghley in some distress. This was because de Vere had accused him of fiduciary mismanagement and he needed to protest his innocence.

The incident appears to have been resolved since he remained in his post. In spite of his success with the two *Euphues* books Lyly was unable to find preferment in any of the court positions he applied for, most notably the prestige post of Master of the Revels. This was held by Edmund Tilney from 1579 until his death in 1610, over thirty years. The Master had complete authority under the Lord Chamberlain to censor plays, as well as providing entertainments for the court. Lyly never gave up hope but died poor.

So long as de Vere had the wealth to support his band of male follow-ers, and could pull rank to extricate them from brushes with the law, all went well. As he grew short of money, and the authorities grew short of patience, his relations with his serving men began to sour. The oldest of his retainers was Thomas Churchyard, an educated man, a minor poet and a former soldier. In 1590, having sold Fisher's Folly after the death of his wife in 1588, de Vere needed somewhere to live, plus accommodation for servants. Acting on his behalf Thomas Churchyard rented rooms in expensive central London, assuming that de Vere would cover his costs. For whatever reason de Vere defaulted on the deal and the sixty-seven year old Churchyard ended up financially disadvantaged, living out a penurious existence thereafter.

Another who never got his money was the joiner Edward Johnson, employed by de Vere to refurbish his house in Plaistow, Essex. As a result Johnson went into debt, had to borrow to get out of it, was arrested for non-payment and forced, 'to lay most of his goods to pawn to his great loss and hindrance'.[2] Another servant William Ruswell, whose duties included tailoring, was owed £500 when he died, a huge sum in those days, accounted for by the value of the cloths he stocked. His widow Judith pursued the debt through the courts. De Vere's lawyers argued that the materials in question belonged to their client and not to the servant, and the widow's claim failed.[3]

Two more of de Vere's long-serving henchmen had already got their come-uppance in 1591, although at the hands of Burghley rather than de Vere. His rent collector in Essex, Thomas Hampton, had been keeping some of the money for himself, betraying a position of trust. Israel Amyce (Amiss) had worked for de Vere's father, Earl John, but he was colluding with the owner of a property sold by de Vere while still retaining possession. In a letter dated 18th May 1591, de Vere wrote to Burghley thanking him for sacking the two dishonest servants. He addressed his letter 'To the Right Honourable & his very good Lord the Lord Treasurer of England'.

By this time de Vere had married his second wife, Elizabeth Trentham, who was considerably more business-like than he was, and soon sorted out some of the servants who had been swindling him.[4] One of these was Arthur Mills, or 'Milles'. From 1576 onward he had been entrusted to carry out small business transactions but finally parted company from his employer in 1602. Mills did not go quietly and in a spiteful letter to Robert Cecil he accused the new countess of behaving even more maliciously towards him than her husband. They accused him of theft. He accused them of not paying his commissions.

Henry Lock was another of de Vere's long-serving retainers. In a rambling letter[5] to Lord Burghley from Edinburgh dated 6th November 1590, *Henry Lock to my Lord,* he explains with some indignation that his reason for leaving was because he could no longer afford to work for the earl of Oxford. Over the years he had racked up expenses in the discharge of his employer's business, expenses for which he had never been reimbursed. He also claimed that de Vere owed him £80 in back wages, a considerable sum for those days, certainly many thousands of pounds today. Vaguely he seeks to excuse himself for the shady deals he had done on his master's behalf and put the blame on those who had 'despoiled' the earl and reduced him to virtual bankruptcy. There is no record that Burghley interceded on the servant's behalf, or that he was ever paid the money he was owed.

Henry was the nephew of Michael Lock (1532–1620), a London merchant whose name was also spelled as Lok, or Locke. Formerly a director of the Muscovy Company, he had recently been appointed for a six-year term as governor of the Cathay Company, Cathay being the name used for China at that time. Both companies had a vested interest in navigating a polar trade route to China, Japan and the East-Indies, the so-called Northwest Passage. To this end Lock funded three voyages led by the experienced navigator Martin Frobisher (1535–1594).

Although originally to search for trade routes, with a secondary interest in annexing territory for the crown, all those concerned in the Northwest adventures were diverted from these honourable intentions to search for gold instead. French and Spanish expeditions had found gold elsewhere on the north and south continents of America so hopes were high when Frobisher returned from his first voyage in 1576 with promising samples. These had come from the rocky coast of what is now Canada, the southern extremity of Baffin Island.

The second voyage a year later was sponsored by Queen Elizabeth with a grant of £1,000. Frobisher was appointed admiral of all the lands and seas he discovered and authorised to take possession of them in the Queen's name. Bigger ships and a larger complement of men, including miners, returned with a cargo of two hundred tons of ore. First assay reports were favourable so a third and larger expedition was planned for 1578. The fifteen ships for this voyage included a hundred men with sufficient provisions to establish a permanent coastal settlement. This ambitious project required money and because a generous return on the ore was predicted the money was soon raised. Edward de Vere's initial share was for £1,000 but wishing to invest more and lacking properties to sell for ready cash he took out a bond for £2,000 with the organiser Michael Lock, raising his stake to £3,000.

The expedition set sail from Plymouth on 3rd June 1578 and returned in October with a thousand tons of ore. By now the attempts to smelt gold from the first shipment had failed, confirming them to be worthless iron-pyrites, unkindly called 'fool's gold', with more of the same just landed. Everyone lost their money, the Queen, Edward de Vere and most of all Michael Lock who was speedily removed to the Fleet Prison accused of fraud. Two ships had been lost and the settlement had failed to establish itself in such inhospitable territory, so the venture failed entirely. Michael Lock petitioned the Privy Council from prison, asking for assistance and relief as he was held liable not only for his own debts but for the whole debt of the Cathay Company to which he was bound as governor. He was still petitioning from the Fleet three years later but was eventually released. The law suits did not go away however and for the rest of his life Lock was still being sued for unpaid bills, mostly for supplies to the ill-fated 1578 expedition. Martin Frobisher was later knighted for his services in helping to repel the Spanish Armada.

De Vere's loss of three thousand pounds calls to mind *The Merchant of Venice* in which the financier Shylock is owed a corresponding amount. In this play the spendthrift Bassanio, having run through his own money, asks his close friend Antonio (the merchant of the title) for a loan so that he can woo and marry the heiress Portia and begin spending hers. Antonio is financially overstretched at the time but being in love with Bassanio takes out a three thousand ducat loan with Shylock. His treasure ships are believed lost in a storm and he has to default on the repayment, thus invoking the famous 'pound of flesh' penalty clause.

Edward de Vere had spent longer in Venice than anywhere else in Italy and so could have been familiar with the Venetian buildings, landmarks and traditions which feature in *The Merchant of Venice*. Is Shylock a literary incarnation of Michael Lock? Are de Vere's three thousand pounds and Antonio's three thousand ducats more than just coincidence? The disastrous Canadian voyage has another possible reference in a Shakespeare play. This occurs in Act 2 Scene 2 (line 380) of *Hamlet* when the prince ruefully admits, 'I am but mad north-north-west'. So he was, lured like many others before and since into parting with money for a get-rich-quick scheme that failed to deliver.

Servants and other subordinate characters feature in many Shakespeare plays. Edward de Vere was born into a privileged lifestyle, accustomed to having servants around him all day and every day. From infancy onward he knew how to speak to them, and how they should address him in return. In Shakespeare's great households the noble characters, both men and women, speak freely with their senior trusted servants, they seek advice from them, employ them on sensitive missions, and use them as confidantes. Think of the Nurse in *Romeo and Juliet*, or Polonius briefing his servant Reynaldo to spy on his son Laertes in *Hamlet*. Servants can also be duplicitous, Borachio for example in *Much Ado About Nothing*.

The case for Edward de Vere as the writer of Shakespeare is strengthened by the author's grasp of the complex relationships which exist within the household of a nobleman, or between members of a royal court, and the inter-dependency between masters and servants that make such establishments workable. The plays themselves are mostly set in the large houses of the nobility, and in the palaces and castles of royalty, with a high proportion of aristocratic or ennobled main characters. This is hard to miss but less obvious are the walk-on extras who supplement the main players. These are variously described in the cast lists as Attendants, Beadles, Boys, Children, Citizens, Clowns, Drummers, Grooms, Guards, Headsmen, Heralds, Huntsmen, Jailers, Keepers, Maids, Masquers, Messengers, Musicians, Officers, Pages, Porters, Prentices, Serving men and women, Sheriffs, Soldiers, Torchbearers, Trumpeters, Ushers, Vergers, Warders and Watchmen.

These are not day labourers or artisans, which do not figure prominently in Shakespeare. These are the liveried and uniformed below-stairs brigade who keep a big house running smoothly day and night throughout the year. Only someone accustomed to living in the magnificent dwellings of the rich and powerful would be familiar with this class of people or understand their functions and purpose. Edward de Vere was such a person. His Cecil in-laws, William, Thomas and Robert maintained huge domestic staffs, as did his sons-in-law William Stanley and Philip Herbert.

Familiarity with the structured daily life of these opulent households has always set the plays of Shakespeare apart as different from those of other Elizabethan dramatists.

18

Violence

The flash and outbreak of a fiery mind.
Hamlet 2.1.34

At the age of seventeen, at the home of his guardian Sir William Cecil, the young earl of Oxford killed one of the household servants, a cook named Thomas Brincknell. The incident took place on a summer evening in July 1567. De Vere and another man were practising fencing with rapiers when the victim intervened and bled to death after receiving a stab wound in the thigh.

Hamlet's stabbing of Polonius with a single sword thrust (Act 3, Scene 4) was similar in manner to de Vere's killing of the servant Thomas Brincknell. The newly introduced rapier was a long-range stabbing weapon capable of inflicting severe wounds in any part of the body. Brincknell was wounded in the thigh, and since he bled to death it is likely that his femoral artery was pierced. Polonius and the servant were both in the wrong place at the wrong time. Hamlet's contemptuous dismissal of Polonius as a 'wretched, rash, intruding fool' (3.4.30) would have applied equally well to the unfortunate cook.

A jury decided that the servant, believed to be drunk, had in effect committed suicide by running on to the point of de Vere's sword. Raphael Holinshed the historian, also resident at Cecil House in the Strand in London, served on the jury which acquitted de Vere of blame. Why he should have risked practising without a protective ferrule on the point of his rapier has never been explained. Some years later Sir William Cecil, by then Lord Burghley, expressed regret at the suicide verdict. He had hoped instead for *se defendendo*, self-defence, so that the financial consequences would have been less severe for the dead man's family. This belated apology appears in an undated memorandum quoted in full by Nelson, p.152. No action was taken against the young earl at the time but the dead man's widow was made destitute by the suicide verdict as his goods were forfeited and church burial denied.[1] The grave-diggers in *Hamlet* debate the propriety of Ophelia's Christian burial when her death was apparently by suicide. 'It must be *se offendendo*' misquotes the first digger, (5.1.9), a noteworthy allusion if linked to the death of Thomas Brincknell.

When his wardship ended, Edward de Vere entered into a long-running feud with the earl of Leicester over the administration and reclaim of his estates. De Vere sided with the court faction opposed to Leicester and the political power he was able to exert through enjoying Queen Elizabeth's support, which lasted until the end of his life. Considered as part of the case for Edward de Vere as Shakespeare the earl of Leicester would be a close match for the opportunist King Claudius in *Hamlet.* Leicester was reputed to dispose of his enemies by poison, hence the connection to Claudius who was identified by the Ghost of Old King Hamlet as his murderer. The Ghost tells his son young Hamlet that while having his afternoon nap in the orchard his treacherous brother, Hamlet's uncle, had poured poison into 'the porches of mine ears'. (1.5.63).

Following on from this revelation, in Act 2 of *Hamlet,* the prince asks the touring players 'Can you play the murder of Gonzago?' (2.2.539-40). They can, and this sets up the scene on which the play turns, the elaborate device by which Hamlet hopes to 'catch the conscience of the King'. The players act out in dumb-show how an Italian nobleman was murdered by having poison poured into his ears while asleep. The Gonzago family ruled Mantua for four centuries. In 1538, in Venice, Luigi Gonzaga murdered his cousin the Duke of Orbino by pouring poison in his ears. This account of the story was referred to by the Italian humanist Paolo Giovio (1483-1552) in his *Elogia,* first published 1551 in Latin and a year later in Italian. Hamlet says, 'The story is extant, and writ in choice Italian.' (3.2.250-51). Dr Noemi Magri of the University of Mantua has written extensively on the Italian sources of Shakepeare's plays and considers that the author's knowledge of this family feud murder could also have been acquired from an oral tradition during his stay in Venice 1575-76. (*The Italian Renaissance in Shakespeare's Plays and Poems,* p 294) The King's guilty reaction begins the play's downward spiral.

Edward de Vere's antipathy to the earl of Leicester extended to his nephew Philip Sidney who was sent to be educated at Cecil House. He was four years younger than de Vere but the two young men always behaved as rivals and enemies rather than friends. This simmering enmity came to the boil many years later. In 1579, at the royal tennis court in Greenwich, the two grown men clashed violently and had to be separated. Acting on de Vere's behalf Walter Raleigh arranged a duel with Sidney but on the intervention of the Queen it was never fought. Duels between men of widely differing rank were forbidden. The smouldering feud flared up again a year later but eventually subsided. Alan Nelson quotes from the Arundel Libel Documents in which Henry Howard accused de Vere, his cousin, of conspiring to have Sidney murdered at his home in Greenwich, and of supplying a ship at Gravesend that would provide the hired assassins with an escape route to the European mainland.[2]

Nothing came of this plot but a tennis court quarrel is referred to in *Hamlet.* In Act 2 Scene 1, Polonius, in a long exchange with his servant Reynaldo, recites a lurid list of the pleasurable activities that young men get up to when given the chance to misbehave away from supervision at home. The list includes gaming, drinking, fencing, swearing, quarrelling and visiting brothels. Lastly comes 'falling out at tennis'. De Vere's altercation with Philip Sidney at Greenwich makes a plausible reference for this otherwise puzzling addition to the list.

In April 1576, on his return home from travels in France, Germany and Italy, de Vere's ship was intercepted and boarded by sea robbers. These were identified as Dutch, believed to be from the port of Vlissingen (anglicised as Flushing). Not only were his chests and boxes stolen but his expensive clothes were stripped off and he was roughly treated. It must have been a terrifying ordeal. Burghley and the Queen were indignant at this outrage and complained to the Dutch ambassador. The Prince of Orange sent an apology and assured them that the pirates were being rounded up and imprisoned. The French ambassador to London from 1575–1584 was Michel de Mauvissière.[3] He recorded the incident about the pirates in his *Mémoires* published *c.* 1590.

This violent and life-threatening incident appears to be mirrored by another intriguing mention in *Hamlet*. After the Prince murders Polonius he is forcibly exiled by his uncle King Claudius to England, accompanied by two sycophantic former student friends, Rosencrantz and Guildenstern. They carry a letter from Claudius to the English king authorising Hamlet's death but he is alert to the danger and arranges for them to die instead. The King's hopes of having seen the last of his troublesome nephew are dashed when letters arrive from Hamlet announcing his swift return. In Act Four Scene 6, Horatio reads aloud Hamlet's account of the incident, namely that two days out on the voyage to England 'a pirate of very warlike appointment gave us chase'. Hamlet complains that he was captured and roughly treated, 'they have dealt with me like thieves of mercy'. He was released and set ashore back in Denmark.

In the next scene King Claudius receives the letter addressed to him and reads it aloud to Laertes. Hamlet writes, 'I am set naked on your kingdom' and apologises for his 'sudden and more strange return'. This short account of Hamlet's aborted voyage and the pirate sequence have no bearing on the plot and leads nowhere. It is a strange addition to the story but Edward de Vere's real life encounter with pirates provides the Oxfordian case with another link to the text of a Shakespeare play.

The birth on 21st March 1581 of de Vere's illegitimate son Edward Vere by his young mistress Anne Vavasour was a defining event in his life since it led immediately to his severance from the court. He had been forgiven much, considering his irresponsible and often wilful behaviour as a young man, but his affair with one of Queen Elizabeth's Ladies of the Bedchamber was a breach too far. The Queen was infuriated and imprisoned both de Vere and his mistress with her child separately in the Tower of London.

After fourteen weeks de Vere was released into house arrest, followed by a period of exile from the court which lasted for two years. His affair with Anne Vavasour was resented, not only by the Queen but also by her well connected family. Anne's half sister Catherine was married to Thomas Howard, 1st earl of Suffolk. Her uncle Sir Thomas Knyvet (later 1st Baron Knyvet),[4] was a successful career courtier with the rank of Master at Arms and he took the slight personally.

In February 1582 the festering enmity between Thomas Knyvet and Edward de Vere erupted into vicious street fighting between their rival factions. Their first pitched battle took place on 3rd March 1582. Both men were wounded, de Vere more seriously, and one of his men was killed. The vendetta between the Vere and Knyvet factions continued for a year with casualties on both sides. One skirmish between the feuding courtiers and their followers took place at a landing stage by the Thames at Blackfriars. Bystanders took sides and joined in, escalating it to a running battle. Another large-scale brawl resulted in Thomas Knyvet's arrest for killing one of Oxford's men, although he was later released without charge.

The East Anglian landowner Roger Townshend attempted to keep the quarrelling families apart, intervening in the manner of Escalus the Prince of Verona in *Romeo and Juliet*. (Prince Bartolomeo della Scala was the actual prince at the time of the play). Townshend was a lawyer and a Member of Parliament who acted as the London business manager for the Howard family.[5] After the execution of the duke of Norfolk he took charge of the affairs of his heir, Philip Howard the earl of Arundel. In the biographical dictionary of former Members of the House of Commons the entry concerning this incident reads

> Arundel was sometimes impatient with Townshend, as when, in 1582, Townshend hurried him off by boat to Arundel House, to avoid his becoming embroiled in the affray between the Earl of Oxford and Thomas Knyvet.

Roger Townshend's explanation was that he feared de Vere and his brother-in-law Peregrine Bertie were planning an ambush for Knyvet, although this never happened. Peregrine Bertie, Baron Willoughby d'Eresby[6] had married Lady Mary Vere, Edward's sister. He also shuttled back and forth to the castle at Elsinore in his capacity as the English Ambassador to the Danish royal family. On behalf of the Queen he had invested the Danish king, Frederick II, with the Order of the Garter, making in all five visits between 1582 and 1585.

The nature of the wound de Vere suffered at the start of this family feuding has never been established but in a letter to his father-in-law Lord Burghley dated 25th March 1595 he writes, 'I will attend Your Lordship as well as a lame man may at your house.' In other letters to Lord Burghley, and in later letters to his brother-in-law Sir Robert Cecil, he makes similar references to a disabling condition which impaired his movement in later life. The lameness could have been caused by an injury incurred in one of the martial arts tournaments in which de Vere excelled as a young man. It could also have resulted from damage to his knee in a Venetian galley during his travels in Italy.[7] Sonnet 74 mentions 'the coward conquest of a wretch's knife', which would appear to identify the fracas with Knyvet and his supporters as the most likely source of the disablement. There are references to lameness in Sonnets 37, 66 and 89

So I, made lame by fortune's dearest spite	Sonnet 37 line 3
So then I am not lame, poor, nor despised	Sonnet 37 line 9
And strength by limping away disabled	Sonnet 66 line 8
Speak of my lameness, and I straight will halt	Sonnet 89 line 3

The Vavasour baby, and the Knyvet quarrels which followed, did not entirely sever de Vere's connection with the court but afterwards no burdensome civic duties mortgaged his attention, or more crucially, his time. Nor did he spare his wife and children much of his time or attention either. 'By fortune's dearest spite' his lack of mobility provided him with an opportunity, an opportunity which Oxfordians believe was critical to the authorship debate, because it provided him the opportunity to write. Although he was eventually reconciled with the Queen, and readmitted to her court circle on 1st June 1583, he had by then side-lined himself with his literary and theatrical interests. Writers need time to write. Denied advancement at court Edward de Vere now had all the revising and writing time he needed, not only for buffing up early drafts into actable versions but more importantly to write new and more expansive drama, plays that would need months of consecutive composition time to bring to completion.

A shock to the physical system can be the origin of later functional derangement, for example in tremor of the limbs.[8] In the days before antibiotics and modern methods of anaesthesia the big risk from surgery lay in the longer term effects. Patients recovered from the operation but the trauma caused by the knife or the saw often triggered some form of neurological impairment in later life. A battle wound or a serious sword-fight injury could have the same delayed effect. At this distance in time, and with no medical records extant, it is only possible to guess at the nature of the disability, or the cause of the poor health which overcame de Vere from his late thirties onwards. Perhaps arthritis, perhaps a stroke or perhaps a condition which these days would be diagnosed as a form of Parkinson's Disease.

Any physical disability is to be regretted but if it steered him to an outlet for his creative energy in the sedentary occupation of writing it could be viewed as adequate compensation. From his late thirties onwards de Vere features hardly at all in records of contemporary life. Until his death at fifty-four he still had sufficient wealth and status to devote himself if he wished to full-time writing. In addition to the basic credentials of education, experience, talent and inclination, whoever wrote Shakespeare needed these two extra and absolutely essential commodities – an adequate income and free time. Edward de Vere had both.

The disgrace of his failed marriage, his financial mismanagement, the illegitimate child born as a result of his adultery, and the street brawling with the Knyvet and Vavasour clan which followed, removed him from contention. Although he was later treated sympathetically by King James he was never again trusted by Queen Elizabeth or her senior ministers and advisers. His saddened father-in-law could do no more for him. In a letter to Sir Christopher Hatton, addressing him as 'Good Master Vice Chamberlain,' he finally accepts that his erring son-in-law would forever be kept in disgrace.

> *Lord Burghley to Sir Christopher Hatton* '... when our son-in-law was in prosperity he was the cause of our adversity by his unkind usage of us and ours; now that he is ruined and in adversity, we only are made partakers thereof, and by no means, no, not by bitter tears of my wife, can obtain a spark of favour for him, that hath satisfied his offence with punishment, and seeketh mercy by submission; but contrariwise, whilst we seek for favour, all crosses are laid against him, and by untruths sought to be kept in disgrace ... '. *from a letter dated 12 March 1582.*

Neither of de Vere's two American biographers consider the effect on him of his imprisonment in the Tower. Nelson only mentions it in passing when dealing with the Vavasour affair and Anderson dismisses it airily[9]

> For a nobleman, time spent in the Tower meant confinement to a modest but still comfortable furnished space. A courtier even in disgrace, was well fed, allowed access to his servants, and given plenty of wood and coal for the fireplace. He was allowed to take fresh air and to exercise on the Tower's battlements. A well-heeled prisoner could also receive visitors and enjoy conjugal visits with his spouse.

More realistically the Tower of London was a grim place of torture and execution, and even if his imprisonment was short, the effect on a sensitive mind could have been considerable. De Vere's knowledge of history would have enabled him to count up the relatives and friends who had endured a miserable death there. His ancestors the 12th earl, John de Vere, and John's son Aubrey de Vere, were two supporters of the Lancastrian cause who found themselves disadvantaged during a period of Yorkist supremacy. They were both imprisoned in the Tower and executed after a token trial. His cousin the 4th Duke of Norfolk suffered death at the block, his fellow poet Sir Walter Raleigh was to endure a similar fate many years later. In *Richard III*, a play which Oxfordian scholars date to about this period in the 1580s, there are twenty-six references to imprisonment in the Tower of London. Other plays featuring prison scenes would include *King Lear*, *Measure for Measure*, *Richard II* and *The Two Noble Kinsmen*.

In 1585 Edward de Vere was on the jury of peers which condemned to death Philip Howard the earl of Arundel, eldest son of the executed duke of Norfolk, and related as a second cousin both to him and Queen Elizabeth. Howard and his family had attempted to leave the country without permission and he was charged with high treason. The execution was not carried out but as he refused to confess, or to repent his support for the Catholic cause, he was never released and died of dysentery after ten years imprisonment in the Tower. He was canonised by Pope Paul VI in 1970 as one of the Forty Martyrs of England and Wales, and is now known as Saint Philip Howard.

In 1586 Edward de Vere was a prominent member of the commission (third in precedence) which met at Fotheringhay Castle, Northampton in September of that year to examine the long imprisoned Mary, Queen of Scots and to recommend her death to Queen Elizabeth. The commission also included de Vere's classmate and friend Edward Manners the earl of Rutland. De Vere's future father-in-law Thomas Trentham, a former High Sheriff of Staffordshire, had been appointed by the Privy Council to escort the Scots queen from Chartley Manor House in Staffordshire to Fotheringhay Castle. The Catholic hierarchy subsequently regarded Queen Elizabeth and her commissioners as complicit in an act of political assassination when Mary was beheaded on 8th February 1587.

In 1601 de Vere was the senior nobleman at a trial in Westminster Hall which condemned to death Robert Devereux earl of Essex and Henry Wriothesley earl of Southampton after the failed so-called 'Essex Rebellion'. Essex was a descendant of the Boleyn family and also the stepson of Leicester, Queen Elizabeth's long-time favourite courtier. As with de Vere before them both men had been royal wards in Burghley's house. Southampton was reprieved but Essex was beheaded.

Although the unfortunate earl of Essex suffered death at the block this was a mercifully quick end compared with those of his followers who were hanged in public and their bodies mutilated. They were just some of the thousands imprisoned, tortured, burned, hanged or beheaded during the reigns of the Tudor sovereigns. It is reasonable to suggest that only someone born into all this mayhem, and who steered a precarious survival path himself, would be qualified to make great literature out of so much savagery. The blood-drenched revenge tragedies of Shakespeare would take on new significance if known to be from the pen of a man so closely involved in the dynastic and religious feuding of the times.

The English historian Lawrence Stone[10] in his book *The Crisis in the Aristocracy 1558–1641*, explains that the measures taken by King Henry VII (reigned 1485–1509), to limit the powers of the nobility accelerated the changes which eventually brought about the downfall of feudal-minded noblemen such as Edward de Vere. His ancestor John de Vere the 13th earl had been the army commander instrumental in defeating Richard III at Bosworth and establishing Henry VII as the unchallenged sovereign. This did not stop the king fining the earl for not disbanding his large private militia quickly enough into the new regime.

Castles as fortified strongholds of the nobility were abandoned as ruins, including eventually Hedingham Castle, and were replaced by the mansions and formal gardens of the new aristocracy, the merchants, lawyers and administrators forming a prosperous bourgeoisie able to buy up the lands vacated by impoverished noblemen. Henry VII presided over the establishment of an efficient, centralised bureaucracy, a system of meritocratic governance which reached its peak a hundred years later under Queen Elizabeth and the Cecils. Professor Stone charts the decline of the old feudal nobility with reference to the disgraceful de Vere–Knyvet street brawls in the early 1580s

> Both in the brutality of their tactics and in their immunity from the law, the nearest parallels to the Earl of Oxford and Sir Thomas Knyvet in the London of Queen Elizabeth are Al Capone and Dion O'Banion, Bugs Moran and Johnny Torrio in the Chicago of the 1920s. It is against this sinister background of rival court factions with their hired killers, of sporadic murder and violence in the streets of London, and occasional pitched battles in the countryside, that the wisdom of Elizabeth's tactics may be judged.

19

Armed Conflict

He jests at scars, that never felt a wound
Romeo and Juliet 2.1.43

Writing historical accounts of the English monarchy as drama to be acted out on a theatre stage was a genre created and developed by the author known as William Shakespeare. The Tudors and their supporters were well aware of their tenuous dynastical claim to the throne and even after a century of rule feared violent overthrow from within, financed by foreign powers from abroad.

The history plays supporting the Lancastrian faction, and the Tudor regime which ensued, began to appear in the early 1580s, when the threat to England as a Protestant country was under mounting pressure from a mainly Catholic Europe led by Spain. These stirring historical dramas conveyed through the medium of public performance the need to unify the country against a common enemy, and the dangers of disloyalty and dissension. The dire consequences of a politically motivated assassination were also spelled out in the play *Julius Caesar*.

The Pope, Pius V, had issued a papal bull, *Regnans in Excelsis*, dated 27th April 1570 excommunicating Queen Elizabeth, and until her hold on power was consolidated by victory over the Spanish invasion fleet of 1588, she was in constant danger. Her security chiefs, Lord Burghley and Sir Francis Walsingham, uncovered many threats to her life and foiled several actual attempts. The most organised of these were the Ridolfi Plot of 1571, the Throckmorton Plot of 1583, the Babington Plot of 1586 and the Lopez plot of 1594. Dr Rodrigo Lopez was a Portuguese physician long resident in London who attended the Queen and received her favour and confidence even after the earl of Essex had accused him of plotting to poison her. Sufficiently tortured, a confession was obtained from him and the unfortunate doctor was publicly hanged, disembowelled and quartered on 7th June 1594 before a cheering London mob.

Of the ten English history plays attributed to Shakespeare only *King John* and *Henry VIII* are stand-alone plays. The other eight, which chronologically come between them, may be grouped into two sets of four (tetralogies) rather than as a continuous sequence of eight (an octology). The second group, which appears to have been written first, begins with the funeral of Henry V in 1422 and ends with the accession of Henry VII in 1485. These are the three parts of *Henry VI* and *Richard III*. The second group of four prequels the others: *Richard II*, the two parts of *Henry IV* and *Henry V*.

No play was written about King Henry VII, leaving a gap which requires some consideration. Once installed by the Lancastrian alliance of nobles this king promptly set about dismantling the feudal infrastructure which had brought the country to the brink of being an ungovernable failing state. Henry VII deserves recognition for the speed with which he transformed an ailing economy and a fractured society. He achieved this most notably by the establishment of a functioning tax-gathering civil service. The history plays of Shakespeare in contrast were the chronicles of the European high-church militaristic feudalism which was fast disappearing beneath the rise of international commerce and trans-global exploration. It could be conjectured that Edward de Vere was acutely aware of these changes, and sufficiently regretted the passing of the old ways to find in Henry VII an unattractive central character for the main subject of a play.

Henry's granddaughter the childless Queen Elizabeth had an obvious parallel with the childless King Richard II, neither having a direct line of succession. The anecdote of the Queen saying 'I am Richard the Second, know ye not that?' shortly after the Essex Rebellion in February 1601 has been many times repeated. The words were supposedly addressed to her archivist William Lambarde, Keeper of the Records in The Tower of London (*Chambers* I, p 354), and show that the Queen was aware of the frequently performed play *Richard II* and its relevance to her situation.

The contention for King Richard's throne had set in motion a long and bitter conflict between the rival factions chronicled in the plays, mostly led by semi-royal cousins, with many shifting alliances along the way. This destabilising and financially draining civil war later became known as Wars of the Roses, the white rose representing York, the red rose for Lancaster. Samuel Daniel's epic poem *The First Fowre Bookes of the Civile Wars* provided source material for Shakespeare's *Richard II*. A parallel situation arose two hundred years later when the childless Queen Elizabeth[1] declined to bring the Tudor dynasty to an end by naming a successor. The earl of Essex tried to force an outcome but his bid for the throne ended in failure and execution.

The ten History plays, with their ordering of caste and station, draw the medieval way of life in England to a close. In these grim historical dramas of violent regime change the main characters speak to one another in the language of political intrigue at the highest level. They wrestle with the confliction of loyalty and ambition. Subsequently the plays influenced how the history of the period was viewed by successive generations, and how it was taught, and to a lesser extent how it is still taught. Who could have written such well-informed plays? Edward de Vere's aristocratic and military ancestry, his own war service and his academic attainments, if taken together, would confirm him as a credible candidate.

As a courtier in competition with men of his own time for the opportunity to win fame and glory as a battlefield commander, de Vere's

136

military career was, by any standards, modest. Military and naval knowledge is evident in many of the plays even so, something hard to explain unless the author was writing from experience of active service, however limited. Stratfordians maintain that the soldiering and conflict scenes could have been lifted from translations of Greek and Latin drama. This is possible but not convincing. The mustering of troops, the apprehension before the battle with its frightened soldiers, bullying corporals and nervous commanders, followed by the clamour and confusion of the actual fighting, make the case for an author who had himself witnessed armed conflict at close quarters. Knowledge of the surgical treatment of battlefield wounds, including amputation occurs in *Coriolanus* 3.1.296 and *Richard II* 5.3.83–4. The dismal aftermath of a battle in the dressing of wounds and the counting of the dead mitigates the relief of victory but exacerbates the misery of defeat. Wars are never glorious.

The Vere ancestors came over with the Conqueror. They survived the Battle of Hastings in 1066 and when Aubrey de Vere was created the 1st earl of Oxford in 1142 a dynasty was founded that would last 561 years until Aubrey de Vere the twentieth earl died without a male heir in 1703. The historian Lord Macaulay described them as 'the longest and most illustrious line of nobles that England has seen'.[2] Robert the third earl was one of the signatories to Magna Carta in 1215, John the seventh earl fought at Crécy (1346) and Poitiers (1356). Robert the ninth earl was closely associated with his cousin King Richard II who showered him with estates and titles, including Duke of Ireland.

Richard de Vere the eleventh earl (1385–1417) commanded the archers at Agincourt in 1415, or at least he did according to *Famous Victories of Henry Fifth*. This early Shakespeare play was later expanded into both parts of *Henry IV* and *Henry V*. Richard is given the role of a counsellor advising Henry IV, and after his death is shown doing the same for his young son Henry V. This is not substantiated by any of the chronicles of the time but if written by Edward de Vere was a nice tribute to one of his ancestors. That the eleventh earl was written out of the later versions could be attributed to the author's increasing need for anonymity.

The consequences of backing the wrong side in a civil war could be severe. John de Vere the twelfth earl was a Lancastrian supporter, beheaded on Tower Hill in 1461 during a period of Yorkist occupancy. His son the thirteenth earl, also John, reversed the advantage by commanding the right wing of the victorious Lancastrian army at the battle of Bosworth in 1485, the battle which placed the first of the Tudors, King Henry VII, on the throne.

The earl of Oxford as a character is mentioned briefly in *Richard III*, an enduringly popular play, the second longest in the canon, but has a significant speech in the third part of *Henry VI*, proclaiming his devotion to the Lancastrian cause. (3.3.106–07). By implication this extends to support for the Tudor dynasty which was secured by winning the battle of Bosworth.

> While life upholds this arm,
> This arm upholds the house of Lancaster.

The first edition of Raphael Holinshed's *Chronicles* appeared in 1577, in two volumes, with an expanded second edition in three volumes following in 1587. The second edition has the closest links to passages in the plays but as de Vere and Holinshed were fellow residents at Cecil House in London, they could have had equal access to the material available in the extensive Cecil library. This library contained some two thousand volumes in a number of different languages, many of them the dramatic and narrative sources of Shakespeare. This included one volume of Belleforest's *Histoires Tragiques*, the primary source for *Hamlet*. Edward Hall's earlier account of the dynastic feuding also contains information used in the Shakespeare Histories. Edward Hall[3] was another Cambridge man (Eton and Kings), who went on to study at Gray's Inn, as later did Cecil and de Vere. The full title of his great work is *The Union of the Two Noble and Illustre Famelies of Lancastre and Yorke*. The second edition of 1550 is listed as being in Sir Thomas Smith's library and so would have been available to de Vere as an earlier source for the History plays, including *Famous Victories of Henry Fifth*. The indifferent quality of the writing in this play, and the availability of Hall, could make an early date of composition possible, even perhaps before de Vere reached the age of twenty in 1570.

All this was a lot of proud history for a twelve-year-old boy to inherit along with the castle, the titles, the landed estates and a guaranteed place at court. As a military family bound to the service of sovereign and country their tradition was proudly upheld, although alas, not by Lord Edward. The two sons of his Uncle Geoffrey provided the nation with its most renowned soldiers, Sir Horace Vere and his younger brother Sir Francis Vere. They were involved for most of their adult lives in the Netherlands Wars of Independence,[4] fought against the might of the Spanish Habsburgs and their army. This lasted for eighty years before ultimately ending in victory for the Dutch.

As garrison commanders, as diplomats, and as generals leading from the front, the Vere brothers were noted for their professionalism. Calm, capable, utterly reliable and loyal they were in almost every way different from their theatre-loving cousin. Even so Edward was known to be proud of them, and of his close relationship to them. There is a soldier Francisco in *Hamlet*, also a steady friend of Hamlet named Horatio, a major character in the play. A book titled *The Fighting Veres*[5] was later written about these two soldier brothers who share a tomb in Westminster Abbey.[6]

Earlier, in March 1570, at the age of twenty, de Vere was sanctioned by the Queen to join the army which had suppressed an insurrection led by the Earls of Northumberland and Westmorland, the so-called Rising of the North. This uprising by the Scots and dissident northerners revolved around the legitimacy or otherwise of Mary Stuart and her claim to the English throne. Dynastically this was strong. She already had a male heir (the future King James I and VI), and at twenty-eight was still young enough to produce more heirs if a marriage could be arranged between her and Thomas Howard the Catholic duke of Norfolk.

The southern forces were led by Thomas Radcliffe, 3rd earl of Sussex, a battle-hardened campaigner with a track record of military success, appointed by Queen Elizabeth as Lord President of the North. How much actual fighting Edward de Vere saw, or was involved in himself, is not recorded but he had travelled with an army and witnessed the shocking aftermath when Sussex punished the humiliated rebel leaders by burning towns and villages and ransacking castles in the border areas and southern Scotland, being particularly severe on Dumfries. The reprisals went on for many months as participants were hunted down and dealt with one by one.

It was a harsh retaliation, intended as a deterrent to any other dissident group considering a challenge to the Protestant regime in London. The earl of Sussex was also related to the Howard family, as were de Vere and Queen Elizabeth, so the issues were sensitive and the stakes high. The Queen wrote warmly to congratulate Sussex on a mission successfully accomplished.[7] and recalled him to London in the prestigious post of Lord Chamberlain. He remained in close attendance on the Queen until his death in 1583.

In Shakspeare the earlier northern rebellion of the Percy family and their supporters, as chronicled in *1 Henry IV*, bears a close resemblance to the sequence of events in the uprising against Elizabeth in 1569–70. The American historian Conyers Read (1881–1959) wrote extensively about the early years of Queen Elizabeth's reign as his specialist subject. His account of the Rising of the North (*Mr Secretary Cecil and Queen Elizabeth* pp. 455–468) puts William Cecil at the centre of events.

Cecil viewed the old nobility in the north, and their fondness for the 'true religion', as a serious threat to the crown. He prosecuted the war with unrelenting vigour, driving on the earl of Sussex and his commanders to confront the forces of the earls of Northumberland and Westmorland with all the military might available, and when this was successful insisted on the brutal suppression which followed. Conyers Read identifies this as the decisive moment in Elizabeth's hold on power which was never again challenged from within her kingdom. It also consolidated Burghley's position as the Queen's most trusted and reliable adviser. Factions within the court had earlier tried to have him removed from office but his ministerial primacy lasted until his death in 1598. As one of the new breed of university men who had risen through merit, loyalty and diligence he exerted his authority over the aristocrats who had conspired to bring him down.

This brutal suppression of a Catholic insurgency, compounded by Queen Elizabeth's assumption of the governance of the Church of England, and the continued imprisonment of her cousin the Queen of

Scots, was not viewed kindly by the Vatican. In 1580 Pope Gregory XIII confirmed his predecessor's excommunication of Queen Elizabeth, declared her a heretic and released her subjects from their allegiance to her. This set in motion the train of events which culminated in the Spanish invasion fleet of 1588, known as the Armada. An excommunicated queen had nothing to lose by removing a courtier suspected of plotting against her, and anyone associating with Catholics from the continent was at risk. Suspicion fell more than once on Edward de Vere, and on others of his Howard relatives, most of whom he regarded as his enemies rather than his friends.

De Vere's next chance for military experience did not come until August 1585 when he sailed with the army commander Sir John Norris to the Netherlands. The Queen and her senior ministers had decided to send an expeditionary force to try and relieve the besieged port of Antwerp. This was the military headquarters for the Dutch revolt against the Spanish occupiers. Earlier, in November 1576, six thousand had died in the sack of Antwerp, and much of the city was burned. This brutal assault, known as the Spanish Fury, escalated the severity of the conflict.

Some Shakespeare scholars identify the excessive cruelty in *Titus Andronicus* as based around this historical event. Although now seldom staged, *Titus* was regularly performed and popular in the 1580s when hostility to the Spanish regime was intensifying. The English intervention on the side of the Dutch was not a success and it proved a fateful decision. Foreign wars are easy to get into, not so easy to get out of, and this act made certain that the Spanish would retaliate against England. The main invasion force of the Armada headed north three years later.

It must have been obvious to all those who needed to know that the poetry-writing, music-loving earl of Oxford was not cut out to be a soldier, and that the age of thirty-five was too late to learn. But he was keen to go and it helped the cause if senior members of the court were seen to be willing to risk their lives for Queen and country. Appointed as commander of the horse, no records survive of military engagements or victories in which he was named. But if viewed as an author gathering source material, rather than as a career soldier seeking battlefield glory, he stayed long enough to gain experience of real life soldiering. He was eventually recalled to London when Leicester was appointed as commander-in-chief of the allied forces, with his nephew Sir Philip Sidney on his staff. Leicester's last military action was to see off the Spanish Armada as Lieutenant and Captain-General of the Queen's Armies and Companies. He died suddenly three months later, on 4th September 1588 at the age of fifty-six.

If de Vere was disappointed not to have lived up to the military glories of his ancestor earls, he had at least survived. This was not the case with his fellow soldier-poet Philip Sidney who died a year later aged thirty-two from a wound received at the Battle of Zutphen. The long attritional conflict with Spain later claimed the lives of Edward de Vere's two sons.

Henry de Vere died in 1624 aged thirty-one from a gunshot wound received at the siege of Breda. Edward's natural son with Anne Vavasour had become a professional soldier and was knighted in 1607 as Sir Edward Vere. He died at the battle of Bois-de-Luc in 1629, aged forty-eight. Henry the 18th earl had died childless, so the title passed to Robert de Vere, who became the 19th earl of Oxford. He was shot in the head and died at the Siege of Maastricht in 1632 at the age of thirty-seven. He has no known grave. Other casualties of the war were Henry Wriothesley earl of Southampton and his elder son James, who both died of fever soon after joining the army of the United Provinces of the Netherlands in 1624.

Edward de Vere is believed to have sailed against the Spanish Armada in the merchant ship *Edward Bonaventure* which had been converted into an armed sloop. It was captained by James Lancaster, later knighted for his explorations on behalf of the East India Company. The *Edward Bonaventure* was the second largest of a flotilla of thirteen ships commanded by Sir Francis Drake in the decisive phase of the struggle to intercept the Spanish invasion fleet which had set sail from Lisbon. Drake was second in command to the Lord Admiral, Charles Howard,[8] another relative of de Vere and the Queen, later Lord Howard of Effingham. De Vere was on board for the reconnaissance voyages in bad weather[9] and possibly for part of the final encounter when the invading fleet was engaged in August 1588.

It should be remembered that Anne, countess of Oxford, had died on 5th June in the year of the Armada. Her husband's absence from the funeral was most likely because he was at sea on active service for his country. (As Hamlet was absent from Ophelia's funeral service). If the plays are any guide, de Vere never wavered in his loyalty to the Queen, in his support for the Protestant religion, and in his patriotism and love of country. A victory parade followed by a service of thanksgiving at St Paul's Cathedral was held in November later the same year. The events are recorded in John Stow's *Survey of London*, edited by de Vere's former secretary Anthony Munday. In his 1928 biography of Edward de Vere, B.M. Ward quotes from an anonymous ballad marking the occasion:

> *A Joyful Ballad of the Royal entrance of Queen Elizabeth into the City of London, the 24th of November in the thirty-first year of Her Majesty's reign, to give God praise for the overthrow of the Spaniards.*

The ballad was first printed in a book by A. M. W. Stirling called *Life's Little Day* and published by Thornton Butterworth in 1924. It contains the lines

> The noble Earl of Oxford, High Chamberlain of England
> Rode right before Her Majesty, his bonnet in his hand.

This must have been a wonderful occasion, with much colourful pageantry. American authors Alan Nelson and Mark Anderson in their biographies of Edward de Vere play down his role in the fighting, and also belittle the patriotic rejoicing which followed the sea victory. The English had no wish to be occupied by a foreign power and had been determined to beat off the invasion at whatever cost. Only those whose countries have been occupied by a foreign military force, or have lived for years under imminent threat of invasion, can fully appreciate the euphoria that follows the defeat of their enemy.

Even if it was only a ditty, the 'joyful ballad' commemorating the 'overthrow of the Spaniards', clearly describes the earl, 'his bonnet in his hand', leading the victory procession to St Paul's Cathedral in November 1588. This must have offered some consolation to him for the death of his wife Anne earlier in the year. Whatever his misdemeanours and shortcomings Edward de Vere had remained close to the Queen and her ruling elite, and was aptly qualified and worthy to be her cheerleader, as well as the chronicler of the age.

20

Insolvency

Who steals my purse steals trash
Othello 3.3.162

On attaining his majority in 1571 Edward de Vere inherited his father's debts which were not finally paid off for another ten years. He was also racking up debts of his own. One third of a titled ward's estate reverted to the crown and the Queen demanded a down payment of £3,000 and a further £4,000 in management charges. He had to sign an obligation to pay double the amount if he defaulted on the payments. As fast as he sold off lands and property to pay his creditors, the law of diminishing returns ensured that the gap between arrears and solvency was never closed.

Edward de Vere's natural extravagance was combined with a reckless generosity that ensured his adult life would be plagued by debt. Regardless of cost he crammed as many entertainments and new experiences into his foreign travels as was possible in the time at his disposal. To provide himself with a congenial social milieu he gathered around him and generously supported an extended family of stage, musical and literary folk, mostly dependent on his good will. To finance his travels, to live in style, to flourish as a patron of the arts, and to write and produce for the theatre, he sold off his inherited estates until none were left.

Add in his wardship and marriage debts, his losses with the Michael Lock north-west expeditions, and by his mid-thirties he was reduced to pleading for financial assistance from his father-in law. Incredible though it must have seemed at the time, the extensive Vere estates accumulated over five hundred years had disappeared in less than twenty. Although he had contributed to his own downfall by his high maintenance lifestyle, de Vere was so closely bound in to the governing establishment by ties of kinship and marriage that his complete financial ruin would have caused undue embarrassment and had to be prevented. On 21st June 1586 Burghley was so concerned for the welfare of his daughter and three granddaughters that he sought advice from Sir Francis Walsingham, asking for his son Robert Cecil to be involved in any approach to the Queen.

> If you had any commodity to speak with her Majesty of my Lord of Oxford and what hope there is, and if you have any to let Robert Cecil understand it to relieve his sister, who is more troubled for her husband's lack than he himself.

De Vere's rescue came five days later on 26th June 1586 when the Queen granted him an annuity of £1,000, a substantial amount of money at the time. A more prosaic explanation for the award of the annuity could be that the Queen was compensating de Vere for lands or property she had detained during his wardship and which were still owing to him as part of his inheritance. His annuity was later renewed by King James, although he only lived to receive it for one more year. What else he had to provide in return for this princely allowance has never been made clear, although there are vague references to 'mine office' in his later correspondence. Whether it was to act as entertainments officer to the court, or to write propaganda in support of the Tudors and the Church of England, or simply to maintain his status and dignity as Lord Great Chamberlain, is difficult to tell.

Not only London but the entire coastline of England had braced itself for the arrival of a Spanish-led invasion fleet. It is a firmly held tenet of Oxfordian belief that the history plays of Shakespeare were performed throughout the 1580s to privileged audiences in the royal palaces, the two universities and the Inns of Court. Although produced and staged without naming an author their patriotic message was spelled out time and again to the assembled nobles and civic dignitaries. Drama of this quality, emphasising the need for loyalty to an anointed prince, and extolling love of country, could help to explain why, when it finally came, there was such spirited resistance to the Spanish invasion. If Edward de Vere's dramatic talents came at a cost, it was a cost for which the crown was well recompensed.

Even so, to be dependent on a charitable annuity was a big comedown in the world for a seventeenth earl. It was downfall on a grand scale. Downfall of the mighty was the underlying theme running through a collection of stories and poems under the title *A Mirrour for Magistrates*, first published in 1559.[1] It was seen as the sequel to a work by the Suffolk based monk and poet John Lydgate with the title *Fall of Princes*,[2] itself based on Boccaccio's *Concerning the Falls of Illustrious Men*. The entries in the *Mirrour* are written as if by the ghosts of once great men examining themselves before a mirror in the hope that a recital of their mistakes will serve as a lesson to others. The 'downfall of illustrious men' would be an apt subtitle for *The Complete Works of Shakespeare*.

One of the contributors to the *Mirrour* was Sir Thomas Sackville[3] with the poem *Complaint of Henry, Duke of Buckingham*. Sackville was co-author with Thomas Norton of the play *Gorboduc* (in 1561), the first English drama to be written in blank verse. He was a well connected courtier and Queen Elizabeth's second cousin, later ennobled as baron Buckhurst and earl of Dorset. A protégé of William Cecil, he moved in the same social, political and literary circles as Edward de Vere, the other Cecils and the earl of Sussex in an anti-Leicester faction. After her trial in October 1586 Sackville was deputed by the Privy Council to convey to Mary Queen of Scots at Fotheringhay the news of her death sentence.

From 1591 until his death in 1608 he was chancellor of Oxford University. As Lord Buckhurst he appears in Henry Peacham's exhaustive list of English poets, *The Compleat English Gentleman*, published in 1622. This is of interest because the list is headed by Edward, Earl of Oxford but omits any reference to a poet named Shakespeare.

Although Edward de Vere had chafed at his father-in-law's interference in his affairs, no one else had his interests at heart or tried so persistently to steer him out of his difficulties, and even this grudging support was withdrawn after his daughter Anne died in the summer of 1588. Neither of the earl's Cecil brothers-in-law, Thomas or Robert, was disposed to help him out of his financial quagmire, hardly surprising after the troubled marriage to their sister.

Nor is there any record of financial assistance from his other brother-in-law Peregrine Bertie who married his sister Lady Mary Vere. With their father dead, Mary had needed to ask her brother's permission to marry, and to provide the dowry promised for the day of her marriage in the will of their father John de Vere. This permission from her brother was not forthcoming and the marriage was postponed. Peregrine was the soldier son of Richard Bertie and the widowed Duchess of Suffolk, all zealous Protestants. The duchess was strongly opposed to the marriage. In a letter to Burghley written 2nd July 1576 she spells out her main objection, 'our religions agree not'. Nor was her belief that the earl of Oxford was a clandestine Catholic her only reason for opposing the marriage. In two long letters to Burghley she deplores that Lady Mary was as headstrong and sharp-tongued as her brother. Mary Vere could be perhaps described as 'feisty', to use a modern term for a spirited woman. She was also very determined. The young couple were adamant in their wish to marry, were engaged in 1577 and married early in 1578. De Vere's objection to the marriage having been overtaken by this *fait accompli,* he and his new brother-in-law Peregrine Bertie, later Baron Willoughby d'Eresby, were soon on friendly terms.

There are some Shakespeare links to these events. In yet another letter to Burghley, this one written in December 1577, Peregrine's mother proposed a stratagem whereby a reconciliation between Edward de Vere and his wife Anne might be procured. This was by confronting de Vere with his infant daughter Elizabeth, a ruse that failed. In *The Winter's Tale* a doughty female character named Paulina similarly tried to bring King Leontes and his infant daughter Perdita together but this attempt also met with failure. As a rumbustious soldier Peregrine Bertie would seem a good role model for Petruccio in *The Taming of the Shrew*. His stormy courtship and marriage to Mary Vere could be seen as a close family match to the warring lovers in the play, Petruccio and Katherine the Shrew.

On 15th June 1580 de Vere purchased from the Genoese-born merchant Benedict Spinola a tenement and seven acres of land in Aldgate, paying £2,500 for the property. It was known as the Great Garden of

Christchurch and was situated in the parish of St Botolph, Bishopsgate, close to de Vere's house known as Fisher's Folly, and where he maintained a pew in the church.[4] Benedict Spinola in London, and his brother Pasquale Spinola in Antwerp, had supplied de Vere with transfers of money to fund his continental travels 1575–76. Benedict, born Benedetto, was a naturalised citizen who spent his entire adult life in London. As a merchant in the country's largest seaport his trading skill as an exporter of cloth and an importer of wine made him rich. Trusted by the Queen and Burghley, he acted as an agent and financier for the crown, dealing in large sums of money.

There was some previous history to the sale of the Great Garden. In return for his help in negotiating a divorce from Catherine of Aragon, King Henry VIII rewarded the lawyer Thomas Audley (1488–1544) with a forfeited monastic estate in London. This was the Priory of Holy Trinity in Aldgate, also known as Christ's Church, with its seven acres of garden. Thomas Audley, later Baron Audley, donated it to Magdalene College, Cambridge in 1542 to provide it with a source of income in perpetuity. The gift came with conditions, and these not being met, on 13th December 1574 the property reverted to the crown. On 29th January 1575 the Queen conveyed the premises to the financier Benedict Spinola as a residence for himself and his family.

Magdalene College brought several unsuccessful court actions over a long period of years, suing for the return of the Great Garden on the grounds that Spinola was a tenant, not the owner, and therefore could not have legally sold it to the earl of Oxford. A duty levied on Oxford and his heirs (a usual practice at the time) ensured that as the purchaser in 1580 he obtained a clear title to the Garden property. The College lawyers were also critical of the Queen's complicity in facilitating a deal for the court financier Spinola in 1574 when this prime site just outside the old city walls was ripe for development. A judgment in the Court of King's Bench for the Easter term of 1615

Gargoyle of Benedict Spinola on the Quayside wall of Magdalene College, Cambridge. Designed by Peter Fluck & Roger Law (of Spitting Image fame)

brought by the Master and Fellows of Magdalene College recorded that the site originally worth only £15 per annum had now been extensively developed and produced £800 per annum. The College remained financially disadvantaged by the permanent loss of this lucrative income-producing property but had their revenge four hundred years later. In 1989

the Quayside development of Magdalene College included a representation of Benedict Spinola as an ugly gargoyle on the college wall,
spouting water into the Cam.[5]

Acquiring and developing this valuable property in London had been a
shrewd investment by the earl of Oxford. It was also a transaction he had
been able to make without oversight from the Cecil family, and showed
some unsuspected business acumen. On 4th July 1591 he sold the Great
Garden of Christchurch to Francis Trentham[6] a businessman from
Staffordshire. The new owner contracted that the rents of the Great
Garden property should be to the advantage of his sister Elizabeth
Trentham, for life. This association with the successful Trentham family
marked a dramatic turn-around in Edward de Vere's fortunes, cemented
by his marriage to Elizabeth early in 1592, the exact date being unknown.

Elizabeth was born at Rocester Abbey in Staffordshire, the daughter of
Thomas Trentham, a wealthy landowner. A maid of honour to Queen
Elizabeth, she became the new countess of Oxford and whether de Vere
managed it by himself, or whether the Queen facilitated the match, the
twelve years of his second marriage finally restored his life to domestic
stability. From her few surviving letters, written to Robert Cecil,
Christopher Hatton (nephew of Sir Christopher Hatton) and Fulke
Greville, among others, from her well-written will, and from the vigorous
way she prosecuted de Vere's dishonest servant Arthur Mills, she would
appear to have been highly competent, and a strong-willed asset to her
husband.

Together with her brother Francis, the new countess retrieved a
desperate financial situation. Francis Trentham was a Justice, Sheriff and
later the Member of Parliament for Stafford. In addition to running his
own extensive property portfolio he took over the administration of what
was left of the Vere estates and returned them to order and solvency, if not
to profit, with the result that the earl did not die in debt. From 1591
onward all the legal documents relating to de Vere's financial affairs
carried the signature of his new brother-in-law.

At the same time Lord Burghley was anxious to ensure that his three
Vere granddaughters, Elizabeth, Bridget and Susan were adequately
provided for before he died. He worked out a financial arrangement with
Francis Trentham whereby the girls benefited from the sale of the manor
of Hedingham Castle, which then passed completely into the ownership of
the Trentham family. It was a symbolic ending. After five centuries of
occupation even the ancestral home had gone and nothing was left of the
Vere estates. The plot of *King Lear* has an interesting parallel. Edward de
Vere sold up to provide dowries for his three daughters. The ageing King
Lear parcelled out his kingdom to do the same for his three daughters.

Lady Elizabeth Vere, the eldest daughter, was the first to benefit. At
the age of twenty, on 25th January 1595, she was safely married to
William Stanley the 6th earl of Derby in a lavish court wedding with the
Queen in attendance. This was a successful outcome for Lord Burghley as

her guardian, marrying his eldest granddaughter to an extremely rich landowner. When he died three years later in August 1598 his two remaining granddaughters, Lady Bridget and Lady Susan, were still unmarried. He bequeathed them substantial legacies and ensured that their custody was transferred to his son Robert Cecil. With his father-in-law dead, de Vere made a belated attempt to obtain parental care of his two unmarried daughters but this was firmly rejected by Robert. In an undated letter to his late father's private secretary Michael Hicks he explains succinctly, '… whether he that never gave them groat, hath a second wife and another child be a fit guardian, consider you'.

As a wealthy heiress the new countess of Oxford was able to buy the secluded mansion of King's Place with its 270 acres of farmland in the outlying pastures of Hackney. This more settled way of life could have provided her husband with the daily desk time[7] an author needed, either to write new work or to revise and edit old work for publication. Fifteen quarto editions of Shakespeare plays appeared one by one in the ensuing years, ceasing in 1604, the year in which Edward de Vere died.

In 1601 de Vere wrote five letters to Robert Cecil on the subject of the Danvers estates. Sir Charles Danvers was one of the leading participants in the failed Essex Rebellion and after his execution Queen Elizabeth granted his forfeited lands to Edward de Vere. This was never put in writing and although de Vere pressed his case through the courts he did so without success. In the first letter in the series dated 7th October 1601 he writes, 'I am advised that I may pass my Book (case) from her Majesty if a warrant may be procured to my cousin Bacon'. Francis Bacon, later Viscount St Alban, was a cousin to both men by marriage, his mother Anne Cooke Bacon being an aunt to both Anne and Robert Cecil. By the fourth letter, written to his brother-in-law in January 1602, de Vere finally accepts that for whatever reason the vacant Danvers estates would never be his and expresses his disappointment with an elegant turn of phrase

> I shall bear it by the grace of God with an equal mind, since time and experience have given me sufficient understanding of worldly frailty.

When incidents such as these are taken into account, Edward de Vere as Shakespeare becomes entirely believable. The bitterness of so many failures is written out in the plays for all to see and hear, at length, and in considerable detail. Versions of his own life story, from precociously talented youth to embittered age, are worked through again and again in the tragic literary characters of his creation – Coriolanus, Hamlet, Lear, Macbeth, Othello, Romeo and Timon. All are failures, even if heroic failures, and they all suffer an ignominious death. None more so than the man himself. When he died in 1604 he left no will, having nothing left to bequeath.

Except, as his loyal Oxfordian adherents believe, the Complete Works of Shakespeare, which would be legacy enough for anyone. No one did more to bring this about than his second wife, Elizabeth, who survived her husband by eight years. She deserved at the very least a funeral monument, instead we do not know where Shakespeare's wife, the countess of Oxford, lies buried. These words from Sonnet 81, which many believe were addressed to the earl of Southampton, could have applied to her just as well

> Your monument shall be my gentle verse
> Which eyes not yet created shall o'er-read

21

Love and Sexuality

The course of true love never did run smooth
A Midsummer Night's Dream 1.1.134

Many explicit sexual references are to be found in the Shakespeare plays and poetry. They range from tavern-bar male coarseness to elegant classical allusions. By the standards of the time the author's sometimes bawdy language, and clever punning on body parts, bodily functions and sex acts would not have been considered unduly offensive. The two narrative poems, *Venus and Adonis* and *The Rape of Lucrece* handle erotic material with sensitivity, skill and charm. There are some relationships of a homosexual nature in the plays, as there are adulterous heterosexual liaisons, but both are written without prejudice. In fact a feature of the canon is the absence of moralising and the ability to write from a range of perspectives. Shakespeare as an author is non-judgmental and mostly sympathetic to the predicaments in which his characters find themselves.

Courtship and abstinence also feature in the plays. Florizel and Perdita in *The Winter's Tale* are two young people deeply in love but for dynastic reasons must remain chaste until they are eligible to marry. In Act 4 Scene 4 they speak some of the most sensuously beautiful love poetry in the whole of Shakespeare. For example this compliment by Florizel, spoken to Perdita, who is bedecked for a country festival as Queen of the Feast. (4.4.135–146)

> What you do
> Still betters what is done. When you speak, sweet,
> I'd have you do it ever; when you sing,
> I'd have you buy and sell so, so give alms,
> Pray so; and for the ord'ring your affairs,
> To sing them too. When you do dance, I wish you
> A wave o'th'sea, that you might ever do
> Nothing but that, move still, still so
> And own no other function. Each your doing,
> So singular in each particular,
> Crowns what you are doing in the present deeds,
> That all your acts are queens.

There is an enduring worldwide appreciation for the love poetry. In *Romeo and Juliet* it can be heard at its most dazzling, in *Antony and*

150

Cleopatra at its most impassioned. The 154 exquisitely crafted sonnets are written in the first person tense and seem to speak directly to the reader. Many are suffused with intense personal pain and suffering. First published in 1609 these evocations of love and longing have been much admired and extensively researched and studied. The allegorical poem *The Phoenix and Turtle*, if by Shakespeare would serve as an example of the author's elegiac capability. This poem was contained in Robert Chester's *Love's Martyr* published by Edward Blount in 1601.

In plays featuring pairs of lovers the author elevates sexual attraction to the highest levels of human love and spirituality. But the play *Romeo and Juliet* opens with a street brawl between the rival factions of the Montagues and the Capulets, two Veronese families locked in a bitter vendetta. Edward de Vere's street brawls with Thomas Knyvet and his followers in 1581 would offer an authorship parallel.[1] This date would also fit in with the earthquake mentioned by the Nurse which devastated the area around Verona in 1570. ''Tis since the earthquake now eleven years'. (1.3.25)

Romeo and Juliet begins when Romeo, an adult man in the throes of a deep mental depression, infiltrates a Capulet gathering hoping to see a woman named Rosaline. He is a Montagu and is involved in an unreciprocated love affair with Rosaline, who never appears. Her indifference and his anguish recall the Dark Lady cluster of sonnets. While at the party Romeo, in a violent mood swing, falls obsessively in love at first sight with the thirteen year old Juliet. (In an earlier version with the title *Romeus and Juliet* her age is fifteen). In spite of the disparity in age, the briefest of courtships, and the complication that a marriage has been arranged for her with a rich merchant, Juliet returns Romeo's love. They are hastily married, spend a night together and then go to their ill-fated deaths.

Pivotal to the tragic outcome of the play is Friar John's detention in a suspected plague house. This ensures that he cannot deliver to Romeo the letter from Friar Lawrence explaining the deception over Juliet's suspended-state death. Friar John cites civic fear of the plague as his excuse for not being able to deliver the letter. (5.2.8–11)

> the searchers of the town,
> Suspecting that we were both in a house
> Where the infectious pestilence did reign
> Sealed up the doors, and would not let us forth

Edward de Vere similarly suffered inconvenience from letters delayed by the plague. In a letter to his father-in-law from Venice dated 24th September 1575 he writes '... having looked for your Lordship's letters a great while, at length when I grew to despair of them, I received two. Three packets which at sundry times I had sent this summer to England were returned back again by reason of the plague, none were suffered to pass.' The plague was rife in Italy during the years 1575–76 when de Vere was on his continental travels. Venice was particularly badly affected with many thousands of deaths. Special officials known as 'searchers' were authorised to enter properties, and if infected victims were found within, to quarantine the house, up to forty days if considered necessary.

Shakespeare's competence and versatility as a writer can be judged by his adaptation of an earlier account of the story, a long narrative poem published in 1562, with the authorship attributed to one Arthur Brooke.[2] Not much has ever emerged about Brooke as a writer whose only other known publication was a translation from the French with the title *Sundry Places of Scripture*. The full title of the poem was *The Tragical History of Romeus and Juliet*. In his notes to *Romeo and Juliet* in the *Oxford Shakespeare* Professor John Jowett writes that although the story was known in French and Italian as well as English, 'Shakespeare owes most to Arthur Brooke's long poem.'

The close similarity to which Professor Jowett refers prompts the suspicion that the same author may have had a hand in both. Could a precocious twelve-year old earl have written or contributed to the earlier poem? The young de Vere was sufficiently well educated to make it possible although Oxfordians are reluctant to press the claim. Even so, borrowing whole scenes and numerous word clusters from *Romeus and Juliet* would not count as plagiarism if the same author revised and rewrote it as *Romeo and Juliet* some twenty years later.

Comparing the play with the earlier version written in poetic form demonstrates the mature author's consummate literary skill and inventiveness in working up unpromising material into world class drama. The leaden-paced original is outclassed by miles in his lively adaptation. Touches of genius include making the Nurse and Mercutio into significant characters. Mercutio's violent death flips the play in an instant from a romantic comedy to stark tragedy. The narrative poem covers a period of nine months. Shakespeare compresses it into five days.

So if Edward de Vere wrote *Romeo and Juliet* along with the rest of Shakespeare, how and when did he acquire the extensive range of sexual knowledge apparent in the plays? As an underage earl with a considerable inheritance he had been closely guarded in the strict Protestant households of Sir Thomas Smith and Sir William Cecil, which makes early sexual experience unlikely. As a law student with other privileged young men at Gray's Inn in London he would not long have remained in ignorance of such matters, and combined with access to bookshops and libraries would have been well aware of courtly love in literature.

For converting knowledge into practice his travels with the army sent to subdue the Rising of the North may have provided him with opportunities to acquire sexual experience. Soldiering as an occupation for young men has always included the need for sexual relief, mostly obtained as the spoils of war. De Vere also saw active service in the Low Countries in the Dutch wars against Spain, and on board ship in the year of the

Armada, 1588. These expeditions could have widened his knowledge of sex in all its manifestations. In his mid-twenties he had spent sixteen months journeying on the continent, in France, Germany and Italy. Travel broadens the mind and offers delights less easily obtainable at home. For many a young nobleman finally free of restraints and intent on making up for lost time, a continental tour could have provided eagerly sought opportunities for acquiring the etiquette and conduct of sexual behaviour.

Once safely returned from his Italian tour de Vere began gradually distancing himself from the court, embarking instead on the literary and theatrical activities that would engage his attention for the rest of his life. His salon in Bishopsgate attracted many educated young men similarly disposed, some still little more than students, revelling in what we might now describe as a bohemian way of life in a city where all forms of vice were readily available.

For Edward de Vere this involved taking a mistress, Anne Vavasour, with whom he had a son. His wife Countess Anne died in 1588 at the age of thirty-one. Four years later de Vere took a second wife, the heiress Elizabeth Trentham, and this appears to have been a more satisfactory marriage as well as producing the long awaited male heir. These cumulative experiences of marriage and fatherhood, continental travels, service in the military followed by tavern and theatrical life in London, if taken together, could be sufficient to account for the richness of sexual imagery contained in the Shakespeare plays and poetry.

De Vere's adulterous liaison with Anne Vavasour in his early thirties had other long-term consequences with relevance to the authorship case. Anne's uncle Thomas Knyvet, a courtier, strongly disapproved of the affair and with other male relatives initiated a violent feud with the earl and his supporters. There were casualties on both sides and the swordfight injury de Vere incurred in their first battle may have resulted in the loss of limb function which incapacitated him in later life.

The deterioration in his health which followed, and the need for effective treatment and medication, may have forced him into contact with the apothecaries who could provide them. The leading physician in London (from 1597 Master of the Company of Barber Surgeons), and also the Vere family doctor, was George Baker, an exponent of the new Paracelsian approach to medical treatment based on pharmacology. George Baker, and others, dedicated medical treatises to de Vere, further strengthening his knowledge of medical conditions and their cure. This would account for the numerous references in the plays to diagnostic categories of illnesses, many of them serious conditions. These included sexually transmitted diseases, their symptoms, treatment and outcome.

The Arundel–Howard Libels of 1580 implied that de Vere had become infected with syphilis during his stay in Italy 1575–76.[3] Nothing supports this directly but references to venereal diseases in the plays exhibit a surprisingly detailed knowledge of the condition. Brothels and prostitutes feature in several plays. Audiences have always found amusing and condoned the lively Falstaff tavern scenes in the two parts of Henry IV, even with their edgy borderline proximity to London's criminal underclass. Mistress Quickly and Doll Tearsheet are sufficiently good-natured to awake sympathy for their lot as women working in the sex trade area of a seaport capital city. The less pleasant consequences of prostitution and syphilis feature in *All's Well, King Lear, Measure for Measure, Pericles* and *Troilus and Cressida*. The gruesome ravages of tertiary syphilis are retailed most explicitly in *Timon of Athens*.

The two final sonnets Numbers 153 and 154 do not fall into any of the main sequences and have as their subject matter the therapeutic benefits of immersion in hot baths. Hot mercury tubs used to treat those infected with syphilis were available in most big cities of Europe at the time, including London.

> I, sick withal, the help of bath desired,
> And thither hied, a sad distempered guest.
> But found no cure ...

There is no evidence that Edward de Vere was syphilitic and these lines from Sonnet 153 could refer instead to the warm spa waters in the city of Bath where he visited in 1595. From Roman times the steaming spring water was believed to have therapeutic properties. London was an insanitary place in which to live, invalids hoped to recover their health by bathing in the warm spring-water, although apparently without success in de Vere's case. The Town Chamberlain of Bath made a gift of poultry to the earl. Alan Nelson in *Monstrous Adversary* (p. 358) quotes from the Chamberlain's Account Roll in the Bath Record Office which lists this civic gift to a visiting dignitary.

Incestuous relationships are rare in Shakespeare. The Syrian king Antiochus and his daughter in the first act of *Pericles* is the most obvious pairing. The frequent mention of incest in *Hamlet* refers to the 'Table of Kindred and Affinity' objection to the marriage of in-laws, in this case Gertrude's marriage to her brother-in-law Claudius, rather than to Hamlet's unhealthy fixation with his mother's sex life. Queen Elizabeth's father Henry VIII had obtained his divorce from Catherine of Aragon by claiming that their marriage was incestuous and therefore invalid because she had been previously married to his brother. In *King Lear* (3.2.55), Lear speaking to Kent says, 'Thou art incestuous.' In *Measure for Measure* Isabella rebukes her brother Claudio, 'Is't not a kind of incest to take life / From thine own sister's shame?' (3.1.140–41).

Although de Vere was never charged with any of the libellous allegations levelled against him in 1580 by his former friends Charles Arundel, Henry Howard and Francis Southwell they were not entirely dispelled either. De Vere had informed on them to the authorities as Catholic plotters. In revenge they accused him of sedition, atheism, necromancy, disloyalty to the Queen, hiring men to commit murder, lying and persistent drunkenness. Mark Anderson in *Shakespeare by Another Name* cleverly spotted that the manner in which the accusations were phrased is mocked by the speech-mangling Dogberry in *Much Ado About Nothing*. (5.1.208–212). In 1584 a polemic written in a more literary style of language, *Leicester's Commonwealth*,[4] claimed to expose the earl of Leicester's manifold crimes and character flaws along similar lines.

More specifically Charles Arundel unsuccessfully pursued a charge of pederasty against the earl, meaning sex with young boys, a criminal offence which would have incurred severe penalties if proved. He accused de Vere with the sexual misuse 'of so many boys that it needs must come out'.[5] To support his case he supplied names of victims, dates, times and locations where the offences had occurred. In 1576 de Vere had brought home from Italy a seventeen year old singer and altar boy named Orazio Cuoco and employed him as a page. This was offered as evidence of his homosexual practices, claiming that the young Italian had complained of being abused by him.

Interrogated by the Venetian Inquisition on his return to Italy a year later (a routine procedure for those returning from non-Catholic countries), the young man said that he had sung before Queen Elizabeth who had tried to convert him from Catholicism to Protestantism but he disclosed nothing of a derogatory nature about his employer. When asked if Oxford had tried to convert him he replied, 'Sirs, no. He let each person live in his own way'. Cuoco also testified that the earl was a fluent speaker of Italian and Latin.[6]

A nobleman's household would of necessity have employed many boys in various capacities, as pages or messengers, or as cheap labour in the scullery and kitchens. De Vere, now in his thirties, had mostly freed himself from a restrictive court. He was actively involved in writing and producing for the theatre where there were a great many boys and young men engaged in the entertainment trades of singing, dancing, juggling, acrobatics and of course, acting. The temptation and the opportunity were there for anyone so inclined but de Vere's only known indiscretion was adultery with a young woman, Anne Vavasour.

Modern productions of *Richard II* have mostly shown the king as overtly homosexual. His men Bushy and Green are described as 'caterpillars' (catamites) and sentenced to death by Bolingbrooke for their 'pernicious lives' (2.3.165) and their corruption of King Richard (3.1.11–13).

> You have, in manner, with your sinful hours
> Made a divorce betwixt his queen and him,
> Broke the possession of a royal bed.

In other mainstream plays there is an implicit homosexual content in some of the conversation exchanges, for example between Romeo and Mercutio, between Othello and Iago, and between Antonio and Bassanio in *The Merchant of Venice*.

In *Troilus and Cressida* the hero Achilles and his companion Patroclus follow Homer as being in an established same-sex relationship. Shakespeare's characters seldom speak disparagingly about such couples, or use derogatory terms to describe promiscuous homosexual men. An exception would be Thersites who accuses Patrocles of being Achilles' 'male varlet' and when challenged spells it out, 'his masculine whore'. (5.1.15–16). Two other soldier combatants, Coriolanus and his deadly enemy Aufidius, embrace and grapple in a surprisingly frank expression of manly love between warriors. (*Coriolanus* 4.5.110–119).

Valentine and Proteus in *Two Gentlemen of Verona* are introduced as young male lovers who then seek marriage partners in heterosexual relationships. Antonio the sea captain and the youthful Sebastian in *Twelfth Night* are also portrayed as male lovers in modern productions of the play. In the same play Olivia and the male-disguised Viola are examples of intense female passion in Shakespeare, as to a lesser extent are Hermia and Helena in *A Midsummer Night's Dream* and Celia and Rosalind in *As You Like It*. Palamon and Arcite, the two noble kinsmen in the co-authored (with John Fletcher) play named *The Two Noble Kinsmen* are more interested in one another than wooing Emilia, for whom they are rivals in matrimony. In return Emilia laments the loss of her 'true love 'tween maid and maid' with her childhood friend Flavinia. (1.3.66–82).

Contemporary writers of openly homoerotic poetry included Richard Barnfield, Michael Drayton and Christopher Marlowe. Many Shakespeare analysts have been troubled by the ostensibly homoerotic nature of some of the first sequence of sonnets 1–126. Written in the first person, seemingly as advances or reproaches to a male lover, the object of the writer's affections is generally thought to be Henry Wriothesley, the third earl of Southampton.

De Vere was twice married, had a mistress and fathered at least seven children, so citing him as a writer of homosexual poetry presents difficulties. An alternative theory could be advanced that de Vere was the younger earl's father. Southampton was born on 6th October 1573 and so was twenty-three years younger than the earl of Oxford. His father the second earl of Southampton, also Henry, was suspected of Catholic sympathies which included complicity in the Ridolfi plot to assassinate Queen Elizabeth. He was arrested in June 1570 and imprisoned in the Tower, eventually 'allowed more liberty' and released on 1st May 1573.

Before this he had been estranged from his wife Mary Browne, daughter of the first Viscount Montagu, another reason why he may not have been the boy's biological father, as well as being incarcerated in the Tower at a time when his heir would have needed to be conceived. Although there is no record of Oxford having an affair with Mary, the second earl's wife, the circumstances existed which could have made this possible.

The so-called 'procreation' group of sonnets 1–17 would not seem so bizarre if the two men were father and son. Awkward phrases such as 'my lovely boy' for example, would fall into place. If viewed as a disabled father addressing a comely young son some of the earlier sonnets would make more sense than if construed as homosexual advances from a middle-aged poet to a younger man. The first two lines of Sonnet 37 would apply

> As a decrepit father takes delight
> To see his active child do deeds of youth

The number of ennobled persons at Queen Elizabeth's court was very much smaller than in the courts of later monarchs. This small tightly-knit circle of aristocrats serving the Queen all knew one another as a kind of extended family, much-interrelated, and were mindful of the obligations of caste which required infidelity to be kept among themselves. These affectionate lines from the third sonnet suggest at least the writer's fondness and admiration for the earl of Southampton's mother

> Thou art thy mother's glass, and she in thee
> Calls back the lovely April of her prime

Stemming from the dedications of the long poems *Venus and Adonis* and *The Rape of Lucrece*, to Henry Wriothesley the earl of Southampton there seems to be a scholarly consensus that this literary connection extends to the Sonnets. The dramatist Bernard Shaw wrote a short play with the title *The Dark Lady of the Sonnets*. It takes the form of a dialogue between Queen Elizabeth and Master Will Shakespear, with contributions from Mary Fitton. She was one of the Queen's maids of honour and included among her many lovers William Herbert, later third Earl of Pembroke, by whom she was made pregnant. Mary Fitton featured in early candidate lists for the Dark Lady but is rarely mentioned now.

Shaw wrote a long Preface separate from the play, examining the twenty-six Dark Lady sonnets in relation to the preceding 126 sonnets. He was disturbed by the apparently homoerotic content of some of these lower numbered sonnets but forcefully rejected any suggestion that the man who wrote Shakespeare was a practising homosexual.

> Shakespear was a man of normal constitution sexually, and was not the victim of that most cruel and pitiable of all the freaks of nature: the freak which transposes the normal aim of the affections. The normality of Shakespear's sexual constitution is only too well attested in the whole mass of his writings.

In the plentiful literature on Shakespeare the problem of the homo-erotic content in the Sonnets is often neatly sidestepped by conceding that the author may have been bi-sexual. This begs the question of whether or not such a condition exists. It may be socially expedient and acceptable to offer the defence of bi-sexuality as an explanation or excuse for a homosexual lifestyle but it still fails to convince. Being gay is a bit like being pregnant, you either are or you aren't, and retrospectively Bernard Shaw's verdict that Shakespeare wasn't would hold true for the earl of Oxford. At worst Charles Arundel accused him of pederasty, sex with boys, not loving relationships with other adult men.

The world of literary scholarship remains permanently intrigued by the Shakespeare sonnets, guessing that they conceal a mystery yet to be discovered, and that somehow Henry Wriothesley the earl of Southampton was involved. The poor physical condition of Edward de Vere at the time of his second marriage to Elizabeth Trentham early in 1592 may be pondered on when considering the birth of his heir the following year. Was he capable of fathering the child himself? Did he knowingly condone a proxy impregnation by a younger and more vigorous aristocrat? Either way Henry de Vere the 18th earl was the result and everyone was pleased with such a successful outcome.

In 1624, twenty years after Edward de Vere's death, an engraving by Thomas Jenner showed side by side in armour, mounted on galloping chargers, two 'Heroes of the Protestant Cause'. It was titled 'The Two Most Noble Henries'. They were Henry de Vere the eighteenth earl of Oxford and Henry Wriothesley the third earl of Southampton. Were the two Henries half-brothers? Or father and son? We shall never know.

And it doesn't matter because a year later both had died on active service abroad, in the Protestant cause against Catholic Spain, and the answers died with them.

Inscription at top left: *The Portraiture of the right honorable Lords, the two most noble HENRIES revived the Earles of Oxford and Southampton*

22

Medicine and Medication

> From his outlays on drugs and care ... nearly one fifth of his total
> expenses, and from his subsequent patronage of apothecaries, we may
> infer that Oxford was chronically sickly, hypochondriacal, or both.

This quotation from *Monstrous Adversary*, Alan Nelson's life of Edward
de Vere, goes some way to answering a frequently asked question. How
did Shakespeare acquire his medical knowledge?

The legal content of the plays is more easily accounted for since de
Vere owned land and property on a large scale and received at least some
formal legal training at Gray's Inn. His surviving letters to his lawyer
father-in-law contain mentions of property rights and the transfer of funds
so the use of legal terms arises naturally in their correspondence.
Landowners were expected to be familiar with the law as it obtained to tax
and property so de Vere's knowledge in this area was not exceptional. But
the impressive level of detailed medical knowledge occurring in the plays
adds a clause to the Shakespeare enigma. The book *Shakespeare and
Medicine* by the Scottish surgeon R. R. Simpson[1] identifies over seven
hundred medical references in the plays. There needs to be an explanation.

Orthodox Stratfordian opinion points to the marriage in 1607 of Susan
Shakspere to the Stratford-upon-Avon physician Dr John Hall, thus
providing her father William Shakspere with a possible source for his
medical knowledge. This is rather late in the day even for orthodox dating.
The American scholar Professor Stephen Booth,[2] although writing from
the Stratfordian corner, considers that the published works of the
Elizabethan physician George Baker provided the main medical influence
on Shakespeare, in particular his 1576 book *The Newe Jewell of Health*.
Professor Booth is an expert commentator on the Shakespeare sonnets.
His 600 page book *Shakespeare's Sonnets*, a line by line and word by
word analysis, is a marvel of diligence, although he avoids being drawn
into the authorship debate.

George Baker wrote several medical works and translated others.[3] He
was an advocate of the new Paracelsian approach to health and medication
based on pharmacology. (As opposed to the Galenic system of medicine).[4]
He was one of the first to realise the therapeutic potential of chemical
compounds for conditions previously resisting treatment. He was also
house physician to the Vere family and his famous book *The Newe Jewell
of Health* was dedicated to Countess Anne, Edward de Vere's wife: 'To
The Right Honourable, Vertuous, and his singular good Lady the Noble

Countess of Oxford'. This was a translation based on the botanical writings of Konrad Gesner,[5] a professor at Zurich University. A second edition of this book *The Practice of the New and Old Phisicke* in 1599 was dedicated to Edward de Vere himself. In 1592 Baker was appointed as Queen Elizabeth's Sergeant-Surgeon and when King James succeeded to the throne he was reappointed as the King's Surgeon. In 1597 he was elected Master of the Company of Barber-Surgeons, so he was a top man in his profession. With George Baker as his physician Edward de Vere would have had access to the best medical advice available at the time.

Apothecaries were the first dispensing chemists, followers of the medical teachings of the Swiss-born botanist and physician known as Paracelsus.[6] Born Philip von Hohenheim he took his name from Celsus, a first century writer on medicine. His contribution to medical practice was the administration of drugs compounded from herbs, oils and finely ground minerals, which he called 'distillations'. The authorities howled 'alchemy', and 'witchcraft', but Paracelsus was pioneering pharmaceutical science and pointing ahead to therapies such as immunisation and the relief of mental illness. He is credited as the first medical practitioner to apply clinical and scientific methods to the unconscious state of mind. He invented laudanum, a distillation of opium dissolved in alcohol, and used it as a palliative and calming medication for disturbed patients, anticipating the later widespread use of anti-depressant drugs.

Another committed Paracelsian was the London apothecary John Hester who described himself as a 'Practitioner in the Arte of Distillations'. He translated numerous books on medical matters, one of which, *A Short Discourse on Surgerie* published in 1580 was from the Italian. It was dedicated to Edward de Vere and carried the Oxford coat of arms on the title page. The original author Leonardo Fioravanti[7] was a noted doctor and surgeon in Bologna. One of the first to employ Paracelsian methods in England was Sir Thomas Smith, de Vere's early tutor and mentor. In November 1574 he provided some medicine for de Vere's wife Countess Anne to prevent her from miscarrying. Sir Thomas was a Renaissance polymath whose interests included horticulture and gardening which he practised at his manors of Hill Hall in Essex and at Ankerwicke, a former female priory on the north bank of the Thames, not far from Windsor.

Lord Burghley was another keen horticulturalist. He had upgraded his mansion Theobalds House[8] near Cheshunt in Hertfordshire to provide a palace fine enough to accommodate the Queen on her visits. The formal gardens at Theobalds House were modelled after the Château de Fontainebleau in France, the English botanist and herbalist John Gerard acting as their superintendent. John Gerard was also involved with a physic garden in Hackney. This garden belonged to Edward de Vere's neighbour Edward la Zouche, eleventh Baron Zouche, another royal ward who had been fostered out to William Cecil. After Trinity College, Cambridge and Gray's Inn he became a career diplomat with an interest in the New World, later becoming a Commissioner of the Virginia Company. Lord Zouche employed the French physician and botanist Matthias L'Obel to supervise his garden and John Gerard obtained seeds from him. L'Obel had a distinguished career, his clients including William, Prince of Orange and King James I of England. Supervising the Hackney garden was his last commission and he died at Highgate in 1616. The plant genus Lobelia is named after him.

The Swedish botanist Max Rydén listed 775 plant references in his book *Shakespearean Plant Names*, published in 1978. In David and Ben Crystal's glossary, *Shakespeare's Words*, the list of botanical references in the plays runs to three and a half pages. These were mostly the shrubs, flowers, herbs and fruits cultivated in the formal gardens of Elizabethan stately homes such as those mentioned above, and where Edward de Vere spent most of his life. They are classified under Flowers, Herbs, Spices, Trees and Shrubs, with a small section, 'Plants viewed as unpleasant'. This last includes the mandrake plant which folklore credits with emitting a lethal shriek when pulled from the ground. Queen Margaret's lover the duke of Suffolk says to her, 'Could curses kill, as doth the mandrake's groan'. (*2 Henry VI*, 3.2.314). In Juliet's long soliloquy on death before drinking from the vial she says, 'And shrieks like mandrakes torn out of the earth'. (*Romeo and Juliet* 4.3.46). Powerful imagery. Two other Shakespeare plays contain female characters given a potion to induce a temporary death-like state, Hero in *Much Ado About Nothing* and Innogen in *Cymbeline*. All three recover, although with tragic consequences in Juliet's case.

How de Vere acquired his knowledge of plants and their therapeutic applications can only be speculative but his known association with apothecaries, and the books dedicated to him and his wife on medical subjects, could offer a reasonable explanation. Also his access to well-stocked libraries, possessing an enquiring mind, and having the time to read and study matters of interest to him. Even so the depth of knowledge about physical and mental illnesses revealed in the plays is not easily explained. The remarkable extent of the author's medical knowledge may be judged by his reference to the 'pia mater'. This is the innermost layer of the meninges, the membranes surrounding the brain. The eccentric scholar Holofernes in *Love's Labour's Lost* says, (4.2.66–71)

'This is a gift that I have, simple, simple – a foolish extravagant spirit, full of forms, figures, shapes, objects, ideas, apprehensions, motions, revolutions. These are begot in the ventricle of memory, nourished in the womb of pia mater, and delivered upon the mellowing of occasion.'

In Shakespeare there are several references to the possession of a pulse, and to the rapid palpitation of the heart in stressful situations. In *The Winter's Tale* (1.2.112–13) an agitated Leontes, believing his wife to have been unfaithful, says

> I have tremor cordis on me, my heart dances,
> But not for joy

An hallucinating Hamlet having just killed Polonius assures his mother that he is sane and in a normal state of mind

> My pulse as yours doth temperately keep time,
> And makes as healthful music

It was not until 1707 that the English physician John Floyer (1649–1734) invented a device for measuring pulse rates. This took the form of a portable clock with a rotating second hand that could be stopped by a push-down switch. The general accuracy of clocks and other timing mechanisms did not improve much until the coming of the railways in the next century. The need for published timetables made reliable timepieces a vital necessity, with medical applications also benefiting.

Although not substantiated by evidence, the degenerative condition that impaired Edward de Vere's limb function in his later years could have originated with the wound sustained in his affray with Thomas Knyvet in 1582. An undisclosed injury from the tiltyard could be an alternative explanation. As a young man de Vere excelled in the tourneys which were a popular form of court entertainment, and which were fiercely contested. In 1571 at the age of twenty-one he won a big tournament at Westminster in which one of the contestants was the Queen's Champion Sir Henry Lee. Other possible causes of his disability may have been the knee injury he sustained in Venice, or the long term after-effects from a disease or infection picked up during his foreign travels or in his military campaigns.[9]

Malaria contracted in Italy could have been the cause of the debilitating condition responsible for de Vere's weakened health in the last half of his life. The term 'malaria' is compounded from two Italian words *mal aria* meaning 'bad air', the atmospheric conditions in which mosquitoes thrive, commonly associated with low-lying swampy or marshy ground. It was also known as 'Roman fever' from a deadly strain of malaria that almost wiped out the Roman army in the fifth century, and by implication may have contributed to the fall of the poorly defended city of Rome that followed. The fever that Edward de Vere recovered from in Venice in September 1575, mentioned earlier, could have been malaria, even though a virulent strain of the bubonic plague was rampant at the same time. Malaria continues to ravage large parts of the world, sub-Saharan Africa in particular, where the humid conditions prevail that sustain large populations of mosquitoes. The earl's recurring periods of illness after his return to England could be symptomatic of malaria rather than syphilis, as implied by the Arundel libels.

In 1606 one of de Vere's earlier continental travelling companions,

Nathaniel Baxter, wrote a poem to honour the earl's daughter Lady Susan Vere's marriage to Philip Herbert, soon afterwards ennobled as the earl of Montgomery. This contains some interesting information, for example that the Queen had ordered de Vere to return to England because of the mounting disease risk. She most likely had the plague in mind but Baxter refers instead to the deadly bite of the mosquito, 'Hopping Helena with her warbling sting... Like as they poisoned all Italy'. This poem also mentions the party's interception by sea pirates on the return journey.

> Naked we landed out of Italy
> Inthralled by pirates, men of no regard:
> Horror and death assailed nobility

The word 'malaria' does not occur in Shakespeare but numerous references to the symptoms of 'ague' confirm them as the same medical condition. Malarial fevers which recur daily are known as quotidian, longer intervals as tertian. King James I died in his sixtieth year from a stroke preceded by a tertian ague. The death of Falstaff is also recorded as caused by the ague. The Hostess of the Boar's Head tavern, now married to Pistol, summons his friends to the bedside. (*Henry V* 2.1.111–14)

> Come in quickly to Sir John. Ah, poor heart, he is so shaked of a burning quotidian-tertian, that it is most lamentable to behold.

Even for aristocrats London was an insanitary place in which to live. Overcrowded and rat-infested, few of its citizens would have been free of body lice or intestinal worms. An outbreak of smallpox in 1562 ravaged the city, with the thirty-year-old Queen Elizabeth one of the unfortunate victims. She recovered but was left with facial scars that had to be concealed under thick white make-up. The Queen was also made bald by the smallpox and wore wigs for the rest of her life.

Recurrent outbreaks of the bubonic plague were an ever-present danger, most grievously in 1563 and 1603 with great loss of life in both years. Places of assembly and entertainment were closed by order of the crown when another ferocious outbreak of the plague erupted in 1592. This lasted until 1594 when the ban was lifted but this long closure adversely affected financially the bear-baiting houses and the public theatres.

The previously unknown but ghastly venereal disease known as syphilis spread rapidly throughout Europe in the sixteenth century, with the inference drawn that it had been brought back from central and south America as trade with that region developed. Not until 1910 when the German physician and haematologist Paul Ehrlich (1854–1915) developed the arsenical compound known as Salvarsan was there any hope of relief from the most distressing symptoms. The only treatment available to sufferers in the period covered by the Shakespeare plays was the inhalation of vaporised mercury salts in an enclosed vessel, most commonly a large wooden tub. This practice was mentioned earlier in relation to Sonnets 153 and 154 but is also quoted with some distaste by Timon in *Timon of Athens* (4.3.84–88).

> Be a whore still; they love thee not that use thee.
> Give them diseases, leaving with thee their lust.
> Make use of thy salt hours. Season the slaves
> For tubs and baths; bring down rose-cheek'd youth
> To the tub-fast and diet.

Typhoid fever was rife in crowded places, municipal hygiene and sanitation being virtually non-existent. A prison sentence could be a death sentence in London's disease-ridden jails. The rebel Dick the Butcher makes the release of prisoners a priority in the second part of *Henry VI* (4.3.14–15).

> If we mean to thrive and do good,
> break open the jails and let out the prisoners.

In a letter to Lord Burghley dated 4th June 1595 de Vere ends, '... pardon my scribbled hand. I have been this day let blood'. Drawing blood was a common treatment for many ill-health conditions, although most likely by opening a vein rather than by applying leeches. In another letter to Lord Burghley written from the village of Byfleet in Surrey and dated 7th August 1595, he writes, 'I most heartily thank your Lordship for your desire to know of my health which is not so good yet as I wish it. I find comfort in this air'.

There are many references in the sonnets to his failing health, and to lameness specifically in Sonnets 37, 66 and 89. 'I will attend Your Lordship as well as a lame man may at your house', de Vere wrote to Lord Burghley in a letter dated 25 March 1595. In another letter to Lord Burghley he writes, 'I would have been with your Lordship before this but I have not had my health'. In another letter dated 8th September 1597 he admits, 'I have not an able body'. To his brother-in-law Robert Cecil he makes the excuse, 'by reason of my sickness I have not been able to write'. By 1602 his tone is even more pathetic, 'by reason of mine infirmity I cannot come among you as often as I wish'.

There is a literary reference to de Vere as deaf in his last years. In the political vacuum between the death of Queen Elizabeth on 24th March 1603, the arrival in London of King James on 7th May and his coronation on 25th July, courtiers split into factions, all competing for royal favour. A document was issued on 20th May with the title *Anagrammata in Nomina Illustrissimorum Heroum*. The heroes in question were nine lords and four knights, and the broadside took the form of Latin epigrams based on their individual names and titles. The earls of Oxford and Southampton were included among the lords. The anagram heading the entry for Oxford was *Edouarus Veierus* per anagramma *Aure Surdus Video.* In the translation by Dr Dana F. Sutton[10] this converts to *Edward Vere – deaf in my ear, I see.'* There are no clues elsewhere suggesting deafness as 'mine infirmity', although there are some textual references. Julius Caesar says to Antony, 'Come on my right hand, for this ear is deaf'. (*Julius Caesar* 1.2.214). In *The Comedy of Errors* (5.1.318) the merchant Egeon laments the ageing process, 'My dull deaf ears a little use to hear'.

The clinical detail of Shakespeare's medical knowledge has aroused the curiosity of many doctors, surgeons and more recently, psychiatrists. Professor Aubrey Kail in his book *The Medical Mind of Shakespeare*[11] examines at length the text of *Timon of Athens* and lists the symptoms of late stage syphilis which occur in this play. Professor Kail was puzzled that for a dramatist with no history of medical training the description and nature of Timon's afflictions are not only extensive and accurate but contained medical knowledge only recently discovered at the time when the play could have been written.

Because insanity and suicidal despair figure so prominently in the plays it is possible to overlook references to other less dramatic forms of illness or disease. These often come shielded behind seemingly innocuous words and phrases, particularly those of a sexual nature which need expert annotation to pick up. The plays feature a wide range of medical conditions and procedures including bone setting and geriatrics, clinical descriptions of the large organs in the body and their functions, therapeutics, sex, sexually transmitted diseases, the plague, pregnancy and childbirth, death and dying.

Whoever wrote the plays of Shakespeare possessed an impressive grasp of the human predicament.

23

Genius and the Hurt Mind

O, full of scorpions is my mind, dear wife
Macbeth 3.2.38

Shakespeare's plays have been exhaustively analysed, receiving word-by-word scrutiny from specialists in almost every known field of human endeavour. These would include the many branches of medicine, with early psychiatric interest aroused when this area of medical science began to be developed in the late nineteenth century.

Insanity in its various forms features prominently in many plays, certainly in the plays commonly referred to as the great tragedies. The gothic horrors of madness, suicidal despair, hallucinations, insomnia, hearing voices, ghosts, nightmares and the supernatural not only runs through them but could even be a reason for the awed fascination they have exerted on audiences over many years, not only in this country but elsewhere, in many lands around the world.

Violent deaths punctuate the Histories and Tragedies. Hotspur is slain and punishment duly meted out. King Henry orders, 'Bear Worcester to the death, and Vernon too'. If the faces of the actors reflect the horrible fate awaiting them it is indeed history brought to life before an awestruck audience. King Richard III is butchered as we watch, Julius Caesar stabbed in the back, Gloucester's eyes gouged out. The wholesale slaughter in *Titus Andronicus* and *Hamlet* leaves the stage littered with corpses. Shakespeare is not for the faint-hearted.

Which forces the question, who could have written this large body of work of such interest to psychiatrists? And secondly, what were the circumstances in the author's life that compelled him to write them? The case for Edward de Vere as Shakespeare is predicated on this assumption: that the known details of his family background, education and life experiences match very closely the psychological profile of the author which can be extrapolated from the texts of the Shakespeare plays and poetry.

Consider these incidents in his early life. Edward was separated from his mother at a young age, possibly in 1554 when only four. Mary Tudor had succeeded to the throne the year before and soon afterwards began her purge of prominent Protestant men and women. Edward was sent to be sheltered and educated at the home of Sir Thomas Smith and even if for his own good, this early separation from his mother could still have affected him in his later years.

If children need a secure identity then the unpleasant family dispute over his legitimacy must have been unsettling. John de Vere died in 1562 so Edward inherited his title at the age of twelve. His half-sister Lady Katherine Vere (twelve years his senior) and her husband Lord Edward Windsor, disputed his right to inherit, claiming that John de Vere's sudden second marriage to Margery Golding, Edward's mother, was illegal because his estranged first wife Dorothy Neville was still living. The suit was rebutted but the accusation of bastardy, and the mental turmoil which would have ensued, if proved, may have inflicted a psychological open wound that never quite healed.

Edward de Vere was brought to London to become a ward of court. His mother remarried but died six years later when Edward was eighteen. At nineteen he suffered a long unexplained illness and went into solitary retreat, renting rooms in Windsor. Even though he does not appear to have had much in the way of maternal affection it is possible that his mother's death could have triggered an episode of depression. Six months later Edward joined the army sent to suppress the so-called Rising of the North. This campaign was led by the earl of Sussex who was particularly hard on the Scots, burning castles and whole villages and carrying out reprisals with appalling severity.

At the age of twenty-one Edward de Vere was released from wardship and faced with the problem of reclaiming his estates and paying off family debts. This presented many difficulties and he was vexed with financial problems for the rest of his life. Also at twenty-one he married Anne Cecil but the marriage was far from happy. His erratic and often violent behaviour began to manifest itself at around this time, in his twenties. A childhood and adolescence spent in two stern Protestant households, where many hours of every day were spent in compulsory study, might explain his high-spirited over-reaction at being finally released into the real world at the end of his tenure as a royal ward.

When he was twenty-two his cousin the duke of Norfolk was executed by beheading in the Tower of London. Bearing in mind the political, religious and dynastical turmoil that beset Queen Elizabeth's first thirty years on the throne (only victory over the Spanish in 1588 finally consolidated her hold on power), this was just another death from within his circle that Edward de Vere had to cope with throughout his life. Other family casualties included his ancestor the twelfth earl, and his uncle the sonneteer Henry Howard, earl of Surrey, both beheaded. As a senior courtier sitting on juries he was himself closely associated with the imprisonment of Philip Howard the earl of Arundel and the executions of Queen Mary Stuart and the earl of Essex.

The court chronicler Gilbert Talbot, in a letter dated 11th May 1573 written to his father George Talbot the 6th earl of Shrewsbury (for eighteen years the custodian of Mary Stuart) referred to de Vere's 'fickle head', predicting that his wayward conduct would not be tolerated indefinitely. So it proved and only impending bankruptcy in his mid-thirties brought him under any measure of control from the Queen and her principal ministers and advisers.

In 1580 de Vere was interrogated in the Tower of London while serious charges against him by his cousins Henry Howard and Charles Arundel were investigated. He was released but the following year was back for a longer stay in the Tower after fathering a child with Anne Vavasour. At the age of thirty-five Edward served with the military in the war against Spain which was being fought in the Netherlands, and at thirty-eight he took to sea against the Armada. Even if not a top commander or war hero himself he had at least witnessed battlefield scenes and felt the throes of war at close quarters. As a music lover and poet the effect of these experiences on a sensitive mind could explain how the brutality of witnessed conflict lives on as great literature.

As he moved into his forties Edward de Vere, a clever, restless man, retreated into a gloomy private life. The cumulative depressive effects of the death of his baby son in 1583, his infant daughter Frances in 1587, and his wife Anne in 1588, would have been sufficient reason for melancholy. His mother-in-law Mildred Cecil died in 1589 and was entombed in Westminster Abbey together with his wife Anne, in a lavish monument placed by Lord Burghley. Many of the people close to him began to pass away at the same time. His two most supportive older friends had died, Sir Thomas Smith in 1577 and then Thomas Radcliffe the earl of Sussex. His cousin, classmate and friend Edward Manners the third Earl of Rutland had died at thirty-eight. Sir Philip Sidney was killed on active service in 1586 followed two years later by his uncle Robert Dudley. George Gascoigne, Roland York, Sir Christopher Hatton and Sir Francis Walsingham, even if not exactly friends, might still have been missed.

With no wife at the time, no son and heir, no proper home and insufficient money, de Vere had good reason to be troubled and unhappy at a bleak period in his life. Many of his sonnets reveal the mind of a melancholy recluse. Contributory factors could have been the bitter memory of an unhappy marriage, his loss of favour with the queen, his lack of advancement at court, his financial ruin, his failing health and his physical disability.

At the age of fifty, although by now more securely remarried, he wrote a resentful letter to his brother-in-law Robert Cecil in July 1600 complaining that his lack of success 'in former suits to her Majesty, after so many trials made in vain, and so many opportunities escaped ... have given me cause to bury my hopes in the deep abyss and bottom of despair.' Any man who can describe himself as in 'the deep abyss and bottom of despair' is a man suffering from mental health problems. What these problems were, what caused them, and the amount of medical help he was given to overcome them is not known.

Whether or not alcohol addiction could be largely to blame is moot but throughout recorded history men and women of undisputed renown have been identified as excessive drinkers. A primary form of creativity such as script-writing, although carried out as a mostly solitary occupation, would still exert stress, the so-called 'agony of creation'. The list of famous writers (and painters, sculptors and composers) who have succumbed to death or dementia from prolonged alcohol misuse is a distinguished parade of talent.

As a young man Edward de Vere could be charming, and persuasive when it came to getting his own way, which he did for most of the time. But he was restless, he travelled at great expense, gambled heavily on a shipping venture that failed, borrowed huge sums of money, subsidised and supported actors and writers, underwrote theatre productions and squandered his inherited fortune by the age of thirty-six. Reckless and grandiose prodigality is typical of an alcoholic's irresponsible attitude to money. He had not only run through his inheritance, alienated his in-laws the powerful Cecil family by the mistreatment of his wife, but also made enemies of just about everyone else he encountered in everyday life, from the Queen to his servants. His long-running feud with Thomas Knyvet added violence to the case history. With no other explanation available the question may be asked whether his predisposition to self-destructive behaviour had been exacerbated by so many adverse experiences in childhood and adolescence.

Alcoholism is known to conceal or to mimic psychological disorders, making it difficult to work out which is causing the other. Those who know the plays and poems will be aware of the manic-depressive symptoms displayed by characters considered autobiographical, Hamlet, Leontes and Romeo as examples, all exhibiting mania and obsession, with violent mood-swings between anguish and elation. The Shakespeare sonnets for all their beauty of language are steeped with a sense of melancholy, alienation and despair. The first four lines of Sonnet 29 are among the most frequently quoted

> When, in disgrace with fortune and men's eyes,
> I all alone beweep my outcast state,
> And trouble deaf heaven with my bootless cries,
> And look upon myself and curse my fate.

Common side-effects that torment the long-established alcoholic would include psychotic symptoms such as seeing ghosts, hearing voices and experiencing terrible nightmares. Also insomnia, the theme of Sonnets 27 (black night ... no quiet find) and 28 (... debarred the benefit of rest.) If writers write from experience then the author of *Macbeth* knew something about sleepless nights. In Act 2 Scene 2 Macbeth describes it in sombre awfulness

> Methought I heard a voice cry 'Sleep no more!
> Macbeth does murder sleep' – the innocent sleep,
> Sleep that knits up the ravell'd sleave of care,
> The death of each day's life ...

The extent to which the author of Shakespeare was familiar with texts in Greek has been much debated by critics and scholars but *Macbeth*[1] would surely qualify as a Greek-style tragedy. The way in which the murder of Duncan is announced would be typical of a Greek report by a messenger. The German scholar and Shakespeare translator August Schlegel wrote of *Macbeth*, 'Since Aeschylus, nothing so grand or terrible has ever been composed.'[2]

In his book *The Medical Mind of Shakespeare* the Australian psychiatrist Aubrey C. Kail concentrates on mental illness, and the characters who suffer from depression or dementia. Characters with a case history of mental disorder come to a long list, with depression as one of the most common conditions. Antonio (*Merchant of Venice*), Hamlet, Jaques, Orsino, Richard II, Romeo and Timon would serve as examples of characters suffering severe depression. Suicides include Brutus, Cassius, Cleopatra, Mark Antony and Romeo. The somnambulist Lady Macbeth goes mad, as does Ophelia. Those who hallucinate or see apparitions in dreams and visions include Brutus, Calpurnia, Hamlet, Queen Katherine, Macbeth, Posthumus and Richard III. Falstaff is a cheerful alcoholic. More than enough to fill a psychiatrist's waiting room.

Characters afflicted with epilepsy include Julius Caesar, Macbeth and Othello. King Henry IV dies following an epileptic fit (*2 Henry IV*, 4.3.110–11).

> … my brain is giddy. O me! Come near me now. I am much ill.

In the whole of literature there is no more harrowing study of an elderly man in mental distress than Shakespeare's King Lear. Symptoms of senile dementia are exhibited by King John, Shylock and Polonius, who struggles with short term memory loss (*Hamlet* 2.1.49-51).

> And then, sir, does a this – a does –
> what was I about to say? By the mass, I was about to say something.
> Where did I leave?

Sir John Bucknill (1817–1897)[3] founded the *British Journal of Psychiatry* in 1853. It is still published monthly. He wrote three books on the Shakespeare plays, *The Psychology of Shakespeare* published in 1859, *The Medical Knowledge of Shakespeare* in 1860 and *The Mad Folk of Shakespeare* in 1867. He was fascinated by the plays and impressed by their forcefulness of language, most of all by the 'extent and exactness' of their psychiatric knowledge.

> That abnormal states of mind were a favourite study of Shakespeare would be evident from the number of characters to which he has attributed them. On no other subject has he written with such mighty power.

In *The Medical Knowledge of Shakespeare* he expresses amazement that the author's descriptions of the 'diseases of the mind' were comparable with 'the most advanced science of the present day'. He writes that Shakespeare used medical terms with 'scientific strictness'. In *The Psychology of Shakespeare* he deals with specific characters in the plays and writes long case-study notes about them, calling them 'psychological essays'. These include studies of Constance, Hamlet, Jaques, King Lear, Macbeth, Malvolio, Ophelia and Timon,

Yet Sir John Bucknill could not explain how the son of a 'wool-comber' (his term for John Shakspere) acquired such extensive medical knowledge. He concluded that Shakespeare must have been 'an insatiable devourer of books', which he says at that time would have needed to include medical treatises written in French. It never seems to have occurred to Sir John that someone other than the son of the 'wool-comber' might have written these extraordinary plays.

The nature of genius, and how to identify people who possess it, is a subject of enduring curiosity. In his book *Autism and Creativity* the psychiatrist Professor Michael Fitzgerald[4] makes the case that genius is a form of mental abnormality and therefore diagnosable. Many people with one or other of the various forms of autism can also be creative and to this group Professor Fitzgerald applies the term 'high functioning autism'. Edward de Vere's irresponsible and often violent behaviour, his financial recklessness and egocentricity, if considered in tandem with his unique mastery of the English language, might well bring him within this medical definition of high function autism.

The Canadian psychiatrist Dr François Martin Mai[5] in his book *Diagnosing Genius* writes, 'The psychology of creativity and its relationship to psychiatric and medical illness is an area of great interest for researchers'. He goes on to explain that many of the people with a generally accepted record of extraordinary accomplishment in music, art or literature exhibited symptoms of morbid depression, mania or psychosis. These encompass a range of conditions that would include impulsive, irrational or delusional behaviour, suicidal thoughts, narcissism and personality disorder, poor judgement, aggression, obsession, emotional coldness and the inability to form or make progress in human relationships. Alcohol and substance abuse featured prominently in the case histories of those studied, yet these were all people capable of externalising the most profound and beautiful ideas in their chosen art form, in words, paint or music.

Another study into the nature of genius, *Cognitive Processes in Creativity* by John R Hayes and Carnegie Mellon found,[6] among other evidence, that thoroughness of preparation is the single most necessary factor in any form of high attainment. Even the most naturally gifted composers, writers and painters had to start early and undergo at least ten years of specialised study and training before they began to produce the work for which they later became famous. Continuous editing and revision were also evident in case history studies of the highest achievers. This would apply to Shakespeare, whose plays cannot be accurately sequenced for this reason. There is sufficient textual evidence to demonstrate that the plays were reworked and refined many times before reaching their definitive versions in the 1623 First Folio. Wells and Taylor in their *Textual Companion* write, 'Editors and critics have long resisted the obvious conclusion, that Shakespeare occasionally, perhaps habitually, revised his work.'[7]

The opening paragraph of Alan Nelson's biography of Edward de Vere, with the title *Monstrous Adversary*, is a disparaging indictment of his character and lack of *noblesse oblige*. Those fortunate enough to be born into the nobility were expected to behave in an honourable and generous way to those less privileged. Nelson believes that de Vere defaulted on this obligation

> He held no office of consequence, nor performed a notable deed. Oxford neglected to serve others for the simple reason that his first aim in life was to serve himself.

Professor Nelson's strongly held conviction that de Vere was self-absorbed to an unusual degree runs through his book from beginning to end, identifying it as a defining character flaw. Although his exhaustive research into de Vere's life and literary activities were written specifically to counter the claims of Oxfordian authorship supporters, his findings are not that far apart. The heartfelt Sonnet 62 could well have been penned by the earl, a vain man saddened by the ravages of time he sees in his mirror

> Sin of self-love possesseth all mine eye,
> And all my soul, and all my every part;
> And for this sin there is no remedy,
> It is so grounded inward in my heart.
> Methinks no face so gracious is as mine,
> No shape so true, no truth of such account,
> And for myself mine own worth do define
> As I all other in all worths surmount.
> But when my glass shows me myself indeed,
> Beated and chopped with tanned antiquity,
> Mine own self-love quite contrary I read;
> Self so self-loving were iniquity,
>   'Tis thee, myself, that for myself I praise
>   Painting my age with beauty of thy days.

Although such egocentrism may tell against de Vere as a human being it does not necessarily disqualify him from also being a writer of genius. There exists a wealth of biographical literature where extreme single-mindedness of purpose features prominently in the life histories of those who possess extraordinary intellectual powers and are able to express them in an art form, or as advanced mathematics. Lord Acton's aphorism, 'Great men are almost always bad men' might usefully be applied.

If the case for Edward de Vere has merit then the length, range and intensity of his education and career preparation could have provided the secure platform on which his working life as a writer was launched and sustained. The underlying causes of his asocial and often unacceptable behaviour as a young man are unclear but the pairing of psychiatric disorder with artistic creativity could be advanced as a feasible explanation. Professor Fitzgerald's term of 'high function autism' might well be applicable if more details of his medical case history were known.

Although Edward de Vere's second marriage to Elizabeth Trentham was happier than his first marriage to Anne Cecil his final years still seem to have been blighted with poor health and depression. This is reflected in the dark nature of the plays generally supposed to be among the last revised or written, the epic tragedies which made the name of Shakespeare one of the most famous in the history of the world. These have assumed a timeless quality, allowing them to be performed in a wide variety of costume and period settings, even set in the future. Nor is it just for dexterity of language that Shakespeare's reputation remains undimmed. No writer of philosophy has so sensitively explored the dark midnight of the soul or taught us what it means to be human.

For new and old readers alike, to study Shakespeare can still be a transforming experience.

24

Death and Legacy

For restful death I cry
from Sonnet 66

In a letter dated 25th April 1603 to Sir Robert Cecil, Edward de Vere eloquently expresses his grief at the death of Queen Elizabeth a month earlier. From the age of twelve he had spent his life as a member of her court and from the tone of the letter he was still deeply distressed by her death. He speaks well of her successor King James, the son of Mary Stuart, whose execution he had helped to arrange. His tribute to the dead queen is pleasingly cadenced with some nice turns of phrase, including a nautical simile of riding out a storm. The long lamentation ends

> I cannot but find a great grief in myself to remember the mistress which we have lost, under whom both you and myself from our greenest years have been in a manner brought up; and although it hath pleased God after an earthly kingdom to take her up into a more permanent and heavenly state, wherin I do not doubt but that she is crowned with glory, and to give us a prince wise, learned and enriched with all virtues; yet the long time which we spent in her service, we cannot look for so much left of our days as to bestow upon another, neither the long acquaintance and kind familiarities wherewith she did use us, we are not ever to expect from another prince as denied by the infirmity of age and common course of reason. In this common shipwreck, mine is above all the rest, who least regarded, though often comforted, of all her followers, she hath left to try my fortune among the alterations of time, and chance, either without sail whereby to take the advantage of any prosperous gale, or with anchor to ride till the storm be overpast. There is nothing therefore left for my comfort, but the excellent virtues and deep wisdom wherewith God hath endued our new master and sovereign lord, who doth not come among us as a stranger but as a natural prince, succeeding by right of blood and inheritance, not as a conqueror, but as the true shepherd of Christ's flock to cherish and comfort them.

Your assured friend and unfortunate Brother in Law,
E. Oxenford.

This must be one of most sincere and generous tributes ever paid to Elizabeth. There is no reason to suppose that the earl had any expectation that his letter would be read by anyone other than the intended recipient and so it could be considered as a fitting valediction to his own life as one of her courtiers. The religious tone of the letter is surprisingly heartfelt and would serve to discount any theory that his death a year later was by suicide. In the early seventeenth century no Christian with any hope of heaven would have risked dying by his or her own hand.

Edward de Vere died on 24th June 1604. He was not buried until 6th July which makes plague as the cause of death unlikely, as plague victims were routinely disposed of quickly. No reason was given in the parish register but from the decline in his health, as gleaned from his surviving letters, it would seem to have been from natural causes. That he had long suffered from the debilitating effects of recurring ague, malaria in modern terms, could be offered as a speculative explanation for his terminal illness. Dying at the age of fifty-four would not have been a cause for concern in an age where the life expectancy of men, even well-cared-for aristocrats, was considerably less.

It is the absence of a funerary monument for such a high profile nobleman that has provoked curiosity ever since. A distant relative on his mother's side, Percival Golding, left a brief note to the effect that the earl had been buried in Westminster Abbey but this has never been authenticated from the Abbey records. It must be almost certain that he was interred in the church of St Augustine in Hackney, even though no memorial exists to confirm this.

Eight years later, on 25th November 1612, his widow Countess Elizabeth signed her will. Her exact date of death is unknown but she was buried in the same church on 3rd January 1613. It is believed that she succumbed to typhoid fever. In her will she asks that a suitable monument should be made for herself and her husband, which implies that no monument had been provided after the earl's death in 1604. There is no record that her nineteen-year-old son Henry de Vere provided such a monument, nor her brother Francis Trentham, one of the executors of her will.

In 1720 the ecclesiastical historian John Strype published a survey of 67 tombs and inscriptions in St Augustine's Church, Hackney. No monument for the Earl and Countess of Oxford was included but an empty and unmarked tomb of grey marble was listed which may have been the missing memorial. An earlier and less comprehensive survey was made in 1633 but again no Oxford monument was listed. This survey was made by Anthony Munday, for many years a literary associate of Edward de Vere, who would surely have included his monument if one existed. In 1798 St Augustine's Church was demolished to make room for a larger church, renamed St John-at-Hackney. A small narrow table-monument was found when pulling down the old church. A drawing of it made at the time is kept in Hackney Council Archives in Dalston Square, London. This is the most that can be offered as a possible last resting place for the 17th earl of Oxford and his Countess.

So for the man who was Shakespeare no earthly memorial exists. What then of Edward de Vere in person, a man who died not knowing whether his plays, his life's work, would be saved? And if they did, and were performed, how they would be received? To die without the praise and recognition that was due to him for his great body of work was to die a sad and demeaning death. Of his many residences only the forbidding keep of Hedingham Castle survives. The apartment at the Savoy, the house in Bishopsgate where his literary talents flourished, the family seashore retreat at Wivenhoe, the house at Stoke Newington and the final home of King's Place in Hackney, are all long gone. Somehow or other Lord Edward himself also slipped through the net, vanished like his houses from the face of the earth.

Perhaps this was how it was intended to be from the start. For those who subscribe to the inexorable laws of mischance there is a grim symmetry in the absence of a grave and the denial of authorship. Anonymous, invisible, incognito in death as in life, the literary earl was doomed to live and die in obscurity. For his ancestors there were marble monuments in plenty. They can be viewed in the collection contained in the secluded private chapel at Bures in Essex, in the splendid East Anglian wool-wealthy churches of Earls Colne and Castle Hedingham, and in the abbey cathedral of Westminster. But for the man who was Shakespeare, the nation's favourite son, their Man of the Millennium, for this man there is no tomb, no pilgrimage, no acknowledgement of a superhuman genius, no worldly fame.

Shakespeare's great tragedies are acclaimed as masterworks of world literature, unmatched for their profundity of thought and feeling, and for their grandeur of language. No other writer has stripped his emotions so bare, perhaps an explanation for the fascination these chronicles of mental disintegration, love, jealousy and thwarted ambition have exerted over readers and playgoers ever since. Those who believe that the Sonnets are by the same hand as the plays must themselves sorrow at the anguish of unrequited love so deeply felt and so frankly expressed. As an author bound into the strife and circumstance of Renaissance Europe the patrician Edward de Vere emerges as a character as tragic as any in his plays, a vulnerable and misunderstood man of infinite complexity and pathos.

Most mysterious of all, and the hardest part of the authorship mystery to understand, is how staunchly the orthodox position is still defended. The literary establishment (academia, criticism, publishing, theatre) strenuously maintains that William Shakspere, the businessman from Stratford-upon-Avon, was also the poet and dramatist known to the world as William Shakespeare. No doubt a good man, but hardly the chronicler of kings. Nevertheless many eminent and well-meaning scholars from centuries past until the present day persist in this belief. Many writers have put their names (well-known names, some of them) to lengthy biographies and studies of the unlettered Stratford grain hoarder. Equally complicit are the literati who obligingly provide kind words for the back covers of such books.

There is something quintessentially British in this obdurate support for the wrong man, something much to admire in its eccentricity, and in its loyalty to past scholars. Yet still to insist, in the face of all evidence and reason, that the world's most widely acclaimed literary genius was an illiterate small-town trader, and to continue lauding him and worshipping his memory, is not easy to understand or explain.

The Shakespeare authorship mystery is also the Shakespeare authorship tragedy.

Appendix A

William Shakspere of Stratford-upon-Avon

There is no record of anyone named William Shakespeare receiving payment for any form of writing. The Elizabethan theatre impresario Philip Henslowe maintained records of payments made to writers of plays, twenty-seven of them in all, but does not include anyone named Shakespeare. Henslowe also kept a diary, 1592–1609, in which some versions of plays by Shakespeare receive a mention. These include *Titus Andronicus, The Taming of a Shrew* [*sic*], *Hamlet* and *The Mawe*, which could refer to *Othello* (The Moor). Two history plays are mentioned, one is believed to refer to *Henry VI*, although which part is unknown, the other to *Henry V*. Shakespeare is not named by Henslowe in his diary entries, either as an actor, an author, or as a person known to him.

Nor does anyone else mention meeting such a person, no letter written to him survives, no one apparently ever received a letter from him in return. There are no records of anyone named William Shakespeare holding any office or attending court. The hyphenated version of the Shake-speare name appeared on the title pages of quarto and poetry editions, and in the prefatory pages of the First Folio. A hyphen was often (although not consistently), used by publishers to indicate a pseudonym. None of the original manuscripts survived and the identity of the author became obscured in the lapse of time.

Shakespeare authorship research has always been complicated by the existence of a man with a similar name. The man's name was spelled or abbreviated in several different ways but mostly as Shakspere, (lacking the 'e' after the 'k'), leading some to think it was pronounced as written, that is as 'Shackspere'. Almost nothing is known about this man except for his name on legal documents, most of them in Stratford-upon-Avon.

In London his name appeared on a lease for the Globe Theatre. The original lease between the landowner Sir Nicholas Brend and six shareholders was signed on 16th May 1599. The Burbage brothers, Richard and Cuthbert, took a quarter share each, the other four owned an eighth each, these being John Heminges, Augustine Phillips, Thomas Pope and William Shakespeare. William Kempe was supposed to be the seventh partner but sold his share in advance to the four minority holders. The original lease has never been found so it is not known how Shakespeare's name was spelled. It is only referred to in a Court of Requests action in 1619, *Witter versus Heminges and Condell.*

William Shakspere was born in the small agricultural town of Stratford-upon-Avon in 1564 and died there in 1616. He was married in 1582 at the age of eighteen, had a daughter in 1583 and a twin son and daughter in 1585. He was in business as a maltster and grain trader. He was also a successful investor in land and property, able at the age of thirty-three to purchase New Place, a large house in his home town. There are no records of him receiving any form of education.

The entrenched orthodox authorship position is still insistent that this man was not just a provincial businessman with property interests in London but that he was also an actor, a poet and a dramatist, in fact the transcendent literary genius known to the world as William Shakespeare. It is the lack of evidence to support this notion that has always fuelled the search for a more believable author. The literary establishment (academia, criticism, publishing, theatre) remains firmly behind William Shakspere from Stratford-upon-Avon as the poet and dramatist known as William Shakespeare. To express doubt about this openly can still prejudice a student or jeopardise a career. The print media and the nation generally also incline to the orthodox view and are mostly dismissive of any suggestion of an alternative author.

The reasons underpinning the Stratfordian position are complex, bound up with national pride and patriotism. Admiration for Shakespeare was widespread in late Victorian times. It was a confident age, always ready to praise the self-made man who prospered by his own ability. Opinion formers and educationists identified strongly with the affluent burgher from Stratford-upon-Avon and staunchly defended his right to be hailed as a literary genius.

This belief is enshrined in the Droeshout portrait from the First Folio, an iconic depiction so deeply embedded in the national subconscious that it is virtually impossible to dissociate it from any discussion of the plays. This curious picture shows a large mask-like face out of proportion to the body, which is much smaller. In an age when the Sumptuary Laws regulating appropriate dress were still enforced it is apparent that the man in the picture wears a richly embroidered doublet, a way of dressing that would only have been allowable for a person of the highest social status. The cut of the sleeves indicate that the sitter has his back to

*Droeshout portrait from
the First Folio*

the artist, and the ear partially shown on the left side of his face looks more like the back of his right ear. The strangely lifeless face mask appears to be attached to the rear of the sitter's head. Martin Droeshout's First Folio engraving remains an unsolved puzzle.

Nothing can be stated with certainty about Shakspere's business trips to London, his age at first arrival being unknown. This has relevance when matching the appearance of the plays in the 1580s to his date of birth in 1564. This does not allow much time for a young man from a small country town to establish himself in a large capital city, find employment in the theatre, learn his craft and then launch his career as a poet and dramatist. Even allowing for exceptional talent it is hard to believe that a young countryman with no known education could achieve so much so quickly while simultaneously fathering children and maintaining a family and a business in rural Warwickshire. Nevertheless many eminent scholars have subscribed to this version of events.

The first use of the famous name came in 1593 with the publication of a narrative poem, *Venus and Adonis*. This was followed in 1594 by a second long poem, *Lucrece*, later reissued as *The Rape of Lucrece*. Both poems carried the name William Shakespeare in their dedications. In 1598 a book was published listing six comedies and six other plays as the work of 'Shakespeare', omitting 'William'. This book was written by Francis Meres, a thirty-three year old clergyman who left London soon afterwards for a rectory in Rutland. It was published as *Palladis Tamia*, roughly translated from the Greek as *Wit's Treasury*, which was used as the book's subtitle. It was a cultural review by an amateur enthusiast, a 'comparative discourse', aligning contemporary writers with their classical counterparts.

Meres published examples rather than complete lists for the poets, playwrights and painters featured in his book, grouped in that order. Some seventy contemporary writers are featured, mostly with full names and titles, 'my friend Master Richard Barnfelde' (a poet), as an example. Shakespeare receives nine mentions, all minus 'William', with no indication that the author knew anything about him other than his surname. At the time of publication in 1598 the Stratford man would have been thirty-four so it was certainly possible for him to have been the author of the twelve plays listed in the review. The possibility also exists that he was the author of other plays not listed. One of the comedies ascribed to him was *Love's Labour's Won*, a play of which there is no trace.

Supporters of the orthodox authorship position (Stratfordians) cite the case of Christopher Marlowe who was a close contemporary, being just two months older than Shakspere. Marlowe became an established playwright in his twenties, producing five highly regarded plays before his untimely death at the age of twenty-nine. (*Tamburlaine, The Jew of Malta, Dr Faustus, Edward II* and his first work *Dido, Queen of Carthage*). If Marlowe could write great plays as a young man, why not Shakspere? The difference lay in Marlowe's formal education which provided him with the literacy required of an author. He was educated at The King's School in Canterbury and received a Bachelor of Arts degree from Corpus Christi College, Cambridge in 1584.

Shakspere from Stratford-upon-Avon had no such qualifications. Apart from the registration details of his own baptism, his marriage, and the birth of his children, nothing at all is known about him until he was almost thirty, and not much even then. This position has never changed and all subsequent attempts at biography from that time to this have been mostly conjectural or invented. In the many books written about 'The Bard' his early adult years are commonly described as the 'lost years'. They were a vacuum waiting to be filled and filled they have been, many times over in film and fiction, with little risk of challenge or contradiction.

The first authorship doubters were even more puzzled by the awkward break at the other end of Shakspere's supposed literary career. Fifteen quarto editions of Shakespeare plays were printed between 1594 and 1604 but then came to a stop, only two more appearing in print before Shakspere's death in 1616 (*King Lear* in 1608 and *Troilus and Cressida* in 1609). No new play can be found to date definitively after 1604. This meant there was a second and even longer vacuum of empty years to be filled, obliging Stratfordians to fall back on the excuse of early retirement, and it is this which has always failed to convince. Why a successful dramatist in his early forties, presumably with his mental faculties intact, should choose to leave cosmopolitan London and spend the rest of his life in obscurity in a remote small Warwickshire town is never satisfactorily explained. Artists in all mediums commonly exhibit a compulsive creativity, even more so at this highest level of achievement. Rarely do they give up in middle age and try something else.

Nor was Shakspere's conduct in the latter part of his life consonant with that of a refined man of letters. Public Record Office documents show that he was a tax defaulter in Bishopsgate Ward in London on four occasions between 1597 and 1600 and could not be traced by the authorities. (Samuel Schoenbaum, *William Shakespeare: A Documentary Life*, pp. 161–63). As well as being a tax delinquent in London he was listed in Stratford on 4th February 1598 as illegally holding ten quarters of malt at a time of shortage. (E. K. Chambers, *William Shakespeare: A Study of Facts and Problems*, Vol II, pp. 99–101). In 1602 he purchased 107 acres of land in Stratford and a cottage in Chapel Lane. In 1604 he was listed in the Stratford records as having substantial holdings of malt and in 1605 he made sufficient investment in tithes to qualify for burial inside Holy Trinity Church. He acquired more land in 1611 and in 1614 became embroiled in a dispute over proposed enclosures of common land in the neighbouring parish of Welcombe.

Throughout this retirement period he was an aggressive litigant, suing over property rights, pursuing defaulting tenants, and to recover small sums of money owed to him, but in Stratford he staged no plays and committed nothing to writing. In his detailed will he made no mention of owning a single printed book, no mention of unpublished manuscripts in his possession, nor any of the artefacts associated with writing such as pens, ink and paper.

No one in Stratford seemed aware that one of their residents had become a famous writer, or if they did never thought it worth mentioning. Local Warwickshire worthies included the poet Michael Drayton, the historian William Camden, the poet and dramatist Fulke Greville and Shakspere's son-in-law Dr John Hall, a physician. None of them apparently knew or even suspected that Shakspere had been engaged in any form of artistic or intellectual activity during his business trips to London. His death and funeral in April 1616 passed without a single recorded mention, either in his home town or in London.

Neither of Shakspere's parents, John and Mary, nor his two surviving married daughters Susanna Hall and Judith Quiney, could read or write. Samuel Schoenbaum, in *Shakespeare: A Documentary Life*, publishes facsimiles of the marks made by John and Mary Shakspere on several legal documents. John signed with a cross and also the outline of compasses, a symbol of his trade as a glover. On p. 238 Shoenbaum doubts whether Susanna Hall could do more than sign her name, being unable to recognise her husband's handwriting when called on to do so. On p. 241 Schoenbaum quotes from the Shakespeare Birthplace Trust Records Office MS. ER 27/11 showing that Judith Quiney signed twice with a mark when witnessing a deed of sale on 4th December 1611.

Shakspere's own six barely legible signatures surviving on legal documents suggest that he was scarcely more than semi-literate himself.

1.

    Willm Shakp
    Bellott–Mountjoy deposition 12th June 1612

2.

    William Shaksper
    Blackfriars Gatehouse conveyance 10th March 1613

3.

    Wm Shakspe
    Blackfriars mortgage 11th March 1613

4.

    William Shaksper
    Page 1 of will 25th March 1616

5.

Willm Shakspere
Page 2 of will 25th March 1616

6.

Shakspeare (preceded by 'Mr William' in a different hand)
Last page of will 25th March 1616

In 1634 a funerary monument in Holy Trinity Church, Stratford-upon-Avon, was sketched by the historian William Dugdale (1605–1686). This showed an elderly man with drooping moustaches clasping a woolsack and may have referred to John Shakspere, William's father. He was a wool merchant and civic dignitary, a former High Bailiff of Stratford who died in 1601. Dugdale made hundreds of similar sketches in other churches and comparing these with monuments which have survived proves that he was an accurate draughtsman, careful over details of heraldry and costume. The engraving below by Wenceslaus Hollar appeared in William Dugdale's book *The Antiquities of Warwickshire* published in 1656.

Funerary monument in Holy Trinity Church, Stratford-upon-Avon

A six-volume collected edition of Shakespeare plays appeared in 1709. The actor Thomas Betterton having seen the original monument in Stratford was able to confirm to the publisher Nicholas Rowe in London that the Dugdale drawing was accurate. A hand-drawn copy of the Dugdale book illustration was made for the Shakespeare new edition. In 1730 a second edition of Dugdale's *The Antiquities of Warwickshire* was published, with revision by Dr William Thomas (1670–1738). Although the text contained additions and alterations from the first edition no change was made to the depiction of the Stratford woolsack monument. The transition from woolsack to cushion, and the appearance of a middle-aged man wielding a quill pen, must therefore have been made at some time after 1730.

No person in history can have been the subject of such exhaustive research as the author known as William Shakespeare. For diligence and accuracy nothing so far published exceeds the Clarendon Press folio edition of Samuel Schoenbaum's *Shakespeare: A Documentary Life* published in 1975. Dr Robert Bearman the former head of archives at the Shakespeare Institute is the author of *Shakespeare in the Stratford Records* (1994). Between these two books and the Public Records Office all that is ever likely to be known about William Shakspere of Stratford-upon-Avon has long since been published. Yet after all this research nothing links him to the plays, and paradoxically serves to disqualify rather than confirm him as the author.

In fairness to the Stratford man it must be pointed out that he never claimed to have written the plays, nor after his death did any members of his family make such a claim on his behalf, or try to obtain commercial benefit from them. Shakspere seems to have been an astute businessman, a resourceful and successful man of his times, but no evidence has ever been produced to show that he pursued any of the scholarly activities and interests normally associated with high achievement in art, music or literature.

Investing in theatre property hardly proved that Shakspere was an actor, still less a writer. Identifying him as the great poet and playwright William Shakespeare rests mainly on posthumous evidence. Praises conferred on the author many years after his death are vague and ambiguous, they express admiration for the works but never specifically refer to his actual identity, nor is there any indication that the writers knew him personally.

With this meagre amount of information available as source material it is truly astonishing that so many thousands of pages of detailed literary biography have been written lauding the life and memory of the enterprising businessman from Stratford-upon-Avon.

Appendix B

Dramatis Personae

Alençon

François de Valois, Duke of Anjou and Alençon (1555–1584) was the youngest son of Henri II of France and Catherine de Medici. He became heir to the French throne in 1574 and in 1579 came to London as a suitor to marry Queen Elizabeth. Deformed and eccentric, and twenty-two years younger than the Queen, the suit failed but on friendly terms. The Duke died prematurely at the age of twenty-nine and was replaced as heir by Henry of Navarre, a Huguenot.

Ariosto

Ludovico Ariosto (1474–1533) Italian poet and dramatist. His epic romance *Orlando Furioso* is a possible source for *The Tempest*, and his play *Suppositi* for *The Taming of the Shrew*.

Arundel

Charles Arundel (1539–1587) was a nephew of the executed Catherine Howard, fifth wife of Henry VIII. Together with Henry Howard and Francis Southwell they were denounced as Catholic conspirators by Edward de Vere. In revenge Charles Arundel pursued a bitter vendetta against the earl, alleging a wide range of offences which would have incurred imprisonment if proved true.

Ascham

Roger Ascham (1515–1568), scholar and writer, was Queen Elizabeth's Greek and Latin tutor 1548–50. A fellow of St John's College, Cambridge he is associated with his mentor Sir John Cheke, and colleagues Sir Thomas Smith and Sir William Cecil, in promoting vernacular English as an expressive literary language. He collaborated with them on the reform of spelling and pronunciation of English.

Bacon

Francis Bacon (1561–1626), later viscount St Alban, was a Renaissance polymath and career courtier who rose to be Lord Chancellor in 1618. His uncle by marriage was Sir William Cecil, de Vere's wife Anne Cecil was his cousin. (Bacon's mother Anne Cooke was the sister of Mildred Cooke, Cecil's wife). In a letter to his brother-in-law Robert Cecil dated 7th October 1601 Edward de Vere refers to 'my cousin Bacon'.

Baker

George Baker (1540–1612) was a physician attached to the court of both Queen Elizabeth and King James. As a practitioner of the new Paracelsian approach to medicine he was the doctor attending on Edward de Vere and his family. He translated many books on botany and medicine, among them *The Practice of the New and Olde Physicke* dedicated to de Vere and *The Newe Jewell of Health* dedicated to his wife Anne.

Bandello

Matteo Bandello (1480–1562) was an Italian writer whose collection of tales published in 1554 as *Novelle*, provided plot material for *Romeo and Juliet* and *Twelfth Night*. No English translations existed at the time so the author either read the original in Italian or in the French translation by François de Belleforest.

Barnes

Robert Barnes (1495–1540) was a Cambridge educated historian and divine who became a Lutheran. He was burned at the stake by Henry VIII for complicity with Thomas Cromwell in procuring Anne of Cleves to be his fourth wife, and for denying royal supremacy in church matters.

Beaumont

Francis Beaumont (1584–1616) was a poet and dramatist mostly remembered for his collaboration with the more successful John Fletcher.

Bedingfield,

Thomas (1545–1613) was commissioned by Edward de Vere to translate the book *Cardanus Comforte* into English.

Belleforest

François de Belleforest (1530–1583) was a French writer and translator. His seven volumes of collected and edited stories from various sources, *Les Histoires Tragiques*, were issued from 1564 until 1582. Volume V contains the story of Amleth, retold by Shakespeare as Hamlet.

Bertie

Peregrine Bertie (1555–1601), later the 13th Baron Willoughby d'Eresby, was married to de Vere's sister Mary. A soldier and diplomat he was ambassador to the Danish royal court at the castle of Elsinore 1582–85. In 1582 he invested King Frederick II of Denmark with the Order of the Garter, a gift from Queen Elizabeth.

Blount

Edward Blount (1565–1632) was a London stationer and publisher, associated with the publication of the First Folio in 1623. Among his other publications were the six Court Comedies of John Lyly. Orthodox scholarship allows that Lyly's employer and patron Edward de Vere earl of Oxford may have collaborated in writing these plays of which *Endymion* is the best known.

Boccaccio

Giovanni Boccaccio (1313–1375) was an Italian writer and poet. As the author of the *Decameron* he achieved fame in his lifetime and exerted influence over subsequent writers who used his book as source material, Chaucer and Shakespeare among them. The *Decameron* is a collection of stories about human love. Some are tragic but mostly they are erotic and salacious.

Byrd

William Byrd (1543–1623) was the most prolific and highly regarded

Elizabethan composer, across a range of musical forms, all of which he extended and developed, notably keyboard music. This included *The Earl of Oxford's March*, for the virginals. Queen Elizabeth and the earl of Oxford were Byrd's two principal patrons. Although a Catholic his sacred pieces for Anglican settings are still considered as Renaissance masterworks.

Cecil, Anne

Anne Cecil (1556–1588) was the daughter of Sir William Cecil and his wife Mildred, the sister of Robert Cecil and the half-sister of Thomas Cecil. She married Edward de Vere in 1571 and became the Countess of Oxford. It was an unhappy marriage and the couple were separated from April 1576 until the last days of 1581. Francis Bacon was her first cousin by marriage.

Cecil, Mildred

Mildred Cecil (1526–1589) was the eldest of five daughters of Sir Anthony Cooke, a Protestant scholar who tutored King Edward VI. She was educated to a high standard, able in adult life to translate texts from the original Greek. She was the mother of Edward de Vere's first wife Anne Cecil. Mildred's sister Anne Cooke was the mother of Francis Bacon. Another sister Elizabeth Cooke was the wife of Sir Thomas Hoby the translator into English (from the Italian) of *The Courtier* which provided source material for *Hamlet*. Her epitaph in Westminster Abbey on the tomb shared with her daughter Anne, and written by her husband William Cecil, testifies to her great learning, in particular her translations from the Greek of the writings of Saint Basil the Great (330–379). The royal wards fostered out in Cecil House, Edward de Vere among them, came under her influence as an uncompromising Protestant intellectual.

Cecil, Robert

Robert Cecil (1563–1612), later the earl of Salisbury, was Sir William Cecil's second son and on his death in 1598 succeeded him as the highest placed politician in Queen Elizabeth's court, a position he consolidated under King James. As Edward de Vere's brother-in-law he rejected all his appeals for grants or favours.

Cecil, William

Sir William Cecil (1520–1598), first Baron Burghley from 1571, was the father of Edward de Vere's first wife Anne Cecil. He was a trusted adviser to Queen Elizabeth for most of her reign, twice Secretary of State (1550–1553 and 1558–1572) and Lord High Treasurer from 1572. Born in Stamford, Lincolnshire he went up to St John's College, Cambridge at the age of fourteen as a Greek scholar and stayed for six years, completing his education at Gray's Inn in London. In 1559 he was elected Chancellor of Cambridge University and from 1592 until his death was also Chancellor of Trinity College, Dublin. On his two establishments at Burghley House in Lincolnshire, and Theobalds in Essex, he lavished the best in art, architecture and horticulture that money could buy. His library at Cecil House in the Strand (later Burghley House) was the most extensive collection of books in London at the time. When dispersed in 1687 it was found to contain many of the books now known to have provided source material for Shakespeare's plays.

Cheke

Sir John Cheke (1514–1557), was an enthusiastic advocate of the English language. Among his students at St John's College, Cambridge were Roger Ascham, later a tutor in classics to Queen Elizabeth, and Sir William Cecil who became her principal private secretary. Together with his colleague Sir Thomas Smith he exerted a lasting influence on the refinement and standardisation of English as a scholarly and literary language worthy of comparison with Latin and Greek. Sir William Cecil's first wife was his sister, Mary Cheke.

Chettle

Henry Chettle (1564–1607) was listed by Francis Meres in his *Palladis Tamia* as one of the 'best for comedy'. He collaborated with other dramatists including Thomas Dekker and may have contributed to the play *Sir Thomas More* which some Stratfordian scholars believe to have been written in part by Shakespeare.

Churchyard

Thomas Churchyard (1523–1604), a soldier and literary man, was employed as a servant by Edward de Vere. As a boy he had been a page in the service of de Vere's aunt Frances de Vere, and her husband Lord Henry Howard.

Cinthio

Giraldi Cinthio (1504–1573) was an Italian prose writer whose collection of stories the *Hecatommithi* provided plot material for two Shakespeare plays, *Measure for Measure* and *Othello*. There was a French translation in 1584 but no English translation until 1753.

Clerke

Bartholomew Clerke (1537?–1590). His books included a translation into Latin of *The Book of the Courtier* from the Italian original *Il Cortegiano* of Baldassare Castiglione. It first appeared in early 1572 prefaced with commendatory Latin epistles by Edward de Vere earl of Oxford, Thomas Sackville Lord Buckhurst, and John Caius (co-founder of Gonville and Caius College, Cambridge). Thirteen years older than Edward de Vere he seems to have been one of his tutors at Cecil House, and held in high regard.

Coverdale

Miles Coverdale (*c* 1488–1569) produced the first complete printed translation of the Bible into English. To avoid persecution he spent many years in exile.

Cranmer

Thomas Cranmer (1489–1556) was prominent in the English Reformation and became Archbishop of Canterbury during the period of Protestant supremacy. He was tried for treason and heresy and executed when the Catholic religion was restored under Mary Tudor. *The Book of*

Common Prayer and the *Thirty-Nine Articles of Religion* were his lasting contribution to the Anglican Church.

Cromwell

Thomas Cromwell (1485–1540) enthusiastically prosecuted the break from Rome and the establishment of the Protestant religion. He sponsored Miles Coverdale and ensured his protection while translating the Bible into English. Cromwell incurred the displeasure of Henry VIII after recommending Anne of Cleves as a suitable bride and was executed on Tower Hill.

Daniel

Samuel Daniel (1562–1619) was an English poet and historian, the protégé of Mary Sidney. His long poem on the Wars of the Roses, *The First Fowre Bookes of the Civile Wars*, published in 1595, contained similar historic references to those used in Shakespeare's *Richard II.* Whether the two writers knew one another, or were aware of handling the same material at the same time, and whether one influenced the other, is not known.

Dekker

Thomas Dekker (1572–1632) was listed by Francis Meres as a notable dramatist and for most of his career was associated with Philip Henslowe and the Admiral's Men company of actors. Among his many collaborative works is a suspected involvement with *Sir Thomas More*, a play with dubious Shakespeare connections.

Devereux

Robert Devereux (1565–1601), later the earl of Essex, led an unsuccessful coup d'état and was executed. Edward de Vere was on the jury of peers which condemned him to death.

Dowland

John Dowland (1563–1626) was an English Renaissance composer, singer, and lutenist. He is best known today for the melancholy nature of his many songs. He is mentioned by name in Poem VIII of *The Passionate Pilgrim.*

Drake

Sir Francis Drake (1540–1596) was second in command to Charles Howard (Lord Howard of Effingham) , in repelling the Spanish Armada. Edward de Vere's armoured sloop *Edward Bonaventure* was in the flotilla commanded by Drake.

Drayton

Michael Drayton (1563–1631) was a prolific writer of poetry, and a versifier of history. Of his twenty-three plays only a co-authored *Sir John Oldcastle* survives, having been subsumed into *I Henry IV*. Drayton was featured more prominently than Shakespeare by Meres in his *Palladis Tamia* and was a major literary figure in Elizabethan & Jacobean England.

Dudley

Robert Dudley (1532–1588), later the earl of Leicester, had a long personal attachment to Queen Elizabeth. Some of Edward de Vere's estates were held in trust by Dudley and never fully restored, a source of friction between them. Dudley's military campaigns against the Spanish on the mainland of Europe ended in failure but he was in overall command against the Armada which ended more successfully.

Dyer

Sir Edward Dyer (1543–1607) was a courtier poet whose best known poem 'My mind to me a kingdom is' has also been attributed to Edward de Vere the earl of Oxford. The writer Alden Brooks proposed Dyer as the author of Shakespeare in a book with the title '*Will Shakespeare and the Dyer's Hand*', published in 1943. One of many outside candidates for the authorship.

Edwards

Richard Edwards (1525–1566) edited the poetry anthology *The Paradise of Dainty Devices* which contained Edward de Vere's earliest verse.

Farmer

John Farmer (*c*1564–*c*1601) was an organist and composer of the English Madrigal School. He was active in Dublin before moving to London where he came under the patronage of the earl of Oxford. A collection of four part madrigals published in 1599 was dedicated to the earl.

Fénélon

Bertrand de Salignac Fénélon, seigneur de la Mothe (1523–1589) was the French ambassador to England from 1568–1575. His various writings contain anecdotes of life at the Elizabethan court, most notably *Memoires touchant l'Angleterre*.

Fiorentino

Ser Giovanni known as The Florentine was an anonymous Italian author who compiled an anthology of fifty stories known as *Il Pecorone* (The Dunce). This was written *c*1378 but not published until 1558, in Italian. The first English translation was made in 1632. *Il Pecorone* contains the story of the bond for human flesh which provided the pivotal plotline for *The Merchant of Venice*. Another story in the collection contains a possible link to the tricking of Falstaff in *The Merry Wives of Windsor*.

Fleming

Abraham Fleming (1552–1607) was a prolific journeyman writer and translator who was a member of Edward de Vere's literary circle. An ordained priest he acted as chaplain to Charles Howard the Lord High Admiral and also preached at St Paul's Cross.

Fletcher

John Fletcher (1579–1625) was a popular and successful dramatist who bridged the gap between Elizabethan and early Restoration drama. For many years attached to the King's Men company of actors, his collaboration with Shakespeare is assumed for *Henry VIII* and *The Two Noble Kinsmen*, also for *Cardenio*, a play now lost.

Fowle

Thomas Fowle (*c*1530–*c*1597) was a Church of England clergyman and a Fellow of St John's College, Cambridge. He received payment as one of Edward de Vere's tutors.

Frederick

Frederick II, King of Denmark (1534–1588). In 1582, at Elsinore Castle, Edward de Vere's brother-in-law Lord Willoughby d'Eresby invested the king with the insignia of the Order of the Garter. The knighthood was a gift from Queen Elizabeth; the king had been one of her unsuccessful suitors.

Frobisher

Sir Martin Frobisher (1535–1594) was a mariner and explorer. He was knighted for his services in helping to repulse the Spanish Armada in 1588. De Vere lost heavily by investing in his earlier unsuccessful attempts to navigate a north-west passage to Asia. ('I am but mad north-north-west.' *Hamlet* (2.2. 378).

Gascoigne

George Gascoigne (1535–1577), a distant relative of de Vere's by marriage, had plays performed at Gray's Inn. He edited an anthology *A Hundred Sundry Flowers* to which de Vere contributed.

Golding, Arthur

Arthur Golding (1536–1606), was the younger half-brother of Margery Golding, Edward de Vere's mother. A Cambridge graduate and classical scholar he was employed by Sir William Cecil at Cecil House in the Strand, London. De Vere joined the household as Sir William's ward in 1562. Golding's translation of Ovid's *Metamorphoses* was published in 1567 and dedicated to the earl of Leicester. Another translation from the Latin was dedicated to his nephew, Edward de Vere. Although no Shakespeare plots originated from *Metamorphoses*, literary allusions drawn from it occur in many of the plays.

Golding, Margery

Margery Golding (1528–1568) was the wife of John de Vere the 16th earl of Oxford and mother of Edward de Vere. When Queen Mary Tudor died it was John de Vere who escorted Princess Elizabeth from house arrest at Hatfield to London. Margery became a maid of honour to the new young queen and spent the year 1559 at court.

Grafton

Richard Grafton (1513–1572) was a printer and historian forced to flee when reprinting Coverdale's Bible in Paris. He was imprisoned but later released, returned to England and continued printing religious texts, including the first Book of Common Prayer.

Greene

Robert Greene (1558–1592) was one of a group of poets and playwrights loosely known as the University Wits. He was a member of de Vere's literary salon which met at his house, Fisher's Folly.

Greville

Sir Fulke Greville (1554–1628), later first Baron Brooke, was a diligent government administrator who rose to become treasurer of the navy and chancellor of the exchequer. Best known today for his biography of his friend Sir Philip Sidney he also wrote some poetry. In 1609 he purchased King's Place in Hackney from the countess of Oxford who had lived there with her son Henry, the 18th earl of Oxford. When he received his barony in 1621 he renamed the property as Brooke House. It remained in his family for the next two hundred years but suffered bomb damage in the 1939–45 war and was demolished in 1946.

Harvey

Gabriel Harvey (*c*1545–1630) was an English writer and a notable scholar. In 1579 he was angry with Edmund Spenser for publishing some satirical verses he had written but without obtaining his authority to do so. These satirical verses with the title *Mirror of Tuscanism* were contemptuous of some prominent people, including Edward de Vere, earl of Oxford, dismissed by Harvey as an Italianate fop.

Hatton

Sir Christopher Hatton (1540–1591) was a career courtier who rose steadily and became Lord Chancellor in 1587. A successful rival to de Vere for the Queen's approval, he wrote verse under the pseudonym *Felix Infortunatus*.

Henslowe

Philip Henslowe (1550–1616) was a theatrical producer whose records are a valuable source of information on Elizabethan dramatic literature. He made payments to twenty-seven contemporary playwrights but the list does not include William Shakespeare. He kept a diary which has been much studied for information on the theatrical world of Renaissance London. This mentions by name plays now known to have been written by Shakespeare but the diary contains no mention of Shakespeare as a person or a writer.

Herbert, Philip

Philip Herbert (1584–1650), earl of Montgomery, was married to Edward de Vere's youngest daughter Susan. On the death of his elder brother William in 1630 he inherited as the 4th earl of Pembroke. He and his brother were joint dedicatees of the Shakespeare First Folio.

Herbert, William

William Herbert (1580–1630), 3rd earl of Pembroke, was the complete grandee – Lord Steward, Lord Chamberlain of the Royal Household, a Garter Knight and Chancellor of the University of Oxford. Broadgates Hall at Oxford was renamed Pembroke College in his honour.

Heywood

Thomas Heywood (*c*1570–1641) claimed to have written over two hundred plays although very few made it into print. Only twenty-three have survived, the most famous being *A Woman Killed with Kindness*.

Hoby

Sir Thomas Hoby (1530–1566), a diplomat and scholar, was married to Lord Burghley's sister-in-law, Elizabeth Cooke. In 1561 he translated *Il Cortegiano* from Italian into English. This book was much admired by Edward de Vere, he commissioned a translation into Latin and contributed a preface, also in Latin. As an exemplar for courtly behaviour *The Courtier* is seen to have an influence on the dialogue in Hamlet, cited by Bullough, among others.

Holinshed

Raphael Holinshed (1529–1580) was the compiler and editor of the book which has come to bear his name, *Holinshed's Chronicles*, first published in 1577 as *The Chronicles of Englande, Scotlande, and Irelande*. It drew together many previous accounts of British history written by a variety of authors. A revised and expanded second edition in three volumes followed in 1587 and is widely credited as providing source material for the Shakespeare history plays. Holinshed's life is not well documented but he was known at some stage to have been a member of Sir William Cecil's household where Edward de Vere was a ward. In 1567 Holinshed was on the jury which acquitted de Vere of the manslaughter of one of Sir William Cecil's servants, a cook named Thomas Brincknell. In 1573 he defended de Vere, who was suspected of a murder on Shooters Hill in London, by issuing a pamphlet which laid the blame elsewhere. As residents of Cecil House both Holinshed and de Vere would have had equal access to the contents of the extensive library, in which case the possibility exists that the History plays may have been drawn, in part at least, from primary source documents rather than lifted from the *Chronicles*.

Howard, Charles

Charles Howard (1536–1624), second Baron Howard of Effingham, was created earl of Nottingham in 1596. As Lord High Admiral he was in command of the fleet which repulsed the Spanish Armada in 1588. Subsequently he became a patron of the theatre with his own troupe of actors, the Admiral's Men. They gave the first performances of Shakespeare's play *Richard III*.

Howard, Henry (Surrey)

Henry Howard (1517–1547), earl of Surrey, was married to Edward de Vere's aunt, Frances Vere. His cousin Anne Boleyn was Henry VIII's second wife and his sister Catherine Howard was Henry VIII's fifth wife. Both were beheaded. Better known as the poet Surrey he achieved lasting fame with his friend Sir Thomas Wyatt for their translations of Petrarch's sonnets. Wyatt and Surrey popularised the sonnet form which became known first as the English sonnet and then as the Shakespearean sonnet. Surrey is credited with establishing the rhyming metre and the division into quatrains. He suffered death at the block when Henry VIII accused him of plotting to prevent his son Edward from inheriting the throne. His own eldest son Thomas was also the victim of royal displeasure, executed for an alleged conspiracy against Queen Elizabeth.

Howard, Henry

Henry Howard (1540–1614), later the earl of Northampton, collaborated with Charles Arundel in laying malicious charges against Edward de Vere, apparently in revenge for being exposed by him as a Catholic conspirator.

Howard, Philip

Philip Howard (1557–1595), later the earl of Arundel, was the eldest son of the executed duke of Norfolk. Edward de Vere was on the jury which condemned him to death for his support of Spanish invasion plans. He died in prison and was later sanctified as a Catholic martyr.

Howard, Thomas

Thomas Howard, fourth duke of Norfolk (1536–1572) was Edward de Vere's first cousin, the son of his aunt Frances de Vere. He was suspected of planning a marriage to Mary Stuart, Queen of Scots. This posed a threat to the throne and led to his execution.

Jaggard

William Jaggard (1568–1623) was a printer and publisher connected with the texts of Shakespeare, including the First Folio. Jaggard died shortly before it was issued in 1623 and the bulk of the work was overseen by his son Isaac Jaggard.

Jonson

Ben Jonson (1572–1637) satirist & poet, was a friend of Henry de Vere the 18th earl of Oxford. He contributed prefatory verses to the First Folio.

Knyvet

Thomas James Knyvet (1558–1622) was born in Wiltshire the son of Sir Henry Knyvet. He attended Jesus College, Cambridge and entered the court as a Gentleman of the Privy Chamber, later promoted to Master at Arms. His niece Anne Vavasour was Edward de Vere's mistress and the mother of his child. This provoked street brawls between the Oxford and Knyvet factions. In 1605 Thomas Knyvet was credited with foiling the Gunpowder Plot and arresting Guy Fawkes. Knighted and made a Privy Councillor he was appointed Warden of the Mint. In 1607 he was ennobled as Baron Knyvet of Escrick in Yorkshire. His home in London, known as Knyvet House, was later renumbered as 10 Downing Street.

Kyd

Thomas Kyd (1558–1594) had success with his play *The Spanish Tragedy* but is now mostly studied by scholars attempting to unravel his connection with Shakespeare. Among his many plays, translations and collaborations are *King Leir* and a possible early version of *Hamlet*.

Lee

Sir Henry Lee (1533–1611) was Queen's Champion and Master of the Armoury. He devised the Accession Day tilts held annually on 17th November, the most important Elizabethan court festival from the 1580s. From 1590 after the death of his wife he lived with Anne Vavasour, the former mistress of Edward de Vere.

Lock

Michael Lock (also Lok and Locke) (1532–1620) was a well-travelled merchant appointed governor of the Cathay Company in 1577. He joined forces with the mariner Martin Frobisher to navigate a north-west passage to China via the arctic but these expeditions ended in failure. Edward de Vere invested and lost three thousand pounds in the third of these expeditions in 1578.

Lodge

Thomas Lodge (1558–1625), one of a group of poets and dramatists known as the University Wits. They formed part of de Vere's literary salon at his house known as Fisher's Folly in Bishopsgate.

Lyly

John Lyly (1553–1606) was Edward de Vere's secretary for most of the 1580s. He attended Magdalen College, Oxford, obtaining a bachelor's degree at twenty and a master's degree at twenty-two. A native of Kent he sought his living in London, applying to Lord Burghley for employment in the government service. He never progressed very far but was compensated by his success as an author. *Ephues, or the Anatomy of Wit* published in 1579, was followed by *Ephues and his England* in 1580, which was dedicated to his employer and patron Edward de Vere the 17th earl of Oxford. Lyly wrote several plays which were performed at the Blackfriars Theatre where he was briefly the stage manager when the lease was held by de Vere.

Manners, Edward

Edward Manners (1549–1587), 3rd earl of Rutland. Was tutored at Cecil House with de Vere and they remained friends.

Manners, Roger

Roger Manners (1576-1612), 5th earl of Rutland, was the nephew of Edward Manners. Married to Elizabeth Sidney the daughter of Sir Philip Sidney, his education, foreign travels and loss of favour with Queen Elizabeth mirror those of Edward de Vere. Roger Manners has received some support as a candidate for the Shakespeare authorship, most persuasively as the true author of the Sonnets.

Mauvissière

Michel de Castelnau, sieur de la Mauvissière, (1520–92) French diplomat and soldier, noted for his *Mémoires* of the Wars of Religion. In the French king's service he made diplomatic missions to England, Germany, Savoy, and Rome. After the death of King Francis II he accompanied the widowed queen, Mary Stuart, back to Scotland. He was a shrewd commentator on life at Elizabeth's court.

Meres

Francis Meres (1565–1647) was a clergyman who secured a place in the history of English Literature with his 1598 book known as *Palladis Tamia*. This title roughly translates from the Greek as *Wits Treasury* and was used as a subtitle. The book takes the form of a cultural review, 'a comparative discourse', beginning with Poets and ending with Painters. In between comes Playwrights and this section includes twelve plays by William Shakespeare. This is the first time the name was used in association with plays. The first play actually published with the name on the title page was *Love's Labour's Lost* in 1598, 'by W. Shakespere'.

Montaigne

Michel de Montaigne (1533–1592) was a French writer who established the essay as a literary form. Although an intellectual he was able to write in an entertaining style which resulted in his collected essays published in 1580 being widely read and admired. His wry judgements and questioning nature make his writing accessible to a modern readership. Scholars have identified Montaigne as a source for Shakespeare's cynical attitudes on love, life and the pursuit of happiness. De Vere would have been able to read the essays in the original French prior to the John Florio translation into English of 1603.

Munday

Anthony Munday (1560–1633), poet and dramatist, served as De Vere's private secretary during the 1580s.

Nashe

Thomas Nashe (1567–1601), one of a group of writers known as the University Wits. Dedicated a pamphlet to de Vere and was a member of his literary salon.

Nowell

Laurence Nowell (1515–1571) was an expert in Anglo-Saxon history and literature, which included *Beowulf*. He was also a map-maker and made cartographic surveys of England and Ireland. He was a protégé of Sir William Cecil and a resident at Cecil House in the Strand. When Edward de Vere arrived in 1562 as Sir William's ward Nowell was appointed as his tutor. A cousin, also named Laurence Nowell, was a cleric who became Dean of Litchfield.

Peele

George Peele (1556–1596), one of a group of poets and dramatists known as the University Wits. With John Lyly and others shared de Vere's activities during his lease of the Blackfriars play-house. He is a possible co-author for *Titus Andronicus*.

Ponsonby

William Ponsonby (1546–1604) was a London stationer who published the works of Edmund Spenser and Philip Sidney. His reputation is for literary discrimination and high quality work.

Puttenham

George Puttenham (1529–1591) is credited with the authorship of the anonymously printed *The Arte of English Poesie*. This is known to have circulated in manuscript form for many years before it was published in 1589. It is in three parts, *Of Poets and Poesie, Of Proportion* and *Of Ornament*. The author was a trenchant critic of many contemporary poets, although praising Wyatt and Surrey (Edward de Vere's uncle). Textual analysts identify the '*Arte*' as having a demonstrable influence on

Shakespeare with many parallel allusions in the plays.

Radcliffe

Thomas Radcliffe the third earl of Sussex (1525–1583) was de Vere's military commander when putting down the so-called Rising of the North in 1570. Appointed Lord Chamberlain in July 1572 he was active in theatrical production as the master of Lord Chamberlain's Men.

Raleigh

Sir Walter Raleigh (c1552–1618) was an English aristocrat, writer, poet, soldier, courtier, and explorer. He acted as Edward de Vere's second when the tennis court quarrel with Philip Sidney escalated into a duel but the Queen intervened to prevent the duel being fought.

Rogers

John Rogers (1500–1555) was a Bible editor and translator, responsible for producing the Matthew Bible which included earlier translations by William Tyndale and Miles Coverdale. Known as *Matthew's Version* and published in 1537 it provided the text on which all subsequent Bibles were based, including the *King James Version*. John Rogers hoped to avoid the fate of William Tyndale by publishing under a pseudonym but still died at the stake on 4th February 1555, at Smithfield. There he was 'tested by fire' and became the first Protestant martyr under Queen Mary Tudor.

Sackville

Sir Thomas Sackville (1536–1608), later Baron Buckhurst and earl of Dorset was Queen Elizabeth's second cousin. A scholar, soldier, diplomat and courtier he became Chancellor of Oxford University in 1591 and Lord Treasurer in 1599. In 1561 he was the co-author with Thomas Norton of *Gorboduc*, a drama about the consequences of political rivalry. It was written in blank verse, the first play in English to do so. He also contributed to the 1563 edition of *A Mirrour for Magistrates*. He is believed to have been a collaborator with Edward de Vere in writing sonnets although there is no direct evidence.

Saxo

Saxo Grammaticus (1150–1220) was a Danish historian. The earliest known reference to the story of a son avenging his murdered father appears in his history of Denmark which was compiled from 1185 onwards. This story is the transcription of an oral tale, and the son seeking revenge was named Amleth, anglicised as Hamlet.

Seymour

Thomas Seymour (1508–1549), first Baron Sudely, was the brother of Jane Seymour and thus the uncle of the young King Edward VI. Seymour was a Garter Knight and Lord High Admiral but was jealous of his elder brother the Duke of Somerset who had been appointed as Lord Protector and was the de facto ruler of the country. Seymour attempted to usurp his brother but was executed for treason. One of the accusations levelled against him at his trial was misconduct with the teenage Princess Elizabeth. He had married the king's widow, the former Catherine Parr, her guardian, and so had access to the princess. That he fathered a child by her, the so-called Prince Tudor, has never been substantiated.

Sidney, Mary

Mary Sidney (1561–1621), the sister of Sir Philip Sidney, was the first English woman to achieve a significant literary reputation. Granddaughter of the duke of Northumberland she was also the niece of Robert Dudley the earl of Leicester who arranged her marriage at the age of fifteen to the wealthy William Herbert, earl of Pembroke. Her eldest son, also William Herbert, and her youngest son Philip (married to Edward de Vere's daughter Susan), were the 'Incomparable Pair of Brethren', immortalised in the First Folio dedication.

Sidney, Philip

Sir Philip Sidney (1554–1586) was a poet, courtier and soldier. He was the eldest son of Sir Henry Sidney, grandson of the duke of Northumberland, and nephew of Robert Dudley, earl of Leicester. His younger sister, Mary Sidney, countess of Pembroke, was a writer, translator and literary patron. Sidney dedicated his longest prose work, the Arcadia, to her, and it is now known as *The Countess of Pembroke's Arcadia*. The Gloucester subplot in *King Lear* was borrowed from the *Arcadia*.

Smith

Sir Thomas Smith (1513–1577), of Theydon Mount in Essex, was a highly educated and widely travelled courtier. Edward de Vere was brought up in his house from infancy until the age of twelve. Sir Thomas was a fellow of Queens' College, Cambridge but took his law degree at the University of Padua. On his return to Cambridge he was appointed Regius Professor of Civil Law in 1544 and vice chancellor of the university later the same year. He collaborated with Sir John Cheke in revising Greek grammar and pronunciation. As a committed Protestant he lost all his offices during the reign of Mary I but later became one of Queen Elizabeth's most trusted advisers, a secretary of state, ambassador to France and chancellor of the Order of the Garter. De Vere studied at Queens' College 1558–59 and received an MA degree from Cambridge in 1564.

Spenser

Edmund Spenser (1552–1599) was an English poet best known for *The Faerie Queene*, an epic poem celebrating the Tudor dynasty and Elizabeth I. This long allegory contains a dedicatory sonnet to 'the Earle of Oxenforde, Lord High Chamberlayne of England'.

Spinola

Benedict Spinola (1519–1580) was a Genoese merchant who lived his whole adult life in the City of London, at that time the principal seaport of England. An exporter of woollen cloths and an importer of wines he also served the English government as an agent and financier. He never married and died of the plague in London.

Stanley, Ferdinando

Ferdinando Stanley (1559–1594) became the 5th earl of Derby in 1593, a year before his death. Until then he had been known as Lord Strange and his company of actors were credited with popularising the plays of Christopher Marlowe. In 1579 he married the heiress Alice Spencer of Althorp with the possibility that *The Taming of the Shrew* was written to be performed at their wedding. Allusions in the play link the bride and groom to Petruchio and Katherine. There were three daughters of the marriage but no son and the earldom passed to his brother William Stanley, married to Edward de Vere's eldest daughter Elizabeth.

Stanley, William

William Stanley, 6th earl of Derby (1561–1642), was married to de Vere's eldest daughter Elizabeth. Evidence in support of his candidacy as the Shakespeare author rests on two letters in 1599 by the Jesuit spy George Fenner in which he reported that Derby is 'busy penning plays for the common players'. As he lived on for nineteen years after publication of the First Folio, and thirty-eight years after the death of Edward de Vere, but published no more plays in all that time, the case is not strong. More likely is his assistance in editing and revising manuscripts for inclusion in the First Folio.

Stuart

Mary Stuart, Queen of Scots (1542–1587). Protestant fear of a Catholic revival led to Mary Stuart's execution. Edward de Vere was one of the peers who recommended her death to Queen Elizabeth. Her claim of descent from King Henry VII was valid and her son inherited as King James I and VI on the death of Queen Elizabeth

Stubbs

Philip Stubbs (1555–1610) was educated at Cambridge and wrote several books of a devotional nature. He is mostly remembered for his savage polemic on contemporary morals, *The Anatomie of Abuses*.

Talbot

Gilbert Talbot (1553–1616), later 7th earl of Shrewsbury, was a member of parliament and a palace insider. His surviving correspondence contains personal observations of life at Queen Elizabeth's court, and of her courtiers, including Edward de Vere.

Thomas

William Thomas (died 1554) was a historian, linguist and translator. A Protestant, he was appointed clerk to the Privy Council under Edward VI but then incurred the displeasure of Mary Tudor by publicly opposing her marriage to Philip II of Spain. He was found guilty of treason and hanged at Tyburn. As a young man he travelled extensively in France and Italy. His *Historie of Italie* published in 1549 provided source material for *The Tempest*, including the names Prospero and Ferdinand.

Townshend

Sir Roger Townshend (1544–1590) was the Member of Parliament for Raynham in Essex. A wealthy owner of land and property he sold the

Manor of Bretts in West Ham (then in Essex) to Edward de Vere and later purchased de Vere's house in Wivenhoe. He acted as an agent for the Howard family and intervened to prevent Philip Howard becoming involved in fighting between the De Vere and Knyvet factions.

Trentham

Elizabeth Trentham (1559–1613) was born at Rocester Abbey, Staffordshire, the daughter of Thomas Trentham a wealthy landowner. A Maid of Honour to Queen Elizabeth she married Edward de Vere in December 1591 and became countess of Oxford.

Tudor, Edward

Edward Tudor (1537–1553) inherited the throne in 1547. He was the son of Henry VIII by his third wife Jane Seymour.

Tudor, Elizabeth

Elizabeth Tudor (1533–1603), Queen Elizabeth I from 1558. She was the daughter of Henry VIII by his second wife Anne Boleyn.

Tudor, Mary

Mary Tudor (1516–1558) inherited the throne in 1553. She was the daughter of Henry VIII by his first wife Catherine of Aragon.

Tyndale

William Tyndale (1494–1536) was one of the earliest translators of the Bible, drawing on original Greek and Hebrew sources rather than working from Latin translations. Although a committed Protestant he incurred the displeasure of Henry VIII as well as the Catholic Church and was pursued to Brussels, imprisoned and later strangled and burnt at the stake. The King James Bible of 1611 was substantially influenced by Tyndale's translation.

Tyrrell

Charles Tyrrell married Edward de Vere's mother Margery, the widowed countess of Oxford, following the 16th earl's death in 1562. Tyrell was a steward for the earl of Leicester's family and seems to have been on good terms with his stepson, leaving him a horse in his will. He died in 1570 which means that de Vere had lost his father at twelve and his mother and stepfather before he was twenty.

Vavasour

Anne Vavasour (c1560–c1621) had a place at court as one of Queen Elizabeth's Ladies of the Bedchamber. Her Yorkshire family were well connected, her maternal uncle being the courtier Sir Thomas Knyvet. Her half-sister Catherine was married to Thomas Howard, 1st earl of Suffolk. In her late teens Anne had an affair with Edward de Vere that lasted from 1579–1582 and resulted in the birth of a son, Edward Vere. Both parents and the child were sent to the Tower. De Vere was released after fourteen weeks although banished from court for a further two years. Anne later married a sea captain named John Finch but left him to live with Sir Henry Lee, Master of the Royal Armouries by whom she had another illegitimate son.

Vere, Aubrey

Aubrey de Vere (1626–1703) was the 20th and last earl of Oxford. His daughter Diana married the duke of St Albans.

Vere, Bridget

Lady Bridget Vere (1584–1620) was de Vere's second daughter. She married Francis Norris, earl of Berkshire (1579–1622).

Vere, Sir Edward

Sir Edward Vere (1581–1629), was Edward de Vere's natural son by Anne Vavasour.

Vere, Edward de, Seventeenth Earl of Oxford

Edward de Vere (1550–1604) was born as viscount Bolbec (anglicised as Bulbeck), inheriting the earldom in 1562 at the age of twelve. He was twice married, first to Anne Cecil with whom he had five children. Two of these, a daughter and an infant son died young. De Vere sold his ancestral home of Hedingham Castle to provide dowries for his three surviving daughters, Elizabeth, Bridget and Susan. (All three daughters married earls, and the earls were all Garter Knights). De Vere's second marriage to Elizabeth Trentham produced a son, Henry de Vere, who inherited the title as the 18th earl of Oxford.

Vere, Elizabeth

Lady Elizabeth Vere (1575–1627) was Edward de Vere's eldest daughter. She married William Stanley, earl of Derby. With the initials W.S., and active in literary pursuits, the earl has been considered as a candidate for the authorship. This is not supported by evidence. However there may have been some form of collaboration between Stanley and other members of the Vere family in revising and editing the Shakespeare plays for publication.

Vere, Frances

Frances de Vere (1516–1577), was a daughter of John de Vere the 15th earl of Oxford and aunt of Edward de Vere the 17th earl. She was married to the poet Henry Howard the earl of Surrey. He was beheaded by order of Henry VIII. Their eldest son Thomas Howard later the fourth duke of Norfolk was beheaded by order of Queen Elizabeth.

Vere, Francis

Sir Francis Vere (1560–1609), career soldier and diplomat. With his younger brother Horatio became known as 'the fighting Veres'.

Vere, Henry

Henry de Vere (1593–1624), the 18th earl of Oxford, was de Vere's son and heir by his second wife, Elizabeth Trentham.

Vere, Horatio

Sir Horatio Vere (1565–1635), was a career soldier and diplomat. With his brother Francis they were known as 'the fighting Veres', upholding the family tradition of service in the military.

Vere, Katherine

Lady Katherine Vere (1539–1600), was Edward de Vere's elder half-sister. She was the daughter of Dorothy Neville, from whom their father the 16th earl of Oxford was separated.

Vere, Mary

Lady Mary Vere (c1554–c1624), Edward de Vere's younger sister, was married to the soldier and diplomat Peregrine Bertie, later the 13th baron Willoughby d' Eresby.

Vere, Robert

Robert de Vere, the 19th earl of Oxford (1595–1632), inherited as a cousin. He was fatally wounded during the siege of Maastricht in 1632.

Vere, Susan

Lady Susan Vere (1587–1629), was Edward de Vere's youngest daughter. She married Philip Herbert (1584–1649) first earl of Montgomery. He later became the fourth earl of Pembroke on the death of his brother William Herbert (1580–1630) the third earl. The two brothers William Herbert and Philip Herbert were the Shakespeare First Folio dedicatees '... *the Most Noble and Incomparable Pair of Brethren'*.

Walsingham

Sir Francis Walsingham (1532–1590) was an efficient administrator and trusted senior minister in Queen Elizabeth's government. From 1573 until his death he was a principal secretary to the Queen, active in foreign affairs and zealous in ensuring that domestic and religious policy conformed to Protestant ideals.

Watson

Thomas Watson (1556–1592), a poet, was the compiler of *The Hekatompathia,*, a collection of sonnets dedicated to de Vere. The book was published in 1582 with the subtitle *Passionate Centurie of Love*. The poems were of high quality and the book contains knowledgeable literary criticism which has been attributed to de Vere, although this is not substantiated.

Webbe

Edward Webbe (c1554–c1620) was the son of Richard Webbe, the Master Gunner of England, and himself originally a gunner before going on extensive travels in the Mediterranean and the north African coast. His memoirs *The Travels of Edward Webbe* were issued in 1590. This included the description of a derelict Jerusalem. He describes the earl of Oxford issuing a martial arts challenge in the Palermo main square, Sicily. According to Webbe no one came forward to meet the earl's challenge.

Wilkins

George Wilkins (died 1618) was associated with the King's Men company of actors. He led a dissolute life and appeared with William Shakspere as witnesses in the case Bellott v. Mountjoy in 1612. As a dramatist he is assumed to be the co-author of *Pericles, Prince of Tyre*. This is attributed to William Shakespeare even though it did not appear in the First Folio of 1623.

Wriotheseley

Henry Wriothesley (1573–1624), the 3rd earl of Southampton, was a royal ward. Wriotheseley refused when coerced by his guardian Lord

Burghley to marry Burghley's granddaughter Elizabeth Vere, Edward de Vere's eldest daughter. He was heavily fined by Burghley for his disobedience. Later he was implicated in the short-lived rebellion of 1601, and with the earl of Essex was condemned to death. Essex was executed but Southampton was reprieved. Edward de Vere was one of the jurors who applied the death penalty. Rumours still persist of a homosexual infatuation by de Vere for the much younger Southampton, although there is no evidence. There seems a consensus of opinion among literary critics that Southampton was the so-called 'Fair Youth' of Shakespeare's sonnets, although again there is no evidence to support this assumption. There is another and slightly more believable theory which makes him the son of Edward de Vere. His mother Mary was separated from the second earl who in any case was imprisoned in the Tower during the period in which the boy would have been conceived, so was unlikely to be the biological father. If de Vere was Shakespeare, and wrote the sonnets dedicated to Southampton, the expressions of affection so hard to explain otherwise would make more sense if addressed by a loving father to his son.

York

Roland York (d 1588), was closely associated with de Vere in the 1570s. Although Yorke was of good family his nefarious reputation made him an unsuitable companion in the opinion of de Vere's relatives and friends. He was suspected of falsely convincing de Vere of his wife's Anne's infidelity, resulting in their estrangement.

Zouche

Edward la Zouche, 11th baron Zouche, 12th baron St Maur (1556–1625) was an English diplomat with links to the New World as a Commissioner of the Virginia Company. He was appointed Lord President of Wales in preference to Edward de Vere who had applied for the position. Lord Zouche had a house and garden in Hackney where de Vere lived in King's Place. His physic garden contained foreign plants and was overseen by the French botanist Matthias de L'Obel. Lord Burghley's horticultural adviser John Gerard obtained seeds from this garden. Knowledge of botany and familiarity with plant names is a feature of the Shakespeare plays.

Appendix C

The 20 De Vere Earls of Oxford, 1141-1703

Alberic de Ver (c1040–1112) was a knight in the service of Duke William who survived the battle of Hastings in 1066. He was generously rewarded by the new King William I with estates close to London in the south-east of the country.

Aubrey de Vere, (c1115–1194), grandson of the above, was confirmed as hereditary Master Chamberlain of England by King Henry I in 1133 and created 1st Earl of Oxford by Empress Matilda in 1141. Until the end of the 16th Century the incumbents were known as the Earls of Oxenford. Hedingham Castle in Essex became their primary seat and residence.

Aubrey de Vere, 2nd Earl of Oxford (c1164–1214). He was engaged in the military campaigns of King Richard I and King John. With no legal heir the earldom passed to his brother Robert.

Robert de Vere, 3rd Earl of Oxford (c1173–1221). He was a signatory at Runnymede and elected as one of the 25 barons charged with monitoring King John's adherence to the terms of the Magna Carta.

Hugh de Vere, 4th Earl of Oxford (c1208–1263). Inherited at the age of thirteen. Was involved in politics rather than the military.

Robert de Vere, 5th Earl of Oxford (1240–1296). He was on Simon de Montfort's losing side in the Second Barons' War, 1264–67. His title and lands were forfeited to King Edward I but soon afterwards restored.

Robert de Vere, 6th Earl of Oxford (1257–1331). The whole of his long life was spent in the military service of King Edward I, Edward II and Edward III, in Scotland and France. With no male heir the earldom passed to his nephew John de Vere.

John de Vere, 7th Earl of Oxford (1312–1360). He was engaged in military activities for most of his life. He fought alongside the Black Prince and was a battlefield commander at Crecy in 1346 and Poitiers in 1356.

Thomas de Vere, 8th Earl of Oxford (1337–1371). He was a soldier closely engaged in the military campaigns of King Edward III.

Robert de Vere, 9th Earl of Oxford (1362–1392) also held the title Duke of Ireland. He was a first cousin by marriage to King Richard II and shared his dynastic troubles. Deprived of his titles and lands in 1387 he fled abroad and died in exile.

Aubrey de Vere, 10th Earl of Oxford (1340–1400) was a career courtier, the third and surviving son of John de Vere the 7th earl of Oxford. The 9th Earl having died abroad with no heirs, King Richard II restored the earldom to Aubrey de Vere in 1393.

Richard de Vere, 11th Earl of Oxford (1385–1417). He was a battlefield commander at Agincourt in 1415, rewarded with a Garter Knighthood. He died at the age of thirty-one.

John de Vere, 12th Earl of Oxford (1408–1462). He pursued a career in politics and diplomacy but was beheaded as a Lancastrian supporter during a period of Yorkist supremacy in the civil wars. His son and heir Aubrey had met the same fate six days earlier.

John de Vere, 13th Earl of Oxford (1442–1513) inherited the title as a second son. As the victorious Lancastrian battlefield commander at Bosworth in 1485 he was generously rewarded by King Henry VII with honours and sinecures for the rest of his life. This patronage by a grateful monarch restored the Vere family fortunes, which had waned. Recorded performances of his play-acting company began in 1492 and he also maintained a chapel choir. He died without an heir and was succeeded by his nephew John, the 12th earl's grandson.

John de Vere, 14th Earl of Oxford (1499–1526). At the age of twenty he attended King Henry VIII at the three-week extravaganza held at Guines near Calais and known as 'The Field of the Cloth of Gold'. He died without an heir at the age of twenty-six and the earldom passed to his cousin John de Vere.

John de Vere, 15th Earl of Oxford (1482–1540). After becoming a staunch Protestant he received the trust of King Henry VIII until the end of his life. He was a senior courtier closely involved with affairs of state, including arranging the King's marriages. He continued to support the company of actors known as Lord Oxford's Men and commissioned the writer John Bale to produce and perform anti-Catholic propaganda. His third son Geoffrey Vere was the father of the two 'Fighting Veres' Sir Francis Vere and Sir Horatio Vere. His daughter Lady Frances Vere, aunt to Edward de Vere the 17th earl, married the Earl of Surrey. He developed the fourteen-line sonnet form of writing poetry, soon afterwards made famous by the writer known as William Shakespeare.

John de Vere, 16th Earl of Oxford (1516–1562) continued to maintain the family acting company known as Lord Oxford's Men. The daughter of his first marriage was Lady Katherine Vere. She contested (unsuccessfully) the legitimacy of his second marriage to Margery Golding, the mother of Edward de Vere the 17th earl. Margery Golding was also the mother of his second daughter Lady Mary Vere. She married Baron Willoughby d'Eresby, ambassador to the Danish royal court at Elsinore. As a Protestant active in regional politics the earl was vulnerable during the six-year reign of Mary Tudor, 1553–1558. He moved his infant son Edward into the safe care of his friend and neighbour, the Cambridge scholar Sir Thomas Smith.

Edward de Vere, 17th Earl of Oxford (1550–1604). Inherited his title at the age of twelve and was brought to London as a ward of court where he lived with the Cecil family. Sir William Cecil was appointed as his guardian until the age of twenty-one. He married William's daughter Anne Cecil the same year, with three surviving daughters of the marriage, Elizabeth, Bridget and Susan. After Anne Cecil's death in 1588 the earl married Elizabeth Trentham who gave birth to his heir, Henry de Vere the 18th earl of Oxford. Edward de Vere revived the family troupe of actors known as Lord Oxford's Men and also maintained a company of singers known as Lord Oxford's Boys. He has no known burial place or funerary monument.

Henry de Vere, 18th Earl of Oxford (1593–1625). He pursued a military career and died on active service after wounds received during the siege of Breda, a Dutch fortified city. With no descendants the earldom passed to his second cousin Robert de Vere.

Robert de Vere, 19th Earl of Oxford (1575–1632). He was the great-grandson of John de Vere the 15th earl and made his home in Holland, married a Dutch wife and served in the Dutch army. He was shot in the head and died during the siege of Maastricht. He has no known burial place.

Aubrey de Vere, 20th and last Earl of Oxford (1627–1703). Inherited his title at the age of six and for the rest of his life remained close to the court. He was a Royalist in the Civil War but supported William of Orange in replacing the Catholic James II. A flamboyant and elegant grandee he died at the age of seventy-six with no heir and thus brought the 562 year line of earls to an end. His daughter Diana married Charles Beauclerk, 1st Duke of St Albans.

Appendix D

Edward de Vere's immediate family

Father   John de Vere 16th earl of Oxford.
Mother   Margery Golding.
Sister   Mary Vere, married to Baron Willoughby d'Eresby.
Half-sister   Katherine Vere, married to Edward, Baron Windsor.
Uncle   Arthur Golding, translator of Ovid's *Metamorphoses*.
Wife   Anne Cecil, daughter of Baron Burghley.
Daughters   Elizabeth, Bridget and Susan.
(An infant daughter, Frances, and a newborn son both died).
Second wife   Elizabeth Trentham.
Son Henry   succeeded as 18th earl of Oxford.

Daughter marriages

Elizabeth married William Stanley the earl of Derby. He was active in literary pursuits and maintained a company of actors. He was on friendly terms with his father-in-law, Edward de Vere, and they visited with one another at their houses in London.

Bridget married Francis Norris the earl of Berkshire but had previously been contracted to William Herbert, earl of Pembroke and Lord Chamberlain.

Susan married William's brother Philip Herbert, the earl of Montgomery. These two brothers William and Philip Herbert were the Shakespeare First Folio dedicatees. Susan's mother-in-law was Mary Sidney the Countess of Pembroke. Mary's brother Philip Sidney who wrote the 'Arcadia' was a fellow scholar of Edward de Vere in residence at Cecil House in London, and a rival suitor for marriage to Anne Cecil.

In-laws

Father-in-law   Sir William Cecil, Baron Burghley.
Mother-in-law   Mildred Cecil, Lady Burghley.
Brother-in-law Sir Thomas Cecil, later earl of Exeter.
Brother-in-law Sir Robert Cecil, later earl of Salisbury.
Brother-in-law Peregrine Bertie, Baron Willoughby d'Eresby.
Brother-in-law Edward Windsor, 3rd Baron Windsor.
Brother-in-law Francis Trentham.
Son-in-law   William Stanley, 6th earl of Derby.
Son-in-law   Francis Norris, 1st earl of Berkshire.
Son-in-law   Philip Herbert, 1st earl of Montgomery.

Cousins

Thomas Howard, 4th duke of Norfolk
Francis Bacon, 1st Viscount St Alban
Edward Manners, 3rd earl of Rutland
Sir Francis Vere, military commander
Sir Horatio Vere, military commander

By the time of the 16th earl's death in 1562 the Vere family had inter-married with almost every other noble family in the land, so the roll-call of distant cousins and relatives could be many times extended.

Appendix E

Some crowned heads in context

British kings and queens

Edmund Ironside	1016
Cnut	1016-1035
Harold I	1035-1040
Harthacnut	1040-1042
Edward the Confessor	1042-1066
Harold II	1066
William I	1066-1087
William II	1087-1100
Henry I	1100-1135
Stephen	1135-1154
Henry II	1154-1189
Richard I	1189-1199
John	1199-1216
Henry III	1216-1272
Edward I	1272-1307
Edward II	1307-1327
Edward III	1327-1377
Richard II	1377-1399
Henry IV	1399-1413
Henry V	1413-1422
Henry VI	1422-1461
Edward IV	1461-1483
Edward V	1483
Richard III	1483-1485
Henry VII	1485-1509
Henry VIII	1509-1547
Edward VI	1547-1553
Mary I	1553-1558
Elizabeth I	1558-1603
James I	1603-1625

Scotland

Duncan 1	1034-1040
Macbeth	1040-1057

Mary 1   1542-1567
Mary succeeded her father James V of Scotland at 6 days old.
She was deposed in 1567 and executed in 1587.
James VI   1567-1625
James succeeded at one year old.
He became James I of England and Ireland in 1603.

France

Henri II	1547-1559
Francis II	1559-1560
Charles IX	1560-1574
Henri III	1574-1589
Henri IV	1589-1610

Notes

1 The Shakespeare Authorship Mystery

1 The four grammarians mentioned were all from Cambridge University. Roger Ascham, John Cheke and William Cecil were from St John's College, Thomas Smith from Queens' College.

2 Gerald Eades Bentley, *The Profession of Dramatist in Shakespeare's Time, 1590–1642*. 1971, p. 95.

3 Sir Edmund Tilney was Master of the Revels from 1579 until succeeded by Sir George Buck after his death in 1610. From 1606 the Master also issued licences for printed texts as well as for performances of plays.

4 Gerald Eades Bentley, *The Profession of Dramatist in Shakespeare's Time, 1590–1642*. 1971, p. 152.

5 Quarto size was nine and a half by twelve inches, Folio was twelve by fifteen inches.

6 William Prynne (1600–1669) was a puritan zealot whose eleven-hundred page polemic *Histrio-Mastix*, subtitled *The players scourge or actors tragedie* was a sustained attack on all forms of theatrical production and the people associated with them. Because Queen Henrietta Maria, wife of Charles I, had acted in masques his condemnation of all women performers as whores was seen as seditious. He was pilloried, branded on the cheeks and had both ears severed.

7 The 1632 edition of the First Folio was printed on high quality rag-based paper imported from France. Dobson and Wells, *The Oxford Companion to Shakespeare, p. 147.*

8 Plays which are believed to be co-authored would include *Henry VIII* and *The Two Noble Kinsmen* (with John Fletcher), *Pericles* (George Wilkins), *Timon of Athens* (Thomas Middleton) and *Titus Andronicus* (George Peele). Several hands were responsible for the collaborative play *Sir Thomas More* which survives in manuscript form.

9 The eighteen previously unknown plays appearing in the First Folio are:

> *The Tempest*
> *The Two Gentlemen of Verona*
> *Measure for Measure*
> *The Comedy of Errors*
> *As You Like It*
> *The Taming of the Shrew*
> *All's Well That Ends Well*
> *Twelfth Night*
> *The Winter's Tale*

King John
Henry VI Part One
Henry VIII
Coriolanus
Timon of Athens
Julius Caesar
Macbeth
Antony and Cleopatra
Cymbeline

10 The quarto edition of *Troilus and Cressida* published in 1609 contained an 'Epistle' addressed to the reader. It referred to the text of the plays as being obtained from the 'grand possessors'. The Herbert brothers, William and Philip, dedicatees of the First Folio, owned Baynard's Castle, a former royal palace in London, and Wilton House near Salisbury. These are two possible locations for the lost Shakespeare archive. Wilton House was partly destroyed by fire in 1647, Baynard's Castle was completely destroyed on 3rd September 1666 during London's great fire.

11 David Garrick (1717–1779) was associated with the Drury Lane Theatre for most of his career as an actor, producer and director. He will always be credited with popularising the plays of Shakespeare and bringing them to an appreciative London audience.

12 Edmond Malone (1741–1812) was a significant editor of Shakespeare but his inability to match the Stratford man to the plays launched the quest for a more credible author. His papers were left to James Boswell Junior.

13 Robert Bearman, *Shakespeare in the Stratford Records*, p. 70.

14 The Elementary Education Act 1870 was drafted by William Forster, a Liberal Member of Parliament. It set out the framework for the education of all children in England and Wales aged between the age of 5 and 12, after years of campaigning by the National Education League to provide the country with a literate workforce.

15 Thomas Howard duke of Norfolk was Edward de Vere's first cousin. The sonneteer Henry Howard earl of Surrey was his uncle. Queen Elizabeth's grandmother was Lady Elizabeth Howard, the mother of Anne Boleyn.

16 A double wedding was performed at Whitehall on 16th December 1571. The first was between Edward de Vere 17th earl of Oxford and Anne Cecil, the second being between Edward Somerset and Lady Elizabeth Hastings, sister of the earl of Huntingdon. Somerset inherited as 4th earl of Worcester in 1589. Two years older than Edward de Vere he was a successful courtier being made a Garter knight and serving as Lord Privy Seal and Earl Marshal.

2 Formative Years

1 Verily Anderson, *The De Veres of Castle Hedingham* p. 158.
2 To avoid punishment John Rogers had unsuccessfully used the pseudonym Thomas Matthew. His translation is known as *The Matthew Bible*.
3 This prestigious chair was founded by Henry VIII in 1540 and the holder is still chosen by the Crown.
4 The Vere estates, manor houses and town properties were located in Berkshire, Buckinghamshire, Cambridgeshire, Cheshire, Cornwall, Devon, Essex, Hertfordshire, Kent, Leicestershire, London, Norfolk, Northamptonshire, Staffordshire, Suffolk, Warwickshire and Wiltshire. Verily Anderson, *The De Vere's of Castle Hedingham*, p. 94.
5 Mark Anderson in *Shakespeare by Another Name* quotes from *The Diary of Henry Machyn* edited by John Gough Nicholls and published by the Camden Society, London. Alan Nelson in *Monstrous Adversary* quotes from John Stow, *A Survey of London*, reprinted from the text of 1603 with notes by Charles L Kingford and published by Oxford: Clarendon Press 1908.
6 Nelson quotes from the Calendar of State Papers 1547–80 that this document was written by Arthur Golding and endorsed by Sir William Cecil.
7 Sir William Cecil was another MA recipient on this occasion.
8 In his *ABC of Reading*, Yale, 1934, the poet Ezra Pound reproduced passages of Golding's Ovid translation, noting, 'Though it is the most beautiful book in the English language, I am not citing it for its decorative purposes but its narrative quality'.
9 Mildred Cecil (1526–1589).
10 Gabriel Harvey (*c* 1545–1630).
11 Edward de Vere's biographers, B M Ward, Alan Nelson and Mark Anderson have drawn on the memoirs of two French ambassadors. These were Bertrand de Salignac Fénélon, seigneur de la Mothe who served 1568–1575 (*Memoires touchant l'Angleterre*), and Michel de Castelnau Mauvissière who served 1575–1585. Their anecdotes of life behind the scenes at Queen Elizabeth's court were published in France and thus escaped the censorship imposed on such material by the Lord Chamberlain's office in London.

3 Troubled Times

1 The Eighty Years War, or the Dutch War of Independence (1568–1648) began as a revolt against Philip II of Spain, the overlord of the Habsburg Netherlands. The revolt was led by Prince William of Orange and ended with the Treaty of Westphalia in 1648.
2 Edward de Vere's two sons were killed in the Dutch wars. These were his heir Henry de Vere the 18th earl of Oxford and his natural son Sir Edward Vere. The 19th earl, Robert de Vere also died. Sir Philip Sidney was an early casualty. Henry Writothesley, 3rd earl of Southampton and his elder son James also died.
3 The most organised of the many plots endangering Queen Elizabeth were the Ridolfi plot of 1571, the Throckmorton plot of 1583, the Babington plot of 1583 and the Lopez plot of 1594. They were foiled by her security chiefs, William Cecil and Francis Walsingham.
4 The nine great officers of state in Elizabethan England:
   Lord High Steward
   Lord High Chancellor – custodian of the Great Seal of the Realm
   Lord High Treasurer – head of Her Majesty's Treasury
   Lord President of the Council – presiding officer of Her Majesty's
      Privy Council
   Lord Privy Seal – responsible for the monarch's personal seal
   Lord Great Chamberlain – bearer of the Sword of State at
      ceremonies.
   Lord High Constable
   Earl Marshal
5 Gaspard de Coligny 1512–72.

4 Early Work

1 Bartholomew Clerke, 1537?–1590.
2 Thomas Bedingfield 1545–1613.
3 Geoffrey Bullough (1901–1982) held a succession of senior academic posts, among them English Literature at Sheffield University 1933–1946 and Professor of English Language and Literature, King's College London 1946–48. He was made a Fellow of King's College in 1964 and an Honorary Doctor of Literature by Manchester in 1969. His eight volume *Narrative and Dramatic Sources of Shakespeare* was published by Columbia University between 1957and 1973. Although in places overtaken by more recent research this remains the standard work on Shakespeare's sources. It does not include either *Two Noble Kinsmen* or *Edward III*.
4 H. Jenkins (editor) *Hamlet*, London: Methuen Arden, 1982.
5 J Thomas Looney, *The poems of Edward De Vere, seventeenth earl of*

Oxford. London: C. Palmer, 1921.

6   Steven W May, *The Poems of Edward De Vere, Seventeenth Earl of Oxford and of Robert Devereux, Second Earl of Essex, Studies in Philology*, 1980.

7   The play *Sir Thomas More* is included in the *Oxford Shakespeare* complete works. The Royal Shakespeare Company staged a performance in 2005. The original manuscript is believed to have been penned by Anthony Munday. One page by an unidentified writer has been claimed by some Stratfordian scholars as possibly penned by Shakespeare. Of the six discernible scripts Munday is identified as Hand S, 'Shakespeare' as Hand D. Anthony Munday was employed by Edward de Vere as a secretary in the 1580s.

8   Shooters Hill is in the London Borough of Greenwich in south-east London. It lies east of Blackheath and west of Welling, south of Woolwich and north of Eltham. It reputedly takes its name from the practice of archery there during the Middle Ages, although the name is also commonly linked to its reputation as a haunt for highwaymen.

5 Continental Travels

1   On 30th January 1575, prior to his departure for Italy, Edward de Vere entailed the lands of his earldom on his first cousin, Hugh Vere, having no children of his own born at this time. If he should die abroad without heirs the lands and property would descend to his full sister, Lady Mary Vere. The indenture also provided for payment of debts in an attached schedule amounting to £9,096 of which sum £3,457 was owed to the Queen through the Court of Wards.

2   Johannes Sturm 1507–1589.

3   Richard Roe, *The Shakespeare Guide to Italy*, Harper Collins, New York, 2011.

4   Nelson, *Monstrous Adversary*, p. 157.

5   Noemi Magri, *Othello's house on the Sagittary*, De Vere Society Newsletter, February 2010.

6   A book, *The Travels of Edward Webbe*, record a sighting of the earl of Oxford in Palermo. Webbe was a master gunner who travelled extensively in Africa and the Middle East. The account of his travels was published in 1589.

7   (George) Bernard Shaw (1856–1950), always dropped the final 'e' when writing about Shakespeare. This was part of his campaign for simplified spelling. (George becomes Jorj etc). Bernard Shaw earned his living by journalism before he began writing plays. He became well known as a drama critic for the *Saturday Review*. As a music critic for the *Pall Mall Gazette* he wrote under the pseudonym 'Corno di Bassetto.'

6 Marriage to Anne Cecil

1 Sir William Cecil had one son by his first wife Mary Cheke, this was Thomas Cecil, later Earl of Exeter. His other son by his second wife Mildred Cooke was Robert Cecil, later earl of Salisbury. Their second daughter was named Elizabeth who married but died childless.

7 Literary Connections

1 Matthew Arnold 1822–1888.
2 Thomas Carlyle 1795–1881.
3 *The Grove Concise Dictionary of Music*, Macmillan, London, 1994, p. 127.
4 Battles Hall is still a Grade II Listed Building.
5 The literary critic J Dover Wilson in his biography of John Lyly cited his comedy *Endymion, The Man in the Moon* as strongly influencing Shakespeare, most obviously in *Love's Labour's Lost* and *A Midsummer Night's Dream*. There was a performance at Greenwich Palace in 1588 acted by the Children of Paul's. Although Cynthia the Moon Goddess represents Queen Elizabeth he discounts other less flattering roles being assigned to members of her court because Lyly as a commoner would not have dared to risk their displeasure. John Lyly was Edward de Vere's secretary for most of the 1580s and dedicated work to him. The six court comedies in which de Vere may have collaborated were *Campaspe, Sapho and Phao, Endymion, Gallathea, Midas* and *Mother Bombie*.
6 Abraham Fleming's manuscript collection passed into the possession of the antiquarian Francis Peck (1692–1743) who included in his list of the items it contained 'a pleasant conceit by Vere, Earl of Oxford'. This may have referred to Sir Christopher Hatton (as Malvolio) and was possibly an early draft of *Twelfth Night*. The manuscript was lost and cannot now be traced.
7 Edward Arber 1836–1912.

8 Family Connections

1 Francis Norris, Earl of Berkshire, 1579–1622.
2 George Russell French, 1803–1881.
3 Sir Israel Gollancz, 1863–1930, Professor of English Literature at King's College, London for almost thirty years, also edited the pocket-sized 'Temple' editions of Shakespeare.

9 A Reader of Books

1 Nelson, *Monstrous Adversary* p. 53.
2 The Folger Shakespeare Library has the world's largest collection of the printed works of William Shakespeare, including 79 copies of the 1623 First Folio, although not all of them are complete. Situated on Capitol Hill in Washington the library was founded in 1928 by Henry Clay Folger, a former president of Standard Oil.
3 Roger Stritmatter holds a PhD in Comparative Literature from the University of Massachusetts at Amherst. Dr Stritmatter delivered a paper to the Shakespeare Oxford Society *An Interim Report on the Marginalia of the Geneva Bible of Edward de Vere*. This was published in the Vol 29 Spring Newsletter.
4 Sir Thomas North 1535–1604.
5 Naseeb Shaheen (1931–2009) taught English literature at the University of Memphis. His 879-page *Biblical References in Shakespeare's Plays* published by the University of Delaware Press in 1999 demonstrates that whichever dramatist wrote Shakespeare had an immense knowledge of the books of the Bible including the Apocrypha. Of the Bibles available at the time (preceding the King James Version of 1611), the Geneva Bible was the most frequently drawn on for scriptural allusions. Professor Shaheen owned over a hundred early printed Bibles.
6 Thomas Whitfield Baldwin was Professor of English at the University of Illinois from 1925 until 1958. His two volume *William Shakespeare's Small Latine and Lesse Greeke* was published by the university press in 1944. Based on a quotation from Ben Jonson the book conjectures at length on the classical education Shakespeare would have received. Professor Baldwin bequeathed his collection of 5,800 books on Elizabethan literature to the university library.

10 A Writer of Letters

1 Stephanie Hopkins Hughes, *Oxford's Letters*, compilation on disc. See Bibliography.
2 Jean-Paul Sartre, 1905–1980, in an essay *Le Regard* uses a similar phrase. 'Je suis ce que je ne suis pas, mais … je ne suis pas ce que je suis.' From *L'Être et le Néant,* 1943.

12 Why the Pen Name ?

1 John Stubbs 1543–1591.
2 In addition to his other perquisites Queen Elizabeth also granted Sir Christopher Hatton the London residence of the Bishop of Ely. The bishopric was vacant at the time, allowing the Queen to make this gift to a favoured courtier. The bishop's large garden was later renamed as Hatton Garden and became the London centre for the diamond and jewellery trade.
3 Dr William Barlow was Dean of Chester at the time of his sermon at St Paul's Cross in 1601. He was one of a panel of divines engaged on a new translation of the New Testament for the King James Bible. He became Bishop of Lincoln in 1608 and died there in 1613. Maclure, M, *The Paul's Cross Sermons*, 1958, p.84.
4 Nicolaus Copernicus (1473–1543) was a Polish born astronomer and mathematician whose work *De Revolutionibus* published in 1543 mapped the solar system as planets orbiting a stationary sun. Clerical opposition to this heliocentric theory was not finally withdrawn until 1835. Vatican displeasure at Galileo Galilei (1564–1642) for embracing and propagating the theory of heliocentrism was not lifted until 2008.

13 Dating the Plays

1 Alan Nelson, *Monstrous Adversary*, p. 53.
2 Kenneth Muir, *The Sources of Shakespeare's Plays*, p. 8–9
3 The play *Sir Thomas More* is included in the *Oxford Shakespeare* complete works.
4 Edward Dowden 1843–1913.
5 E.K. Chambers 1866–1954.
6 Woolley, Benjamin *The Queen's Conjuror: The Science and Magic of Dr. John Dee, Adviser to Queen Elizabeth I.* New York: Henry Holt and Company, 2001.
7 Kenneth Muir, *The Sources of Shakespeare's Plays* p. 206.
8 Wells and Taylor, *William Shakespeare : A Textual Companion*, p. 122.
9 A. L. Rowse 1903–1997.
10 From E.T Clark, *Hidden Allusions in Shakespeare's Plays*, New York, 1931. Eva Turner Clark (1871–1947) was the founder of the American Oxford Society.
11 The definition of these as 'problem plays' was first made by Professor Frederick Samuel Boas (1862–1957), an English scholar of early drama. He characterised them as complex and ambiguous in tone, with

violent shifts between comic situations and dark, psychological drama. F. S. Boas, *Shakespeare and his Predecessors*, published by John Murray, Third Impression, 1910.

12 In his biography of Edward de Vere, *Shakespeare by Another Name*, Mark Anderson follows the hyphenated 'Shake-speare' spelling of the author's name used in early publications of the plays and poems.

13 Sir Israel Gollancz, *The Sources of Hamlet*, p.229. This book includes a translation from the Latin of the relevant section of *Historia Danica* (Saxo Grammaticus) by Professor Oliver Elton, and a translation from the French of Book V of *Des Histoires Tragiques* (François de Belleforest). This is the first translation into English, with the title: '*The Hystorie of Hamblet*, Imprinted by Richard Bradocke, for Thomas Pavier, to be sold at his shop in Corne-Hill, neere to the Royall Exchange'.

14 Printing the Plays

1 Information on printing the plays taken from Wells and Taylor, *William Shakespeare : A Textual Companion*.

2 Baynard's Castle survives as a name in Castle Baynard Street, just south of Queen Victoria Street, and as a local ward in the City of London.

3 Several editions of the Shakespeare plays were published in the 18th century:

1709	Nicholas Rowe, 6 volumes
1710	Charles Gildon, *Poems*, and in 1714
1714	Nicholas Rowe, 8 volumes
1723	Alexander Pope, 6 volumes
1728	Alexander Pope, 10 volumes
1733	Lewis Theobald, 7 volumes
1740	Lewis Theobald, 8 volumes
1743	Thomas Hanmer, 6 volumes
1747	William Warburton, 8 volumes
1765	Samuel Johnson, 8 volumes
1767	Edward Capell, 10 volumes
1773	Samuel Johnson and George Steevens, 10 volumes
1778	Samuel Johnson and George Steevens, 10 volumes
1785	Samuel Johnson, George Steevens and Isaac Reed, 10 vols
1786	Joseph Rann, 6 volumes
1790	Edmond Malone, 10 volumes
1793	George Steevens and Isaac Reed, 15 volumes

15 Family Relationships in Shakespeare

1 Shakespeare's retelling of the closet scene in François de Belle-forest's version of the Hamlet story stays close to the original. In both a troubled young man expresses deep revulsion at the idea of his mother engaging in sexual activity:

> Although the queen perceived herselfe neerly touched, and that Hamlet mooved her to the quicke, where she felt herselfe interested, nevertheless shee forgot all disdaine and wrath, ... hearing her selfe so sharply chiden and reprooved, for the joy she then conceaved, to behold the gallant spirit of her sonne... . She durst not lift up her eyes to beholde him, remembering her offence, and on the other side she would gladly have imbraced her son, in regard of the wise admonitions by him given unto her, which as then quenched the flames of unbridled desire ... and so, overcome and vanquished with this honest passion, and weeping most bitterly, having long fixed her eyes upon Hamlet, as being ravished into some great and deepe contemplation, and as it were wholy amazed, at the last imbracing him in her arms with the like love that a vertuous mother may or can use to kisse and entertaine her owne childe. *The Hystorie of Hamblet*, Translation of Book V of *Les Histoires Tragiques* by Thomas Pavier, 1608, p.219.

16 Tudor Myths

1 Mark Anderson, *Shakespeare by Another Name*, p. 73.
2 Alan Nelson, *Monstrous Adversary*, p. 293.
3 Alan Nelson in *Monstrous Adversary*, p. 95, quotes from the 1791 *Illustrations of British History* by Edmond Lodge, which contains the Talbot papers.
4 *Lady Clara Vere de Vere* is a poem by Alfred, Lord Tennyson, included in the collection *The Lady of Shalott and Other Poems* published in 1842.
5 Mary Fitton (1578–1647). Mary Fitton was one of the Queen's maids of honour and included among her many lovers William Herbert, later 3rd earl of Pembroke, by whom she was made pregnant.
6 Bernard Shaw regularly jeered at Shakespeare's creaky stage directions and absurd plots. He wrote, 'With the single exception of Homer, there is no eminent writer, not even Sir Walter Scott, whom I can despise so entirely as I despise Shakespeare when I measure my mind against his'. *Dramatic Opinions and Essays*, Vol 2.

17 Unruly Servants

1 Nelson, *Monstrous Adversary*, pp. 174–176.
2 Nelson, *Monstrous Adversary*, p. 361.
3 Nelson, *Monstrous Adversary*, pp. 376–79.
4 Nelson, *Monstrous Adversary*, pp. 401–04.
5 Public Record Office, State Papers 12/234, quoted by Mark Anderson in *Shakespeare by Another Name*, p. 250 and by Alan Nelson in *Monstrous Adversary* pp. 325–27.

18 Violence

1 Mark Anderson, *Shakespeare by Another Name*, p. 35–37.
2 Nelson, *Monstrous Adversary*, pp. 199–200
3 Michel de Castelnau, sieur de la Mauvissière, (1520-92).
4 Thomas James Knyvet (1558–1622).
5 Nelson, Monstrous Adversary, p. 281–82.
6 Pergrine Bertie (1555–1601), later the 13th Baron Willoughby d' Eresby.
7 This injury to one of de Vere's knees is mentioned in a letter 23rd September 1575 from Clemente Paretti (a banker) in Venice to Lord Burghley in London, reporting on de Vere's activities on the continent. Burghley also spied on his son Thomas when he was away from home. Burghley and Sir Francis Walsingham presided over an efficient information gathering network extending far into Europe.
8 Former President of the United States Ronald Reagan, Pope John Paul 2 and Adolf Hitler had something in common. All three survived assassination attempts but soon afterwards developed neurological symptoms, Alzheimer's in Reagan's case, Parkinson's for Hitler and the Pope.
9 Mark Anderson, *Shakespeare by Another Name*, p. 173.
10 Lawrence Stone, 1916–1999, was Dodge Professor of History at Princeton University from 1963–1990. His book *The Crisis in the Aristocracy 1558–1641* was published by Oxford in 1965.

19 Armed Conflict

1 In addition to King Richard II, Queen Elizabeth's two predecessors on the throne were also childless, Edward VI and Mary Tudor.

2 Thomas Babington Macaulay (1800–1859), *The History of England*:

> The noblest subject in England, and indeed, as Englishmen loved to say, the noblest subject in Europe, was Aubrey de Vere, twentieth and last of the old Earls of Oxford. He derived his title through an uninterrupted male descent, from a time when the families of Howard and Seymour were still obscure, when the Nevills and Percies enjoyed only a provincial celebrity, and when even the great name of Plantagenet had not yet been heard in England. One chief of the house of De Vere had held high command at Hastings; another had marched, with Godfrey and Tancred, over heaps of slaughtered Moslem, to the sepulchre of Christ. The first Earl of Oxford had been minister of Henry Beauclerc. The third Earl had been conspicuous among the Lords who extorted the Great Charter from John. The seventh Earl had fought bravely at Cressy and Poitiers. The thirteenth Earl had, through many vicissitudes of fortune, been the chief of the party of the Red Rose, and had led the van on the decisive day of Bosworth. The seventeenth Earl had shone at the court of Elizabeth, and had won for himself an honourable place among the early masters of English poetry. The nineteenth Earl had fallen in arms for the Protestant religion, and for the liberties of Europe, under the walls of Maestricht. His son, Aubrey, in whom closed the longest and most illustrious line of nobles that England has seen, a man of loose morals, but of inoffensive temper, and of courtly manners, was Lord Lieutenant of Essex and Colonel of the Blues.'

3 Edward Hall 1498–1547.

4 The Eighty Years War, or the Dutch War of Independence (1568–1648).

5 Sir Clements Robert Markham, (1830–1916) published *The Fighting Veres*, London : S. Low, Marston. From the Americana collection, University of California Libraries.

6 Members of the De Vere family buried in Westminster Abbey are as follows. In the Chapel of St Nicholas – Anne de Vere, countess of Oxford; Elizabeth Stanley, countess of Derby and Susan Herbert, countess of Montgomery. These are Edward de Vere's wife and his oldest and youngest daughters. In the Chapel of St John the Evangelist there are Sir Francis Vere, Sir Horace Vere, Aubrey de Vere, 20th and last earl of Oxford, his second wife Diana and their unmarried daughter Henrietta. In the Chapel of St John the Baptist lie Henry de Vere the 18th earl of Oxford and Lady Anne Bayning de Vere the 20th earl's first wife. In St Andrew's (Norris's) Chapel lies buried Maria Vere an unmarried daughter of the 20th earl.

7 B.M. Ward, *The Seventeenth Earl of Oxford*, p. 46.

8 The office of Admiral of England was created around 1400 in the reign

of Henry IV, although before this there were Admirals of the Northern and Western Seas. The title was changed to Lord Admiral and then to Lord High Admiral, In 1546 King Henry VIII established the Council of the Marine, later to become the Navy Board. Operational control of the Navy remained the responsibility of the Lord High Admiral.

9 The month of June can be cold and blustery with rough seas in the western approaches and the Channel. The D-Day landings on 6 June 1944 were seriously disadvantaged by bad weather and were postponed until the last possible minute.

20 Insolvency

1 One of the stories in the anthology is of Leir and his daughter Cordila, and so a possible source for *King Lear*.
2 John Lydgate, 1370–1451.
3 Sir Thomas Sackville of Knole, 1536–1608.
4 Nelson, *Monstrous Adversary*, p. 295.
5 Benedict Spinola, 1519–1580. The Quayside development of Magdalene College, Cambridge in 1989 included an ugly gargoyle representing Spinola. This was positioned on a wall spitting water into the Cam. The gargoyle was designed by Peter Fluck and Roger Law who made the puppets for the television programme Spitting Image.
6 Francis Trentham 1563–1626.
7 De Vere owned a portable writing desk which accompanied him on his travels. He mentions it in a letter to Lord Burghley dated 6 September 1596. 'The writing which I have is in the country, for I had such care thereof I carried it with me in a little desk'.

21 Love and Sexuality

1 *Romeo and Juliet* was adapted for the Broadway stage as the musical drama *West Side Story*. The music was written by the highly regarded conductor and composer Leonard Bernstein which guaranteed that it would receive serious critical consideration. First performed in 1957 it has remained in the repertoire and is regularly revived, occasionally by opera companies but mostly by regional theatres and amateur productions. The Montagues and the Capulets are represented by two rival New York gangs, the Jets and the Sharks. Tony comes from Jets, Maria from the Sharks. Professor Stone's analogy comparing the Oxford and Knyvet vendetta with American gangsters and turf wars was therefore fully vindicated, although not in a way he would have understood. Romeo and Juliet, Tony and Maria, Edward de Vere and Anne Vavasour – three pairs of star-crossed lovers.

2 Shakespeare scholars seem in agreement that this was based on a translation from the Italian *Novelle* by Matteo Bandello. Arthur Brooke was a nephew of George Brooke, Lord Cobham. He was admitted to the Middle Temple in 1563 but then joined the military before completing his studies. He is believed to have drowned on 19th March 1564 aged twenty when his ship *The Greyhound* was wrecked on the sands near Rye. The ship was bound for Le Havre, crossing to help Protestant forces in France. Oxfordians do not press the claim for the twelve year old Edward de Vere as the author of *The Tragical Historie of Romeus and Juliet* using Arthur Brooke as a pseudonym. (Arthur Brook = Author Ford) ?

3 Nelson, *Monstrous Adversary*, p.217

4 Two tracts issued during the earl of Leicester's lifetime were savage attacks on his character, accusing him of political chicanery and criminal acts. The first and best known of these was *Leicester's Commonwealth*, printed in France and appearing in 1584. Edward de Vere the earl of Oxford blamed Leicester for his financial ruin, with some justification as Queen Elizabeth had put many of his estates in trust to Leicester and they were never fully restored to him. De Vere's lifelong enmity towards Leicester, and his support for anti-Leicester factions at court, have prompted suspicions that he was involved in writing and producing *Leicester's Commonwealth*, and for sponsoring similar pamphlets after Leicester's death in 1588.

5 Nelson, *Monstrous Adversary*, p.215

6 Nelson, *Monstrous Adversary*, p. 157

22 Medicine and Medication

1 *Shakespeare and Medicine* by R.R. Simpson, Ed. E. & S. Livingstone, Ltd., 16 and 17 Teviot Place, Edinburgh, Scotland, 1959.

2 Dr Stephen Booth (born 1933) is a professor emeritus of English literature at the University of California, Berkeley and a noted Shakespeare expert who has written extensively on the sonnets: *Shakespeare's Sonnets, Edited with Analytic Commentary*, New Haven, 1977. Also *An Essay on Shakespeare's Sonnets*. New Haven, 1969.

3 The De Vere family physician George Baker had previously dedicated to Edward a translation from the Spanish of Aparicio de Zubia's *The Composition or Making of the Most Excellent and Precious Oil Called Oleum Magistrale.*

4 Galenic medicine, or Galenism, derives its name from the Greek physician and philosopher Galen (CE 129–c216). Medicine was identified with Galenism for 1,300 years. It was taught in European universities from the eleventh century onwards after Arabic trans-

lations of Galen's writings were retranslated into Latin. Though Galenism was eclipsed in Europe by the rise of modern medicine, it still survives as *Unani* (Greek) medicine in some parts of India and Pakistan.

5 Konrad Gesner 1516–1565.

6 Paracelsus, born Philip von Hohenheim, 1493–1541.

7 Leonardo Fioravanti 1518–1588.

8 In 1607 Theobalds House passed in ownership from Robert Cecil, who had inherited it from his father in 1598, to King James I who exchanged it for the nearby Hatfield Palace. Theobalds House quickly became the King's favourite country seat and he died there on 27th March 1625. Rebuilt on a nearby site as Theobald's Park after the Restoration, the name survives as one of the De Vere chain of hotels.

9 The fever he reported from Venice in 1575 coincided with a surge in plague deaths which continued until 1577.

10 Dana Sutton was the Emeritus Professor of Classics at the University of California, Irvine.

11 Aubrey C. Kail, *The Medical Mind of Shakespeare*, Wilkins & Wilkins, Balgowlah, New South Wales, Australia, 1986.

23 Genius and the Hurt Mind

1 In the notes on *Macbeth* by Professor Stanley Wells in the *Oxford Shakespeare* he writes, 'Shakespeare took materials for his story from the account in Raphael Holinshed's *Chronicle* of the reign of Duncan and Macbeth. Occasionally he closely followed Holinshed's wording.' The Gowrie Conspiracy of 1600, which was an attempt to murder James VI, could be an alternative source of inspiration for the play, or even the earlier murder of Lord Darnley in 1567.

2 August Schlegel's essays on dramatic art and literature were published in 1811 as *Über dramatische Kunst und Literatur*. Schlegel was connected by marriage to the composer Felix Mendelssohn (the nephew of his brother Friedrich). At the age of seventeen in 1826 the young Mendelssohn was reportedly so impressed by his uncle's translation of *A Midsummer Night's Dream* that he composed the famous incidental music which is now as well known as the play.

3 Sir John Charles Bucknill (1817–1897) founded *The British Journal of Psychiatry* in 1853.

4 Dr Michael Fitzgerald was the Henry Marsh Professor of Child and Adolescent Psychiatry, Trinity College Dublin, and Clinical and Research Consultant to the Irish Society for Autism. He is a Fellow of the Royal College of Psychiatrists, a member of the Royal College of Surgeons in England, and an associate member of the British Psychoanalytical Society. His book *Autism and Creativity, Is there a*

link between autism in men and exceptional ability? was published by Brunner-Routledge in 2004.

5 François Martin Mai, *Diagnosing Genius,* McGill : Queen's University Press, 2007. Dr Mai is a Medical Advisor to the Government of Canada and an Adjunct Professor at Queen's University, Kingston. Formerly he was Director of Psychiatry at Ottawa General Hospital.

6 *The Handbook of Creativity* edited by J Glover, New York : Plenum Press 1989.

7 Wells and Taylor, *William Shakespeare : A Textual Companion*, p. 17.

Bibliography

Anderson, Mark, *Shakespeare by Another Name*, Gotham Books, Penguin Group, New York, 2005.

Anderson, Verily, *The De Veres of Castle Hedingham*, Terence Dalton Limited, Lavenham, Suffolk, 1993.

Bearman, Robert, *Shakespeare in the Stratford Records*, in association with The Shakespeare Birthplace Trust. First published in the United States of America, Alan Sutton Publishing Inc, 83 Washington Street, Dover, New Hampshire, 1994.

Booth, Stephen, *Shakespeare's Sonnets*, Yale University Press, 1977.

Boyce, Charles, *Shakespeare A to Z*, Roundtable Press, New York, 1990.

Brazil, Robert Sean, *Edward de Vere and the Shakespeare Printers*, Cortical Output, LLC, Seattle, WA, USA, 2010.

Bucknill, John Charles, *The Medical Knowledge of Shakespeare*, London, Longman & Co., 1860.

Bucknill, John Charles, *The Psychology of Shakespeare*, London, Longman & Co, 1859.

Bullough, Geoffrey, *Narrative and Dramatic Sources of Shakespeare*, Routledge and Kegan Paul, 1957. In five volumes.

Chamberlin, Frederick, *The Private Character of Queen Elizabeth*, John Lane The Bodley Head, London, 1921.

Chambers, E.K., *Shakespeare : A Study of Facts and Problems*, two volumes, Oxford : Clarendon Press, 1930.

Crystal, David and Crystal, Ben, *Shakespeare's Words : A Glossary and Language Companion,* Penguin Books, 2002.

Dobson, Michael and Wells, Stanley, eds, *The Oxford Companion to Shakespeare*, Oxford University Press, 2001.

Elson, Louis C, *Shakespeare in Music*, London, 1901

Erne, Lukas, *Shakespeare as Literary Dramatist*, Cambridge University Press, 2003.

Fitzgerald, Michael, *Autism and Creativity : Is there a link between autism in men and exceptional ability?* Brunner-Routledge, Hove and New York, 2004.

Fowler, William Plumer, *Shakespeare Revealed In Oxford's Letters*, Peter E Randall Publisher, Portsmouth, New Hampshire, 1986.

Fox, Robin, *Shakespeare's Education*, Laugwitz Verlag, Germany, 2012

Gilvary, Kevin, ed., *Dating Shakespeare's Plays : A Critical Review of the Evidence*, Parapress, Tunbridge Wells, 2010.

Gollancz, Sir Israel, *The Sources of Hamlet*, Frank Cass & Co Ltd, London, 1967.

Hayes, John R. and Mellon, Carnegie, *Cognitive Processes in Creativity*. Published in *The Handbook of Creativity* edited by J Glover, New York :

Plenum Press 1989.

Hughes, Stephanie Hopkins, *Oxford's Letters*. Compilation on CD produced by Absolute Audio, 35a Broadhurst Gardems, London, NW6 3QT. *politicworm.com*

Jolly, Margrethe, *The First Two Quartos of Hamlet : A New View of the Origins and Relationship of the Texts*, McFarland & Company, North Carolina, 2014.

Kail, Aubrey C., *The Medical Mind of Shakespeare*, Williams & Wilkins, Balgowlah, NSW, Australia, 1986.

Looney, J. Thomas, *Shakespeare Identified in Edward de Vere the Seventeenth Earl of Oxford*, Published by Cecil Palmer, Bloomsbury Street, London, 1920.

Magri, Noemi *Such Fruits Out of Italy: The Italian Renaissance in Shakespeare's Plays and Poetry,* Laugwitz Verlag, Germany, 2014.

McGinn, Colin, *Shakespeare's Philosophy: The Meaning Behind the Plays.* Harper Perennial, New York, 2006.

Mai, François Martin, *Diagnosing Genius*, McGill-Queen's University Press, Montreal, 2007.

Malim, Richard, *The Earl of Oxford and the Making of Shakespeare*, McFarland & Company Inc, North Carolina, 2012.

Malim, Richard, ed., *Great Oxford, Essays on the Life and Work of Edward de Vere 17th Earl of Oxford 1550–1604*, Parapress, Tunbridge Wells, 2004.

Meres, Francis, *Palladis Tamia; Wits Treasury*, Garland Publishing, New York, 1973 with a preface by Arthur Freeman. A facsimile of the 1598 original.

Moore, Peter R., *The Lame Storyteller, Poor and Despised*, Verlag Uwe Laugwitz, Germany, 2009.

Muir, Kenneth, *The Sources of Shakespeare's Plays*, Methuen & Co Ltd, 1977.

Nelson, Alan H., *Monstrous Adversary*, Liverpool University Press, 2003.

Nelson-Cave, Wendy, *Who's Who in Shakespeare*, Grange Books, London, 1995.

Ogburn, Charlton, *The Mystery of William Shakespeare*, Penguin Group, London, 1984.

Price, Diana, *Shakespeare's Unorthodox Biography : New Evidence of an Authorship Problem*, Greenwood Press, Connecticut, USA, 2012

Read, Conyers, *Lord Burghley and Queen Elizabeth*, Jonathan Cape, 1960.

Read, Conyers, *Mr Secretary Cecil and Queen Elizabeth*, Jonathan Cape, 1955.

Roe, Richard Paul, *The Shakespeare Guide to Italy*, Harper Collins, New York, 2011.

Rouse, W.H.D., ed., *Shakespeare's Ovid Being Arthur Golding's Translation of the Metamorphoses*, Centaur Press, London, 1961. A facsimile of the

1567 original.

Rowse, A.L., *William Shakespeare*, Macmillan, 1963.

Schoenbaum, S. *William Shakespeare : A Documentary Life*. The Clarendon Press : Oxford, 1975.

Shakespeare Oxford Society, *Report my Cause Aright*, Fiftieth Birthday Anthology 1957–2007.

Shapiro, James, *Contested Will : Who Wrote Shakespeare?* Faber and Faber, 2010.

Vickers, Brian, *Shakespeare, Co-Author*, Oxford University Press, 2002.

Ward, Bernard. M., *The Seventeenth Earl of Oxford, 1550–1604, From Contemporary Documents*, John Murray, London, 1928.

Wells, Stanley, *Shakespeare, Sex, and Love*, Oxford University Press, 2010.

Wells, Stanley and Taylor, Gary, eds., *William Shakespeare, The Complete Works*, Second Edition, Clarendon Press · Oxford, 2005.

Wells, Stanley and Taylor, Gary, *William Shakespeare : A Textual Companion*, Clarendon Press : Oxford, 1987.

Wilson, J. Dover, *The Essential Shakespeare*, Cambridge University Press, 1964.

Index

Achilles, character in *Troilus and Cressida*, 156

Acting companies, 50, 70, 75, 84, 101

Acton, Lord, (1834-1902), historian and politician, 173

Adonis of the North (Amleth), 91

Advice for Thomas Cecil from his father, 61

Aeschylus, ancient Greek tragedian, 29, 170

Agincourt, battle of, 1415, 137

Ague, vernacular for malaria, 163, 175

Aguecheek, Sir Andrew, character in *Twelfth Night*, 80

Aldgate, London district, 75, 145

Alençon, duc d', François de Valois, duc d'Anjou, (1555-84), 115, 185

All's Well That Ends Well, Shakespeare play, 38, 94, 104, 211

Amadis de Gaule, medieval French romance, 97

Amiss (Amyce), Israel, servant to Edward de Vere, 123

Amleth, original character of Hamlet, 91, 111, 186, 197

Amyot, Jacques, translator of Plutarch's *Lives* into French, 20, 63, 85

Anatomie of Abuses, The, 1583, polemic by Philip Stubbs, 54, 199

Anderson, Mark, scholar, 90, 115, 132, 142, 155, 213, 219, 220, 221

Angelo, character in *Measure for Measure*, 119

Ankerwicke Priory, near Windsor, 15, 64, 160

Anne of Denmark,(1574-1619), wife of King James I, 75

Annuity, granted to Edward de Vere by Queen Elizabeth, 1586, 13, 144

Annuity, renewed by King James I, 66, 144

Anonymous, a film portraying Edward de Vere as Shakespeare, 117

Antiochus, king of Syria, character in *Pericles*, 154

Antiquities of Warwickshire, The, William Dugdale, 183

Antonio, merchant, character in *The Merchant of Venice*, 64, 125, 155, 170

Antony (Marcus Antonius) character in *Julius Caesar* and *Antony and Cleopatra*, 165, 170

Antony and Cleopatra, Shakespeare play, 33, 38, 63, 85, 94, 98, 151, 212

Antwerp, sack of, 1576, 140

Apocrypha to Christian Bible, 63, 217

Appeal for marital reconciliation by Anne Cecil, 47

Arber, Edward, (1836-1912), literary critic, 53, 216

Arcadia. see *Countess of Pembroke's Arcadia*

Arcite, character in *The Two Noble Kinsmen*, 18, 156

Arden family, 78

Arden of Faversham, a play, 33

Arden, Alice, (1516-51), compared with Lady Macbeth, 33

Ariosto, Ludovico, (1471-1533), Italian poet and dramatist, 30, 39, 185

Arnold, Matthew, (1822-88), poet, 48, 216

Arte of English Poesie, The, George Puttenham, 1589, 82, 196

Made in the USA
Columbia, SC
14 November 2018